Ray,
I hope you find the book interesting & informative. Thanks for your advice.
Dick

To my grandchildren,
Abby, Carter, Henry, Lucy, and Stanley,
that they might make informed decisions about life.

ALL FISH HAVE BONES is
COPYRIGHT © 2017 Richard Sonnichsen

Book Cover Design by Parker Design House, Seattle WA

Manufactured in the United States of America

ISBN 978-1544283-00-5
Library of Congress Control Number: 2017937184

All rights reserved by the author, including the right of reproduction in whole or part in any form. Permission to quote from the book for the purpose of review is hereby granted.

For more information:
Ponder Point Books
410 Ponder Point Drive
Sandpoint, ID 83864

Published for Mr. Sonnichsen by
BLUE CREEK PRESS
Heron, Montana 59844
www.bluecreekpress.com

Book design by Sandy Compton and Blue Creek Press

Also by Richard Sonnichsen

*High Impact Internal Evaluation: A Practitioner's
Guide to Evaluating and Consulting Inside Organizations*

*Evaluation in the Federal Government:
Changes, Trends, and Opportunities*
(Ed. with Christopher G. Wye)

*Can Governments Learn: Comparative Perspectives
on Evaluation and Organizational Learning*
(Ed. with Frans L. Leeuw and Ray C. Rist)

ALL FISH HAVE BONES

ALL FISH HAVE BONES

A Recovering Catholic's Advice
on Living a Good Life Without Religion

RICHARD SONNICHSEN

Table of Contents

i	Introduction
1	Challenging Religious Doctrine
23	Reason and Science versus Faith and Mystery
35	The Decline of Christianity and Rise of Secularization
49	Faith in a Fantasy
73	Sin, Sex, Suffering and Salvation
79	Dubious Dogmas
95	Does God Exist?
119	Women in Christianity: The Theology of Exclusion
133	The God Illusion
183	Living without God: A New Beginning
195	Seeking a Good Life
213	Epilogue
217	Acknowledgements
219	About the Author
221	Bibliography

ALL FISH HAVE BONES

INTRODUCTION

Many years ago in a small logging town nestled in the mountains of the Panhandle of Idaho lived a young Catholic boy who, because of his religion, was required to abstain from meat on Fridays. I was that boy and my memory of the Friday evening fish dinner ritual with my family is the origin of this book.

This is the story of my life sojourn: accumulating experiences, observing human behavior and reflecting on the relationships between nature, humanity and God. This is also the story of a journey toward gradual disillusionment with Catholicism, the benefits of organized religion and the Christian concept of a supernatural deity called God.

When I was growing up in the 1940s and '50s, practicing Catholics were required to abstain from eating meat on Fridays as a means of penance and atonement to acknowledge our sinful way of life and to commemorate the crucifixion of Jesus (Canon Law #1250 of the Catholic Church, since modified to require abstinence from meat only on Fridays during Lent).

ALL FISH HAVE BONES

Living in the Inland Northwest limited our access to fresh fish or shellfish with which to satisfy church requirement for abstinence. My wife, on the other hand, grew up in Baltimore where Catholics had access to the bounty of the Chesapeake Bay. On the Catholic Church's deprivation scale, lobster thermador, oysters Rockefeller, shrimp scampi, and blue crab cakes were considered equal to canned tuna. I believe these East coast meat substitutions pretty much vitiated the suffering concept. One wonders about the origination of this peculiar church doctrine.

When I was growing up, attendance at dinner was obligatory. My mother was fairly indulgent as to my whereabouts during the day as long as I returned home for dinner at five o'clock. Barring a medical emergency, my brother, two sisters and I were expected to remain at the table until everyone had finished eating.

On Fridays, tuna was the common fish du jour; and not Ahi tuna, gently seared on the outside, pink and moist in the middle, served on a bed of quinoa, with sides of haricots verts and baby bok choy with a foie gras and parsley garnish. This was tuna with an aluminum skin, packed in water or oil, cleverly marketed as "Chicken of the Sea."

The Catholic obligation to abstain from meat caused my mother to become a creative genius at preparing and presenting multiple manifestations of tuna casseroles to her family of six. My favorite casserole combined tuna with noodles and mushroom soup and a garnish of crushed potato chips on top! I always believed that a best-selling book for Catholics living in the Northwest would be *101 Ways to Disguise the Taste of Tuna*.

Occasionally, we would have fresh fish on Fridays — caught in our lake or bought at the supermarket — to comply with church doctrine. When this occurred, I would ask my Dad, "Does this fish have bones?" He would invariably reply, "All fish have bones."

What began as an innocent question developed over time into an amusing, routine banter; a Friday night dinner ritual. His reply became predictable, though not particularly helpful. His apparent indifference to answering my question compelled me to discover the bony nature of fish on my own. I

Introduction

learned that it was my responsibility to determine how best to eat the fish and avoid the bones.

Reflecting on this exchange with my dad after seven-plus decades of life, I began to see it as metaphor. My question about fish and bones was an expectation that someone else would make a decision for me. My Dad preferred that I use my own skills to examine the fish and determine the bone content, encouraging me to observe, analyze, decide and act on my own. It was a parental teaching moment I failed to recognize for many years. Our dinner table conversation gave me a recipe for looking analytically at life and seeking answers to difficult questions.

This childhood experience has relevance for exploring thorny questions encountered in life. We will use the "fish and bones" analogy to examine the mysteries of religion and supernatural belief.

Sometime in the last 2.5 million years, *Homo sapiens* became sentient — self-aware — with the ability to perceive existence and to subjectively contemplate the meaning of life. French philosopher Rene Descartes (1596-1650) eloquently declared: "I think, therefore I am." This oft-repeated phrase reinforces the notion that humans have the capacity to ponder existence and the purpose of life and death. Human consciousness enables us to explore a rationale for existence, purpose and meaning; often leading to belief in a supernatural deity or God who created the universe, planet Earth, flora, fauna, and humans; monitors the daily actions of seven billion humans on earth; and sits in final judgment to determine each person's place in the afterlife.

However, after seven-plus decades, I have concluded that there is no supernatural deity — it might be noted that approximately 150,000 persons die each day on the planet earth; a considerable number of daily decisions, even for a deity! A philosophy of life grounded in science, reason, and common sense is more intellectually sustainable, mentally rewarding and explanatory of the universe than a belief system theologically dependent on mystery and faith. On top of that, I've been unable to discover any evidence that leads me to believe in a future life.

ALL FISH HAVE BONES

Having established my philosophical beliefs, I would submit that this perspective is just one of a myriad of facets of who I am and my unbelief does not wholly define me or any other non-believer. I am a composite of many factors, only one of which is unbelief.

I did not arrive at this conclusion easily. Several years of copious reading, research, and considerable contemplation preceded this decision. I have not formally studied theology, except for religion classes in high school, nor do I have access to any special revelation. However, for seven plus decades I have participated, observed and experienced the effects of religion and I believe that background, coupled with research, gives me some standing to write about it.

Skepticism and disillusionment with religion or belief in God was not a childhood experience. I was raised by a Catholic mother and a Lutheran father who eventually converted to Catholicism. My education and early moral influence was from Catholic schools. Religion was not discussed at home; my religious practice was confined to going to school and attending mass on Sunday.

I enjoyed an uncomplicated childhood, apart from the guilt dispensed at school and church. I attended Catholic grade school and high school, taught by Immaculate Heart of Mary nuns. My mother, brother, two sisters and I attended mass every Sunday at St. Thomas Catholic Church staffed by Redemptorist priests. I was an altar boy and received the Boy Scout Ad Altare Dei medal award for service to my church.

I was baptized, took my first Holy Communion, was confirmed, and married in the Catholic Church. I went regularly to confession and communion. I am a 3rd Degree Knight of Columbus. I have received five of the seven Catholic Church sacraments; obviously I'm not a priest, so Holy Orders is out and I'm not in a hurry to receive the sacrament of the sick and dying just yet.

As a youth I was a committed Catholic, a product of my environment. I functioned under the belief that my existence was the result of a supernatural being and if I obeyed the laws of the Catholic Church I would go to heaven when

Introduction

I died. As children, we weren't expected to understand this mystery. Ironically, adults don't understand it either. As an adult, I continued to faithfully attend mass every Sunday until recently. Between us, my wife and I have 28 years of Catholic education and 149 years of attending church services.

I was well educated in Catholic school. I learned reading, writing, math, science and how to speak proper English. The curriculum was sufficiently rigorous to prepare me for college. The downside was the atmosphere of guilt that accompanies a Catholic education.

The nuns in our school, supplemented by priests, regularly dispensed guilt and fear of spending eternity in Hell for even minor transgressions along with the 3 R's. According to them, due to a misunderstanding in the mythic Garden of Eden, we humans had a pre-existing guilt condition. Guilt was never the subject of required courses but rather an integral "stealth" component of a Catholic education. Religious indoctrination included a constant reminder that anything pleasurable was probably sinful. Our "immortal souls" were in constant danger!

The nuns, who had dedicated their entire lives to God, had an appropriate moral aphorism for any situation during the school day. "The road to Hell is paved with good intentions." "An idle mind is the devil's workshop." "God's last name is not dammit." "Offer it up (to God)." This applied to any misfortune that occurred in your life. These moral adages, even after seven decades, still ring in my ears and are indelibly etched in my brain.

Sexuality in a Catholic school was nonexistent; girls wore uniforms: non-form fitting, long, blue dresses and white blouses buttoned to the neck. Boys became ankle guys – that was the only feminine skin showing. Cleavage was a no-no. Girls arriving at dances with even a hint of décolletage were promptly offered a shawl to cover up the offending skin. Boys knew girls attended their school because the girls wore dresses, had long hair and high-pitched voices but it required a vivid imagination to ponder the feminine mystique.

The nuns could and did use physical and mental punishment to maintain control of large classes. Many boys and a few girls received a rap on the knuckles with a ruler for misbehavior, but mental threats had an even greater impact.

I attended early grade school in a converted house. The nuns constantly reminded us that misbehavior would result in banishment to the "rat cellar," a basement under the house that our imaginations embellished. This terrified me. I learned to hate school and devised numerous ruses to get out of class. One of my classics was a request to go the bathroom, which was across the street from the schoolhouse. Once out the door, I walked straight home and told my mother it was a church holiday. She bought it until she noticed there were no other kids in the neighborhood, which led to a prompt return to the classroom.

Looking back on my childhood fears, I should be grateful that I was not schooled by the Sisters of Mercy in Ireland, whose name is the height of irony. Their documented emotional and physical abuse on young children is unspeakable.

Mortal sin was a ticket to eternal punishment in Hell, and even skipping mass on Sunday was considered a mortal sin, requiring a trip to the confessional to be forgiven. Long lines were routine outside the confessional box on Saturday evening since communion on Sunday was unavailable to those "living in mortal sin." The confessional lines symbolized of the fear of Hell instilled by church authorities. Sin removed one from a "state of grace" with God and if you died in this condition purgatory was probable and Hell was likely.

A prevailing characteristic of Catholicism is the number of compulsory requirements to be a member in good standing, requirements which failure to perform was considered sinful. Obligatory church attendance at Sunday Mass, regular attendance at confession, and frequent reception of Holy Communion are but a few of the regulations to be obeyed by the congregation.

As I reflect on my childhood, I have great difficulty comprehending that missing Mass on Sunday was a mortal sin punishable by eternity in Hell! This is a quintessential example of the absurdity of Catholic doctrine. It is illogical that failure to attend church services on Sunday was so egregious

Introduction

that one was doomed for eternity. The church taught deliberate failure in the obligation to attend Mass was a *grave sin* (my italics). A trip to the confessional was required to atone for this flagrant infraction of church doctrine. This preposterous obligation was so ingrained in ardent Catholics that my wife and I, even when on vacation, would diligently seek out a Catholic church to attend Mass.

I am baffled and frustrated that I didn't come to my current religious insights sooner. In hindsight, it is almost impossible to believe that educated adults (myself included), though deceived and manipulated as children, continue believing these bizarre doctrines.

Since childhood, we were exposed to the theological "mumbo jumbo" of our church leaders. The chronic anxiety and confusion created by this religious experience was palpable and unnecessary. The guilt dispensed in school during the week was reinforced by priests on Sunday. We were told we were all sinners and only through contrition, humble obedience to church rules and regulations, and the benevolence of our creator would we ever enjoy a pleasant afterlife. Strict obedience to God was a requirement for salvation. We were continually reminded by priests and nuns that the most important thing in life was to save our souls for the afterlife.

The impact of words uttered by religious authorities has a profound impact on the vivid imaginations of young people and forms indelible impressions. It borders on impossible for a child not to be influenced by adults dressed in bulky, black clerical garb, priests in cassocks and nuns in habits with yards of rosary beads cascading from waist bands, delivering frightening spiritual lectures. They were imposing, intimidating, authoritative figures. In childhood, the opinions of our elders are sacred and we have no past experience to challenge their views. It has been experimentally demonstrated that false beliefs in children may persist into adulthood, particularly where non scientific ideologies are transmitted by trustworthy religious sources (Bloom and Weisberg, 2007).

There are sufficient ugly realities in the world that young people do not need their vivid imaginations burdened with pictorial images of the "burning fires of perdition," yet the tableau of Hell was routinely and dramatically illustrated in school, limited only by the imagination of the speaker. Introducing young children to religion by scaring them with fairy tales of the netherworld; traumatizing pliant, preadolescent minds with spooky religious beliefs and horror stories about the dire consequences of failure to abide by religious rules and regulations is a cruel and subtle form of child abuse. I resent religious authorities who instill fear in impressionable young children with embellished fictions of Hell and eternal damnation for trivial misbehavior and minor infractions of silly man-made religious rules.

My religious upbringing was informed by Catholic priests and nuns who were celibate and lived in cloistered rectories and convents. They were rarely seen away from church and school grounds. I recall two sightings of priests away from church grounds in my youth. A young priest came to the beach one summer and swam with us, and one evening I noticed two priests having coffee in a restaurant downtown. These sightings were remarkable because they were unusual. We never saw nuns away from school or the convent.

Celibacy has not always been mandatory for Catholic priests. It is a senseless doctrine that frustrates the natural sexual expression of males and females and serves no observable spiritual benefit. In fact, priests in the Eastern Rite can marry and many Episcopal priests who convert to Catholicism are married with families. In the early church, priests, bishops and even Popes were married. Jesus never suggested an all-male priesthood. The Council of Trent (1545-63) established that celibacy laws were not Divine laws but Church laws, but celibacy was still a requirement for the priesthood. Prior to celibacy requirements, Church assets could be inherited by the families of priests. A case can be made that celibacy is less a spiritual tradition to imitate Jesus than a pragmatic policy to preserve Church assets. A lifelong commitment living a celibate life in isolation is not normal human behavior.

The environment of one's youth is critically important for intellectual and social development and has a profound impression on judgment and thinking

Introduction

processes. I'm convinced that many unrealistic and illogical ecclesiastical pronouncements issued from the Vatican Curia are the result of the selection and training process that the Catholic church uses to prepare young men for the priesthood.

The first stage of the path to the priesthood is the self-selection by young boys who are apparently unfazed by the prospect of a life of poverty, obedience, isolation, and celibacy in an all-male environment. Young men studying for the priesthood attend high school and college at seminaries, isolated from their families, friends, women and the realities of everyday life. This education and indoctrination — living and learning while insulated from exposure to the real world — has to affect their intellectual maturation process. Isolating future leaders of the Church from reality is a disservice to the individual and the institution.

A monastic existence is hardly proper preparation for administering and leading a parish. Even after ordination, priests live alone or in cloistered communities. Yet they are expected upon ordination to immediately adjust to the real world and manage parishes, counsel parishioners on faith, morals, marriage and sexual issues.

Over the years I was associated with the Catholic church, I met many priests, some likable and some unsociable and unapproachable, but my exit from the church was never contingent on the personality of any single individual. I don't doubt the zeal, virtue, and dedication of the participants but question the practicality of the training protocol. It's difficult to imagine that this preparation is an optimal education strategy for dealing with difficulties encountered in the modern world. It may be responsible in some way for the thinking process that goes into formulating church policy. The contemporary Catholic tradition of only ordaining celibate males reinforces the belief of the laity that modernity is a distant objective of the Church.

During my youth, I had several occasions to go the rectory where the priests lived. The public was not allowed beyond the waiting room. The dim lighting and monotone dark décor provided a melancholy atmosphere. It was a gloomy place to spend one's life.

ALL FISH HAVE BONES

The landscape of twenty centuries of Catholic Church history is littered with shameful illustrations of leadership failures, intellectual ineptness and scandalous misdeeds. Examples of both spiritual and secular blunders abound. The Church has betrayed its followers by ordaining and entrusting corrupt Popes, dishonest bishops, and deceitful priests to guide the Catholic faith community. The Vatican has repeatedly failed to acknowledge and respect major scientific discoveries, persecuting the scientists rather than accepting their findings. In pursuit of heretics, the Church initiated the Inquisition, causing misery and suffering by persecuting and torturing innocent people, and executing or imprisoning those who objected to Church orthodoxy. The Crusades were an unprecedented demonstration of military force employed to further the Catholic faith and combat infidels.

This disreputable past, coupled with the Church's controversial, archaic approach to modern social issues, makes one skeptical of the integrity and objectivity of future ecclesiastical pronouncements. It is astonishing that Catholicism has survived its history.

Discussing religion is always argumentative but, excepting a few solipsist philosophers, there is usually agreement on the existence of the universe and humans as obvious facts. The creation of the universe began with two unlikely scenarios. Was it a random accident of nature or the purposeful creation of a supernatural force that has always existed? Both alternatives seem highly improbable and farfetched. Two explanations of the existence of humans on planet Earth are the mystical, supernatural notion of God, and the rational, scientific solution. This book will examine the plausibility of and the evidence for these two options.

In Ecclesiastes 1:9 (*New American Bible*), we are told there is nothing new under the sun. I believe the advances and discoveries of science contradict this Biblical phrase and diminishes, if not eliminates, the need for a supernatural explanation of the existence of the universe.

Using the "fish question" as a metaphor for life may be asking a lot from a dead fish, but it's a start. My fish-and-bones experience is a challenge to

Introduction

examine life, take nothing for granted, and think for yourself. In our youth, much of what we learn is taught to us by authority figures. Because of our naiveté and limited experience in the world, we come to rely on teachers, clerics, and parents for guidance. Fish bones can represent the obstacles we encounter in life.

Question assumptions. Be skeptical of pronouncements from authority figures. Applying logic and reasoning to examine serious questions both broadly and in great detail can open new intellectual vistas. Research difficult problems.

Detecting the bones requires an examination of the fish. We can ask questions, analyze answers, examine evidence, decide on courses of action, arrive at conclusions, and make decisions. Most of us have sufficient intellect and curiosity to examine life. Let's see what lessons we can learn about life from a dead fish on a young boy's plate.

This book can be viewed as a tool for those seeking spiritual liberation, using the fish and bones metaphor as a template for examining important religious issues. There is irony in this since the fish motif is prominently featured in Bible stories and is one of the central icons of Christianity.

Writing this book was cathartic, but also difficult. This is not because I am uncertain of my beliefs, but because public expression of these beliefs has the potential to alienate family and friends. As a recovering Catholic, I am trying to intellectually reconcile six decades of religious indoctrination, boring Sunday homilies, required confessions, strict obedience to rules about fasting and abstinence and guilt with my current rational view of religion and the supernatural. This documents my disaffection with religion; my pilgrimage from committed Catholic believer to nonbeliever, from religious certainty to skepticism and confusion to conviction. It is an attempt to validate my unbelief and seek reasonable answers to spiritual questions.

I have been a participant in religion and more recently a skeptical observer, as I abandoned belief and began to contemplate my religious experience and those of others. I have the advantage of viewing the religious experience from inside and out. My farewell to God and organized religion was a liberating experience. I have no regrets, except to wish that I had arrived at this decision earlier in life.

A quest for a life with purpose and meaning is a fundamental, lifelong process for most people. We live in a complex world. Our entry and departure from the planet are random events over which we have no control. A philosophical binary confronting humanity is, *can the world be explained by science and reason or do we rely on the metaphysical and supernatural?*

This book is devoted to exploring this topic and explaining my analysis and conclusion. I propose that traditional religious affiliations and doctrine may not be a satisfactory answer for everyone. I hope to motivate readers to examine their current religious beliefs and ask themselves if those beliefs are sufficient to use as guideposts for life.

I write this regretting that I knew not nearly enough about my parents, grandparents, and ancestors. During childhood, you don't have much interest in ancestry details, and in adulthood, it's often too late for inquiry. What I have experienced and learned in my long life may have some value for my children and grandchildren. I'd like to leave them with observations they might read and learn something about me they didn't know. My further goal is to inspire other readers to critically examine life issues and arrive at reasoned conclusions.

At a minimum, I expect that this manuscript will amuse my children and siblings and hopefully inform my grandchildren. It's my hope that these musings will help my grandchildren make informed decisions about religion sooner in life than I did.

There is an old African proverb: "When an old man dies, a library burns to the ground." It's pretentious for me to claim library status, but I may have accumulated enough experiences to be a bookmobile idled by a flat tire on the side of the road. On the shelves is an anthology of observations, events, experiences and philosophical musings accumulated over the years.

This book examines the existential question of human life on the planet earth from two perspectives: science and reason versus faith and mystery. The premise of this book is simple, that by using observation, reason, and science,

Introduction

a plausible conclusion can be reached that God does not exist. Although neither believers in God nor nonbelievers can assemble sufficient evidence to emphatically prove or disprove the existence of God, one can examine the available data and arrive at a reasonable judgment. Hopefully, this narrative will convey a meaningful message that will engage and challenge readers to reflect and examine their own circumstances.

My urge to write this book is twofold: writing gives clarity to my thoughts and it may serve as a catalyst to others who are struggling with their spiritual beliefs and seeking spiritual guidance in their lives. The ideas expressed here are an accumulation of experiences, observations, and doubts coupled with the reading of considerable literature on religion, philosophy, and belief systems. This manuscript may also function as a survey of the literature on the topics discussed leading those interested toward further research.

I am solely responsible for the content of *All Fish Have Bones*. The thoughts, ideas, and opinions expressed here are mine, but they have been considerably informed by authors and books recorded in the bibliography. These writers helped shape and focus my thinking, gave substance to my doubts and musings, and made me feel less of a pariah for questioning conventional religious orthodoxy. My debt to these authors is best expressed by the elegant prose of Henry David Thoreau, who wrote, "I think it will be found that he who speaks with most authority on a given subject is not ignorant of what has been said by his predecessors. He will take his place in a regular order, and substantially add his own knowledge to the knowledge of previous generations."

What I hope to provide is a coherent view of my evolution from believer to nonbeliever over the years. My expectation is that *All Fish Have Bones* will provide a compelling, theoretical framework to examine belief systems for readers at a crossroad in their life who may be frustrated, disillusioned, and struggling with their current religious views and looking for a road map for living the good life without Divine guidance.

ALL FISH HAVE BONES

CHAPTER ONE
CHALLENGING RELIGIOUS DOCTRINE

Don't believe a teaching just because you've heard it from a man who's supposed to be holy, or because it's contained in a book supposed to be holy, or because all your friends and neighbors believe it. But whatever you've observed and analyzed for yourself and found to be reasonable and good, then accept that and put it into practice.

— *Buddha*

This epigraph encapsulates the fish and bones metaphor. It's a logical fallacy to believe something is true just because many people believe it. Even in our information age, it is difficult to be an independent thinker. Our brain appears to understand the modern world yet we cling to ancient myths in the hope that they are true. The rapid advancement in scientific discovery and acceleration of knowledge accumulation, coupled with the capability of social media to rapidly dispense information, dazzles the human intellect. We're bombarded by electronic gadgetry dispensing news, sports, opinion, and entertainment. We have multiple distractions in life that allow us to pursue the trivial while neglecting the meaningful. British philosopher Bertrand Russell (1872-1970) stated it clearly: "Many people would sooner die than think. In fact, they do so."

Today in the U.S., questioning orthodox religion is not a popular pursuit in the religious atmosphere and doing so risks offending some devoted believers. But critically examining religion, affords us an opportunity to choose reason over revelation and reality over fantasy. I don't have access to any special revelation nor do I wish to convince anyone against their will of what I have come to believe. I have no wish to be dismissive, or to insult or critique anyone's religious beliefs or ideology. There is no intent to persuade anyone that my view is an appropriate belief for them, nor to dissuade anyone from their present belief system. I fear that in writing this book some cherished relationships may be damaged beyond repair. This I regret. I hope not to intrude or cause any pain or distress in any reader's life.

Many people find emotional comfort, solace, and fellowship in religious settings and pastoral guidance has been crucial in many lives. For many, religion offers inspiration, hope, and a social affiliation with like-minded people. I have no quarrel with anyone who maintains religious beliefs of any faith. However, for those who may harbor doubts, I suggest looking past the culture of religion and obfuscation of theology and employing science and reason as appropriate tools for discovering the secrets of life.

If this book has a subtext, it is to serve as a template for anyone who may harbor doubts about their current beliefs or disillusionment with their religious affiliation and its doctrines. It can function as a catalyst to aid in analyzing and exploring their own faith. My hope is that there is sufficient empowerment in these pages to assist readers in examining their lives and determining if they are comfortable and satisfied with their religious beliefs. Beginning a dialog with yourself may uncover some overlooked ideas that you have ignored.

Challenging Religious Doctrine

If disbelief finally does become a reality in your mind, it will be a tangible moment in your intellectual maturation process. You will become aware of a significant change in your life, a poignant sense of a discontinuity from your former life, an estrangement from religion and the start of a new adventure.

I believe one of the principle reasons religion has persisted throughout the ages is that many of us are philosophically shallow, reluctant to engage our brain power to question, ponder, and seriously reflect on material dispensed to us by religious clerics. As the Buddha noted, we are influenced by the beliefs of those in our community. *It must be true if everyone believes it.* We accept religious teachings on faith, without question. The result is a shallow understanding of serious philosophical issues affecting our entire existence.

Yet it is imperative to examine the origin of our beliefs and determine if they are in synchrony with our current worldview. Failure as an adult to critically examine and challenge youthful religious beliefs is suggestive of stagnated intellectual development.

Over time, organized religions accumulate calcified laws, rules, regulations, and traditions that reinforce the original concept of the religious belief while obscuring attempts by believers to critically examine the salient issues. Almost from birth, young people in a Christian household are acculturated into these beliefs. Religion can then become an unintentional routine; a habit from childhood that only occupies a few hours a week and never gets closely examined. We become robotic in our religious lives. We fall into a rut. Attending church on Sunday, listening to hymns, prayers, and homilies, becomes a habitual activity, devoid of meaning.

As we continue our affiliation with a religious organization, our religious belief diminishes as a robust intellectual ideology and becomes a mindless social habit. We attend Mass on Sunday, donate money to build a new church, help out at soup kitchens and funeral dinners, deprive ourselves during Lent, all the while attending these functions as habit, forgetting the core concept and doctrine of our chosen church.

ALL FISH HAVE BONES

Most of us in Western society have experienced and been influenced by religion but few have expended the necessary effort to intellectually study and diligently investigate the historical basis and origin of religious doctrine. Rational contemplation of theological questions is not a prominent feature of childhood reasoning.

Young people are occupied with the trivial, pragmatic aspects of life: learning to read and write, passing school tests, discovering the opposite sex, the affects of alcohol on the human body, and obtaining a driver's license. The rut deepens as we mature. We become distracted by career, family, friends and personal pursuits. The underlying religious routines increase in intensity as we age and become very difficult to discard. It's difficult to re-route ourselves in a different direction. Religious dogma, firmly embedded from childhood, is slow to erode. Having a sincere and reflective soliloquy on existential questions may open new vistas on life that have the potential to enrich the human experience.

Childhood beliefs are difficult to eradicate. As an example, let's examine a plant we're all familiar with: the common dandelion (*Taraxacum officinale*). As children living in the U.S., we learn from adult authorities that the dandelion is a pesky weed, not a beautiful flower; and not just any weed, but a noxious weed that needs to be eradicated at any cost. As adults, we grumble and complain when we see this pervasive nuisance in our yards and spend huge sums of money on poison at the hardware store in an attempt to exterminate this plant from our fields of vision. We vigorously hand dig these colorful blossoms from our gardens as soon as they appear.

However, the dandelion is not intrinsically a weed, but a lovely, attractive yellow flower, completely edible, (roots, leaves, and flowers) that appears in our lawns every spring, without human assistance. In some cultures, it enjoys a lofty status and is valued for its medicinal properties. But many of us go through life believing it is an annoying weed, because some authority figure told us it was a weed when we were children.

By altering our perspective now that we are adults, we can reframe our attitude and recognize the dandelion as a beautiful flower, a harbinger of

Challenging Religious Doctrine

spring and a welcome blanket of color in our neighborhoods! Imagine the delight, reverence and respect we might have for the dandelion if we hadn't been indoctrinated in childhood that it was a weed! Let the lovely dandelion symbolize the intractability of childhood beliefs.

Growing up with religion doesn't require growing old with religion. Your childhood history need not be your adult destiny. For many of us, religion has a predictable path. We are born into it, taught as school children to never question its authority, and as adults become apathetic about it. Religion becomes more of a social obligation than a religious experience.

Our adult religious beliefs have considerable ties to our birth circumstances and family environment but do not have to continue to be dependent on these circumstances. You were born as a *tabula raza*, a clean slate without knowledge. Then, if you grew up as I did, just as you reached the age of reason you were informed that you were imperfect and a sinner, even though during the first years of life there is precious little opportunity for egregious acts of bad behavior!

Critical thinking can offer relief from the intellectual bondage of our childhood beliefs. Beliefs are important to analyze because they affect not only how you think, but how you act. A philosophy of life is a vital component in a feedback loop between mind and behavior. What you believe affects how you live, behave, and interact with others. Your religious faith is a major factor in this cause and effect cycle. Critical thinking allows an examination of ideological phenomena and the rejection of principles and doctrines that are flawed and illogical.

Belief in a transcendent deity is not a transient impulse but a life altering commitment. Religion is easily defined as habit, hope and happiness. We are comfortable in our religious rut, harboring hope that our earthly life is not all there is, and maintaining faith in the potential for an afterlife of pleasantness with friends and relatives. Plants are phototropic and tilt toward the sun to fuel the photosynthetic process that gives them life. Humans appear to nurture a spiritual tropism, leaning toward a God figure that promises a life extension.

Disillusionment with religion affects different people at various periods in their lives. I suspect most of us have periods when we vacillate between belief and skepticism. But, it's difficult to sever the comfortable tether to a lifelong dependency on a religion. Questioning religious beliefs held from childhood, instilled by parents and reinforced by religious authority figures, is emotional and intimidating. Children are essentially captives of their parent's dogma. We were taught as children that God was responsible for everything and we believed it. Western civilization — culture, history, art and music — and Christianity are inextricably intertwined and it requires self-assurance to challenge the existence of God in the face of this history. Questioning the existence of God and the value of religion in the U.S., a Judeo-Christian country, can be stigmatizing, with the potential side effect of alienating friends and family.

For many of us, religion is significant in defining who we are. Religion is always a serious topic of discussion. It explores the mysteries of existence. It is a clash of emotion, fact, and fantasy. Disbelief raises complex issues. Weaning ourselves from Yahweh requires addressing topics such as meaninglessness and recognizing that there is no afterlife.

I imagine that most religious folks enjoy believing in their faith, but few are interested in probing deeply into its doctrine. This seems similar to people who fail to see a physician because they're afraid they might learn they have a serious medical condition. Exposure to iconoclastic points of view may be uncomfortable, but life is essentially exposure to competing viewpoints from which you have to choose those that appear rational. I believe it is best to discover if you are sick and begin treatment and to examine your beliefs and begin the process to determine if they are still valid for you.

One should not hesitate to probe disturbing intellectual questions for answers that may aid in discovering a rational and intelligent philosophy of life. It can be intellectually stimulating for a person to occasionally engage in a contrary thought. What a tragedy it would be at the end of life, to realize that you never seriously examined the question of existence or your religious ideology and that you had surrendered your intellectual integrity to religious authorities and their interpretation of a speculative, metaphysical uncertainty.

Challenging Religious Doctrine

The German philosopher Immanuel Kant (1724-1804) believed that we ought to think for ourselves, free from the influences of authority figures. Becoming a religious hostage, chasing someone else's dream, is squandering your life. This problem can be avoided if you allocate some of your time and energy to appraise and question your religious convictions and determine if what you routinely profess to believe is in actuality what you do believe.

A rigorous examination of a long-held belief system is going to require an intense look into the past for answers and a speculative glance at our future. The Roman god Janus, whose two faces look in the directions of future and past, can be a useful and inspirational model as we question the origin of our religious beliefs and look to the possibilities of our future. Janus, who looked both ways, was the god of transformation, beginnings and endings, and was regularly called upon to preside over Roman functions (Wasson).

Our ancestral culture and tradition need not dictate our destiny toward a belief system. Each individual has the opportunity to accept or reject the religious beliefs of his ancestors. Religious culture, although prominent in one's life, is not hereditary. Although it may have been inappropriate and blasphemous to question religious authority as a child, adults can make their own decisions and choose their own beliefs. As adults, it is sensible to examine the theology of our youth, particularly one branding us as imperfect beings prone to sinfulness. *Humans are obviously fallible, but not the moral degenerates that religion teaches.*

Upbringing is a fairly good predictor of adult religious behavior. The incubator for religious belief is our childhood environment. We quickly become able to think and see after birth, but many of us are immersed in a set of values and beliefs at an early age by authority figures that leaves an indelible lifetime impression. No matter how tenaciously you cling to the idea that your religious beliefs reflect a conscious choice, it's highly unlikely that your early childhood religious beliefs were original and the product of robust analytics. I didn't consciously choose Catholicism as my faith. Like most of us, I was born and raised in the religion and tradition of my parents (in this case, my mother). I grew up and was indoctrinated with Augustinian Catholicism: Original Sin, salvation only with the grace of God, Heaven for the righteous, Hell for the wretched, the restorative nature of confession and the power of prayer. Unless you were particularly precocious, the religious beliefs of youth remained with you at least until early adulthood, a result of your parent's beliefs and your community.

The "geography of belief" probably determined your childhood religion. If you were born in Poland, the Philippines, Brazil, Mexico, Ireland or Italy you are likely a Catholic. Scandinavian children are likely to be Lutherans. Children born in Israel are predominantly Jewish. If you were born in Russia or China under Communist rule, you may be an atheist. Those born in the Middle East are likely Muslims. If you were born in the United States in the 20th century, it is probable that you are a Catholic or Protestant Christian. Note that you had little influence on where you were born, but where on the planet the inscrutable sperm and egg dance took place was a major determinant of your childhood religious beliefs and possibly the philosophy that guides your whole life. It was an accident of geography. Your heritage of faith, however, does not have to be the ultimate determining influence in your life.

Blind faith — a God dependency — requires an unthinking allegiance and obedience and inhibits our ability to logically address imbedded religious beliefs. Slavish adherence to traditional models, rules, regulations and customs tends to stifle creativity. Intellectual consciousness, on the other hand, can lead to reevaluating one's belief system as part of a continuing process of interpretation. One avenue to intellectual maturity is reliance on one's own cognitive abilities, life experiences, and common sense.

Perhaps our greatest asset as humans is our ability to wonder. We are an inquisitive species. We are perplexed by our existence and the wonders of the universe and seek answers to why we exist and whether we are alone in the universe. It's a reasonable pursuit to search for meaning in one's life.

Suggestions made here to rigorously examine a lifelong belief may trigger a defensive reaction to protect and preserve an individual's core values and to resist a potential identity loss. A perfectly rational reaction may be to construct an intellectual bulwark as a safeguard against assertions that are contrary to your current beliefs. Rejecting new ideas and retreating to a safe mental place is normal when you are asked to consider a new understanding of who you are. Few of us are comfortable with discarding what we have come to believe is a viable philosophical approach to living.

Many people of faith have never been exposed to factual criticism of their beliefs. Having believed all of our lives that God was lurking like a satellite in the sky, watching and cataloging our activities, may cause some discomfort. Fear of cosmic retribution for questioning God's existence may surface some angst.

I don't suggest that analytical scrutiny of youthful beliefs automatically presages a change in a person's philosophy of life, but a review of this nature should, at a minimum, provide a reaffirmation of those beliefs, and could cause a modification, or complete change. The ideas in this book may offer that opportunity.

To begin the introspective journey into the place of religion in our lives will be intellectually challenging and possibly even disagreeable at times. But it is a necessary step in the process of discovering our true identity. We may be perplexed, astonished, frightened, perturbed, saddened, relieved, joyful or emancipated at what we find. There will be times when you may feel like the yellow fish on the cover, swimming against the rest of the school, questioning long-established traditions and conventional wisdom.

Tommy Dewar (1864-1930), the Scottish whisky distiller who built the Dewar name into an international success, once said, "Minds are like parachutes, they work best when open." Approaching the concept of religion with an open mind may provide a refreshing experience. One of the opportunities in examining one's religious belief is being open to new ideas and not what someone told you to think. A periodic, thoughtful examination of concepts acquired in childhood may unleash refreshing insights and introduce new and stimulating understandings.

Even though we are adults, there is always some childhood residue within us. What seemed logical when we were children may not have the same relevance in adulthood. We may want to consider modification or — in some cases — complete replacement of previously held convictions.

Any pursuit toward a new philosophical belief system begins with an unfettered mind. Relaxing an attachment to a preconceived ideology allows one to objectively contemplate alternative explanations for existential questions. Liberating ourselves from fixated religious beliefs and opening our minds to the possibilities of an alternate explanation to the origin of the universe and the appearance of humans on earth is a powerful catalytic event on the journey to a rigorous examination of long-held beliefs. Buddhists believe wisdom begins with observing, studying and reading, then intellectually examining and reflecting on what you have learned. That is what our "fish" is advocating.

Howard Bloom, writing in *The God Problem* (2012), offers a suggestion for understanding the world. "If you want to know the patterns with which God or cosmic creativity runs the world, if you want to know the rules and laws of our earth and of the heavens above, you have to open your eyes. Facts count more than theory." He continues, ". . . blind faith and a God intoxication inhibits our ability to logically address our imbedded religious beliefs. Real-world experiments reveal more than any letter from St. Paul or Biblical account of the life of Isaiah."

Unlike Newton's instant discovery of gravity, doubt seldom begins with an epiphany, but builds up slowly over time with no discernible beginning and a glacial pace of growth. Disbelief rarely commences with a "Eureka" moment. Its origin is elusive, not an impulsive event, and it is unlikely you will remember when it began.

I don't recall any sudden impulse to forsake Catholicism and discontinue going to Sunday Mass. During young and middle adulthood, the stirrings of apostasy never received my conscious attention. My transformation from committed Catholic to unbelief was the result of slow-crawling skepticism and doubt that eventually overcame my subconscious resistance built up over decades of practicing Catholic ideology. As I matured, I noticed friends and colleagues leading happy and moral lives without any religious affiliation.

Challenging Religious Doctrine

These observations initiated my quest for an authentic philosophy of life that was appropriate for me. It was only after I retired that I had time to address my concerns and think and read about religion.

When I seriously began to explore religious doctrine, my 33-year career as an investigator considerably informed my thinking and provided emotional and reflective skills that were instrumental. My training as a Counterintelligence Agent in the Army and Special Agent in the Federal Bureau of Investigation (FBI) and experience conducting program evaluations supplied me with the tools and aptitude to be skeptical of first impressions, question assumptions, challenge traditions, and seek out facts about important issues. Investigating cases and evaluating the efficiency and effectiveness of programs required collecting evidence and being careful not to rush to judgment after initial observations at crime scenes.

Researching the God question lead me to read Richard Dawkins' book, *The God Delusion*. This book, written by a distinguished scientist, was extremely helpful in reinforcing my skepticism and helping me understand that I was neither alone in my disbelief nor deranged. Beside *Walden*, it's the only book I ever read twice! I also recommend the books of Christopher Hitchens, Sam Harris, Bart Ehrman, and Daniel Dennett for eloquent and scholarly approaches to the belief question. These books were instrumental during my deliberations and quest for certitude on existential questions.

As I reflect on my nascent skepticism of religion, I find the tipping point was the inconsistencies found in the Bible. Skepticism is the first step in the questioning process and mine had its incubation during Sunday sermons on Bible verses that didn't make any sense; passages that were clearly myths, fables or legends offered from the pulpit as foundational material for preaching faith and belief. It was difficult to reconcile the contradictory messages of love, hate, hostility, and vengeance that appeared in some form or another in almost every book. I was exasperated every Sunday listening to time-worn, coma-inducing platitudes and endless puerile homilies that defied logic and reason when contrary information was readily available to any diligent reader. I rarely experienced an informed and eloquent sermon on pertinent church doctrine. Sunday homilies seem disconnected from reality and the everyday life the faithful experience.

I believe most parishioners doze or daydream during boring Sunday homilies. I, on the other hand, began to follow almost every word; seeking inconsistencies, illogical arguments and silly assertions. For me, it became humorous sport. On the way to breakfast after church, I gleefully pointed out to my wife flaws I detected in the sermon. She politely indulged my antics.

It began to appear counterintuitive to live in fear of eternal punishment from a benevolent God who ostensibly had my best interests at heart yet required continuous adulation and obsequious behavior from his followers. God seems to crave attention. In Romans 14:11, he commands, "As I live, says the Lord, 'every knee shall bend before me, and every tongue shall give praise to God.'" "For as heavens are high above the earth, so surpassing is His kindness toward those who *fear* Him." (my italics) (Psalm 103: 11-12).

Genuflecting as you enter and leave a Catholic church is a requirement of the Catholic faith. The first four of the Ten Commandments are obligatory requirements for God's glorification and veneration. I am hard-pressed to understand the convoluted logic of creating humans, subjecting them to pain and suffering, tainting them with sin, and then offering salvation to some and not to others. This is a diabolical God.

My religious upbringing indoctrinated me with the idea that God was responsible for everything. This seemed plausible to a young mind, which suppressed any curiosity to examine alternative explanations. My earliest doubt about my faith was in high school when I began to question Church doctrine. The mother of one of my high school girlfriends got divorced at an early age. Because of the Catholic Church teaching on divorce and remarriage, she remained single for the rest of her life. It seemed insensitive to deprive this woman of the opportunity for remarriage.

The Catholic Church considers itself the one true church and traces its origin to St. Peter, the first Pope. The Catholic Church has always exhibited a sense of spiritual smugness, a certitude that Catholicism was the only true practice of Christianity and all other religious beliefs were either fatally flawed or simply wrong. In my youth, the insular Catholic Church disapproved of

Challenging Religious Doctrine

attendance at religious events — weddings, funerals and other rituals — at other churches since it might bring "scandal" to our Catholic faith!

The challenge to understanding any religious doctrine begins with a knowledge and awareness of the history of the doctrine and the structure of the church organization. Historically, there has been a serious intellectual gulf between church authorities and the laity. The Catholic Church is an authoritarian church with a well-defined hierarchy and a caste system that explicitly outlines the relationship and boundaries between the clergy and the laity. The power of the "Red Hats" (bishops and cardinals) is unquestioned; only the formally ordained can interpret the scriptures and establish Church doctrine. There is no balance in the relationship between the priesthood hierarchy and the laity, no communication, no exchange of ideas, no feedback loop.

"The Catholic Church teaches as a doctrine of faith that Christ gave the Church, in his apostles, a hierarchical structure of an episcopal nature and that within the hierarchy and the Church he established a primacy of authority in the successor of St. Peter" (Rodriguez). The Council of Trent (1545-1563) established the absolute authority of the Pope. This was reinforced at the First Vatican Council (1869-1870), which added the dogma of infallibility, that the Pope cannot err when he speaks on doctrines of faith and morals. The Second Vatican Council (1962-1965) gave increased responsibility to the laity, and lay ministers began serving in some Church posts, but the doctrinal apparatus of the Church remains with the Pope and his bishops.

The Pope and bishops operate under the premise that their authority is derived from the will of God and their role is to promulgate Catholic doctrine, at which the Pope is infallible. Functioning under the absolute authority of the Pope, the Church has an elitist male cadre of ordained bishops and priests, interpreting God's will and developing and maintaining doctrinal discipline. The Pope enjoys supreme power and jurisdiction over the entire church. The Pope and bishops are policy makers while priests and deacons dispense doctrine to the laity.

Nowhere is this separation more evident than in the encyclical *Vehementer Nos (On the French Law of Separation)*. This was written by Pope Pius X in response to the French passing a law in 1905 restricting religious freedom in France and confiscating church properties. The Pontiff is quite clear in the distinction between Catholic hierarchy and the laity.:

> It follows that the Church is essentially an *unequal* (italics in the original) society, that is, a society comprising two categories of persons, the Pastors and the flock, those who occupy a rank in different degrees of the hierarchy and the multitude of the faithful. So distinct are these categories that with the pastoral body only rests the necessary right and authority for promoting the end of the society and directing all its members towards that end; the one duty of the multitude is to allow themselves to be led, and, like a *docile flock* (my italics), to follow the Pastors.

This Papal proclamation certainly establishes the role of the laity and gives new meaning to the biblical notion of shepherds and sheep!

Understanding the theology of the priesthood helps make some sense of the privileges and power afforded to Catholic priests. The current model of Catholic priesthood separates the priest from his constituency — and reality. The act of ordination establishes a cadre of isolated, elitist clerics who minister to congregations with whom they have little contact and even less in common. Most parishioners, besides shaking hands as they leave church after Mass, have little personal contact with a priest.

The rite of ordination in the Catholic Church (the administering of the Sacrament of Holy Orders) has profound implications for both the young seminarian and the Church as an organization. The young man commits himself to a life of celibacy and service to God and the Catholic community. The Sacrament of Holy Orders elevates an ordinary individual to an exalted priesthood where he joins an exclusive, privileged group of men with absolute authority and mystical powers. According to Wilkes, the theology of the priesthood evolved during the Middle Ages. The formality of ordination fundamentally changed the concept of the priesthood from the Biblical notion of service to the religious community to a special status apart and above the people with certain "powers" — changing wine and bread into the body and blood of Jesus Christ — that the lay person did not have. "The priest, with his mystical powers to bring Christ down onto the altar at mass, was set apart from the people, who were obligated to do his bidding obediently. He was their leader; he stood in Christ's place."

A priest's lifestyle — isolated living, clerical garb, special forms of address (Reverend, The Most Reverend, Your Excellency, Your Eminence, Your Holiness,), anointed hands, and the mystical powers to forgive sin and convert wine and bread into blood and flesh — establishes an effective obstacle between the ordained and the laity. The tyranny of the anointed creates a communications barrier between the ordained and the laity. This makes it almost impossible for lay input to Church decisions. There is an abrupt bifurcation between clergy and the folks in the pews, the shepherds and the sheep. The separation between leaders and the led forecloses any constructive dialog on topical issues. The scriptural portrayal of a harmonious and protective relationship between the shepherd and his flock is no longer relevant.

Religion, as it is generally understood, is not a consensus result of the ideological yearnings of the people who adhere to a belief system but rather a package of doctrines developed, refined, and handed down to believers by an ecclesiastical hierarchy. Jesuit scholar and popular novelist, Andrew Greeley, in *Confessions of a Parish Priest* (1986), explains the Catholic version of religion:

> Does religion exist first of all in the heads of theologians, bishops, and priests and then, after it is taught, in the minds of the people? Or does it exist first of all in the experiences of the people and then in the reflections of the elites? In theological Catholicism of the last five hundred years there has been no doubt of the answer. The religious experience of the people is highly suspect. It must be purified, filtered, refined through the thought processes of theologians and Church leaders before it becomes acceptable as a manifestation of the presence of God. The essential mission of

the Church is to impose right doctrine on its people, not to listen to the people for the voice and presence of God.

Are we just pawns in the grand scheme of religious institutions?

There are several concepts of God among believers. Some believe God is a personal God who watches over the human race, answers prayers and is genuinely concerned about His creations. They have a direct relationship with this God. Others feel their God is a remote God who created the universe but allows it to be governed by natural laws, without intervention from above. Atheists don't believe in any mystical, supernatural deity.

Before continuing examination of my belief system, some definitions are in order:

A **Theist** is one who believes in a personal God, a supernatural deity who created the universe, everything in it, and is in control of human and nature's activities. This God will stand in judgment when we die and decide on reward or punishment depending on a person's behavior during their lifetime on earth. (In this book we will refer to God in the conventional mode as male, since we don't really have any idea of God's gender. Given the inconvenience and annoyance of menstruation and the pain associated with childbirth, it is highly unlikely God is female.)

A **Deist** is one who believes in an impersonal God, a supernatural deity who created the world but does not intervene in the operation of the universe, allowing it to function deterministically according to the laws of nature. Many of the founding fathers of the United States were deists.

A **Pantheist** is one who believes that the universe *is* God or a manifestation of God and sometimes many gods. God is seen in the flora and fauna that exists in the world.

An **Atheist** is one who does not believe in a supernatural deity and trusts that reason and science are sufficient to explain the functioning of the universe and its inhabitants.

An **Agnostic** is one who believes that human reason is incapable of determining if God exists; therefore, God is unknowable.

A **Secular Humanist** is one who rejects the notion of God but believes in the goodness of mankind and the capacity of humans for ethical and moral behavior without faith in God. While rejecting the idea of God, Humanists believe in the ability of science and philosophy to explain the world.

Humanism is eloquently defined by British philosopher A.C. Grayling in his book, *The God Argument* (2013):

> ... humanism premises the value of things human, without the assistance of illusions about anything supposedly beyond this world and its realities... It is about human life; it requires no belief in an afterlife. It is about this world; it requires no belief in another world. It requires no commands from divinities, no promise of reward or threats of punishment, no myths and rituals, either to make sense of things or to serve as a prompt to the ethical life.

A **Cultural (Catholic, Jew, or Protestant)** is a person who does not believe in God but because of birth, culture, education, or background has some allegiance to the history and traditions of that faith.

An **Intelligent Design** believer is one who believes that the universe and its inhabitants can be best explained by an intelligent supernatural designer. For them the extreme complexity of nature could not have been the result of pure chance.

Creationists are Biblical literalists who believe in a literal interpretation of the Bible – that God created the universe and everything in it exactly as it is described in the Book of Genesis. Creationists want to supplant evolutionary theory.

Ontology is the branch of philosophy that studies the nature of existence.

The explanation of my belief in the Introduction technically defines me as an atheist. However, "atheist" has a negative connotation and carries sufficient baggage that portrays its adherents in an unfair light. Therefore, I prefer the term secular humanist. The term "atheist" may be an impediment to nonbelievers who would like to publicly declare their non-belief, but do not wish to suffer the opprobrium attached to the term.

In a 2002 TED lecture, Richard Dawkins, a prominent atheist and Oxford professor of biology, suggested "secular humanism" is a more benevolent term than "atheism" and may induce the "outing" of more non-believers.

Religion has an unmatchable magnetism. It is a magic elixir combining imagination, faith, and emotion. We create images of God and Heaven in our imaginations, rely on faith that these images are real, and become emotionally attached and committed to them. Religion offers a continuation of life and an escape from death. Religion is often the default emotional crutch when crisis strikes. Religion also has a powerful stranglehold on its followers and sometimes interferes with commonsense reasoning.

I'm perplexed at the behavior of people at the scene of catastrophic events, such as airplane crashes, hurricanes or tornadoes. We often see a visibly distressed individual in front of a TV camera, standing in rubble and surrounded by abject devastation of what was once their home, thanking Jesus or God for sparing their life. Ostensibly, this God is the same God that just reduced their town to rubble and killed many of their neighbors and friends, yet singled them out to be spared. It's difficult to fathom divine benevolence in these disasters and more difficult to ascertain a rationale for indiscriminate destruction and the loss of life for some but not for others. The incongruous reaction of survivors is difficult to reconcile. God sure does work in mysterious ways! A more rational response might be anger, or better yet recognition, that this is simply the way the universe functions.

This book attempts to answer this question: Why has organized religion continued to flourish when scientific discoveries dispute the plausibility of a supernatural creator?

As we mature, most of us recognize the absurdity of cherished childhood beliefs in Santa Claus, Easter Bunny, Tooth Fairy, stork, talismans, dream catchers, leprechauns, elves, unicorns and pots of gold at the end of rainbows and relegate them to the dustbin of our childhood fantasies. As we mature, the logic and logistics of a jolly old gentleman in a red suit flying all over the world in a single night delivering toys to children by sliding down chimneys crumbles under close examination. A critical examination of religion shows that the concept of the supernatural contradicts the basic principles of the physical and biological sciences and common sense.

Challenging Religious Doctrine

We now know the earth is neither flat nor the center of the universe, blood eclipses of the moon do not signal the end of the earth, Bubonic Plague is not caused by miasmas (invisible vapors that emanated from swamps), and bloodletting is no longer a recommended medical remedy. Yet, with minimal available evidence, we cling tenaciously to belief in an unknowable, transcendent, unexplained, mysterious, invisible entity we call God.

I believe this fascination with the God concept is difficult to relinquish for eight reasons:

We are awestruck by the majesty of the universe, its diversity, and the assumed elevated stature of the human species.

Since the dawn of time, mankind has existed in a state of wonderment. For many, religion answers the hard questions and fills a void where science leaves us perplexed. Unfamiliar with science, we find it difficult to believe the universe is accidental and therefore must have been created by a complex, supernatural force. In the *Atheists Guide to Reality* (2011), Alex Rosenberg humorously points out: "There isn't any rhyme or reason to the universe. It's just one damn thing after another."

Fear of eternal punishment for immoral and unethical behavior.

The God of the Old Testament regularly punished his constituents and the God of the New Testament wasn't much better. We are continually reminded from the pulpit of our incorrigibility and sinfulness and the likelihood of some form of punishment for those transgressions. The ominous possibility of burning in the fires of Hell for all eternity instead of a comfortable lodging in Heaven is a powerful and compelling motivation to maintain a religious affiliation with some church. Religion offers a path to repentance, forgiveness, and opportunity to improve our behavior and attain salvation.

Religion has an irresistible attraction.

It assuages fear and anxiety of death and nourishes man's insatiable desire to live forever. The promise of immortality gives religion a magical allure. No one wants to die and the promise of a jolly life in heaven has an enchanting appeal. There, we are told, we will join all our loved ones who died before us and live happy and worry free for eternity. Without the promise of an afterlife, religion has little to offer to attract followers.

Each of us desires that someone genuinely and unequivocally loves and cares for us.

God fulfills that requirement. For many, religion is an incandescent beacon of hope, offering solace to those living a bleak existence. Religion offers a framework for life and support to those who might otherwise be marginalized in society.

The religious culture of our birth environment affects our early learning experience and indoctrination.

As children, we are respectful of authority figures and also gullible; a fertile environment for developing religious belief. As we grow up we are exposed to church liturgy, music, art, and sacraments. We associate with priests, clerics, pastors, and bishops who are ever present at major events in our lives. They preside at christenings, marriage and funerals — "hatching, matching and dispatching." They console and comfort. We participate in church rituals using vestments, holy water, miters, staffs, robes, music, incense, and candles. As altar boys, we referred to the pageantry that accompanied church services as "bells and smells."

We pray to saints, we pray to our dead relatives, we receive sacraments, we observe Holy Days of Obligation, obey rules of fasting and abstinence. We pray privately and publicly when tragedy and misfortune strikes.

This legacy of religious tradition is a pervasive influence, particularly during our youth, but traditions tend to calcify with age. As we grow into adulthood, our childhood perspectives travel with us. It is easy to become imprisoned in the lore and rubrics of childhood religious culture.

Churches are often central to social activities, including those that assist the less fortunate.

Affiliation with a church offers an opportunity to serve in soup kitchens, clothing outlets, and charitable activities, instilling feelings of accomplishment and an identity as a contributing member of the community. Additionally, churches offer opportunity for members to associate with each other during social and charitable functions. People with similar interests tend to gather together and religious organizations offer that opportunity. Cultural anthropologists tell us our evolution as a species conditions us to be attracted to "tribes," or groups of people with whom we share similar interests and beliefs. The church calendar becomes an indispensable part of life. In addition to Sunday services and baptisms there are rituals and processions associated with Advent, Christmas, Lent, Easter, Pentecost, and always the May Procession.

Divine justice and punishment for bad people has a visceral appeal.
We want inhuman acts, such as immoral crimes against children, punished.

When a concept (belief in God) becomes institutionalized, the organizational bureaucracy acquires a self-serving life of its own, establishing complex rules and regulations, recruiting members, defining doctrine, and developing a mission.
Christianity became a clever fusion of spirituality and statecraft; the promise of the Second Coming of the Kingdom of God and a political infrastructure forming alliances with monarchs and civic institutions. This blending of religion and politics allowed the Christian Church to flourish and become politically influential in the civic and spiritual life of Europe while continuing its obligation to address and serve the religious interests of its membership. An institutionalized idea is adroit at nourishing itself.

Seeking God or an explanation for God is frustrating because of the "unknowability" factor. Theories of God continue to disappoint due to the intangible nature of the deity. Rejecting religious beliefs is a sensitive societal topic, particularly in the United States at this time, yet the more closely you examine Christianity the less clearly defined it becomes. Flaws become more visible. Historically, human civilizations have advanced by incorporating discoveries and innovations into their cultures enabling beneficial change. Religion, however, is essentially unchanged since polytheism was supplanted by monotheism thousands of years ago.

This book concentrates on Christianity with anecdotes from Catholicism since that is my background and experience, however, the material presented herein can be utilized by anyone in any religious setting.

In chapters that follow, we will unpack the trappings and traditions of religion and critically examine the core concept of Christianity and why people continue to believe. There are substantial deviations from the commonly accepted tradition of peace and love preached by Jesus. Christianity is surprisingly hostile toward science, nature, and women.

During research for this book, I was surprised to discover the pervasive anti-feminine (misogynistic) bias still existent in the Catholic Church, had its roots in early Christianity among just a small group of Christian writers. We will explore this important topic in depth in Chapter Eight.

CHAPTER TWO
REASON AND SCIENCE VERSUS FAITH AND MYSTERY

There is a fundamental difference between religion, which is based on authority, and science, which is based on observation and reason. Science will win because it works.
— *Stephen Hawking*

One of the fundamental conflicts in life is the struggle between belief and nonbelief in a supreme cosmic power, a God, a supernatural deity that created the universe and everything in it. Even though evolution of the human mind has enabled humanity to understand the complexities of the world in a more insightful way than in preliterate societies, human history reveals mankind's inability to abandon belief in ancient superstitions and religious doctrines .

Gods were important to preliterate societies because they offered solutions to problems, but I believe faith in some cosmic force is inadequate as an explanation for life and our universe. Fear of the unknown motivates us to seek answers from authoritative religious leaders, but seeking clarity and empirical answers to vexing metaphysical questions is a hopeless endeavor.

Religion has a formidable challenge: to explain and defend a puzzling and opaque ontology; to make the unseen and unknowable relevant, attractive and beneficial to the human condition. This daunting task appears to have been successful. Belief in God provides the Christian framework for understanding the world, and the promise of immortality eclipses all arguments for atheism and science.

Why does religion occupy a privileged position in the panoply of intellectual ideas? Why are religious beliefs different from other beliefs we have about the world? Religion seems intrinsically immune to scientific discovery and explanation. The assertion that religion is a supernatural phenomenon seems to place it beyond challenge. We demand verifiable evidence for scientific discoveries but accept religious beliefs with little evidence.

Religion offers little insight into the reality of the world, yet we discuss transcendental phenomena as if they were reality. We maneuver effortlessly from objective reality to metaphysical fantasy without recognizing the immense differences between the two realms.

The God debate is polarized by the opposing perspectives of the participants. Science and religion are mutually antagonistic; they operate in different paradigms yet compete to explain the same world. Science is impersonal, dealing in experiments and observable facts. Science begins with the presupposition that there is a predictable world, eternal to our minds, that can be observed, studied, measured, and described.

I'm astonished that science has been unable to inform religion, but Catholic Church history reveals a bungling and inept relationship between the Church and the scientific community. The cascade of scientific discoveries has scarcely altered the beliefs of the faith community, which remain steadfastly committed to a supernatural explanation of creation.

Reason and Science Versus Faith and Mystery

Religious folks' beliefs about the supernatural are contradicted by scientific discovery, commmon sense and everything they have personally experienced.

Among atheist writers, it is axiomatic that science and religious belief are incompatible. It's difficult to understand why educated adults can't comprehend the discoveries of science that refute many of the doctrines of Christianity. We are intellegent organisms, but we seem unable to forge a rational vision of how the world works.

Astrophysicist Neil deGrasse Tyson, describes the scientific method in one sentence: "Do whatever it takes to avoid fooling yourself into thinking something is true that is not, or that something is not true that is." As simple as that might seem, science is unintelligible to the majority of people. Even though science is a search for objective knowledge, in the U.S. there is an anti-science hostility. Science is unintelligible to most people; difficult to understand, partially because of its arcane language and mathematical computations. Many people won't or can't take the time to understand it, though it offers an explanation for life on earth and should be an important component in anyone's education. Public illiteracy of science is rampant.

The world we know is bewildering. Few would deny that the human intellect is incapable of a comprehensive understanding of the universe. Yet, we are born with a sense of awe and wonder, and endeavor with our limited intelligence and reason to cope with and understand our existence and surroundings. By marshaling insights from scientific discoveries we can draw some conclusions that help mediate the science-religion conflict.

There is feeble evidence for religious claims. The basic concepts of religion — that the universe was created by a thinking, cosmic, supernatural force, and an afterlife is available for well-behaved people — tend to disintegrate when common sense and lack of evidence are considered.

Science and religion compete for control of the human intellect. They offer two pathways to experience and examine life; two methodologies to seek meaning and understanding in a complex world. Scientists and religious clerics share a similar goal, a yearning to discover answers to existential questions. Both seek verifiable truths.

Embracing science or religion are two options for individuals seeking meaning in life. Challenging religious doctrine is a collision between science and mythology. Scientists accumulate useful data by testing hypotheses and reporting outcomes that are subject to scrutiny by their peers. Religion is restricted to studying and interpreting the meaning of ancient scriptures.

During the Scientific Revolution, which began in Europe during the 16th century, science became the intellectual authority, diminishing reliance on church doctrine to explain natural events in the universe. Science has demystified the world and produced alternative explanations for most events in the Bible. Ancient mysteries have succumbed to scientific explanation and been replaced by empirical narratives. Current scientific understanding of the universe and the origin of humanity eliminates the need for a supernatural force as explanation.

Michael Schermer, publisher of *Skeptic* magazine, writing in the September 2016, issue of *Scientific American*, succinctly and eloquently describes the differentiation between science and the supernatural.

> The history of science has beheld the steady replacement of the paranormal and the supernatural with the normal and the natural. Weather events once attributed to the supernatural scheming of deities are now understood to be the product of natural forces of temperature and pressure. Plagues formerly ascribed to women cavorting with the devil are currently known to be caused by bacteria and viruses. Mental illnesses previously imputed to demonic possession are today sought in genes and neurochemistry. Accidents heretofore explained by fate, karma or providence are nowadays accredited to probabilities, statistics and risk.

Reason and myth do not comingle well. They are contentious and antagonistic, each repelling the central tenants of the other. Religious beliefs are incompatible with empirical reality. Religion is personal, dealing with mystery and faith, unsupported by the evidence; relying on revelation and mystical experience. Science operates from experimentation and reason. Although the scientist and the cleric have the same yearning to discover the truth about life and the functioning of the world, their approach is widely divergent. Both science and religion believe people have value. Religion believes human life has purpose and meaning. Science is dispassionate and posits that human life has no specific purpose.

Science is an objective endeavor seeking verifiable truths, and therefore can't test the concept of the Genesis creation story. Mythical information is unusable for scientists to formulate and test hypothesis predictions. Science is unable to deal with the supernatural since it is impossible to quantify the unknown and there are no data to be tested. Science tells us nothing about the supernatural and has no use for revealed truth. Science is fact. Theology is imagination.

Hope is the foundation of myth. Religion is implausible, unsupported by facts, and contrary to available evidence. The only evidence for theism is scripture. Any other evidence is philosophical.

Atheists argue from a scientific, fact-based paradigm which is antithetical to the theist argument of a metaphysical, faith-based model. Atheists don't credit a deity when good things happen, nor a satanic force when bad things happen. Science reveals answers to difficult and persistent questions; religions raise unanswered questions. Science continually discovers information that is uncomfortable for religious believers. Being faith-based, Christianity does not produce tangible results or outcomes, relying instead on the imagination of believers to interpret God's intentions. Hence the often heard, over used, trite and meaningless expression, "God works in mysterious ways."

This collision between polarized philosophies can preclude rational discourse between believers and non-believers. This controversy has been described as science dealing with unimportant questions that can be solved while religion deals with important issues that are unsolvable!

One commonality between science and theology is that they both seek a "theory of everything." In this religion wins, since it has anointed God as the answer to everything. Science has not yet discovered the answered to everything.

ALL FISH HAVE BONES

The orthodox message of Christianity can be found in John (3:16), "For God so loved the world, that he gave his only begotten Son, that whosoever believeth in him should not perish, but have everlasting life." This sentence set in motion a theistic mythology that has existed for over 2,000 years. The debate over Christ as immortal Savior revolves around this 25-word sentence in the Gospel of John. This scripture has become so universal that you see signs and placards emblazoned with "John 3:16" at public demonstrations, political rallies, and sporting events. Most Christians know this scripture by heart. The sad, puzzling and disturbing legacy of this short verse is that it furnished the justification for two essential doctrines of Christianity: the necessity to attone for sin and the use of bloody sacrifice to appease God. It further established the idea of an afterlife.

So God sent his only son to be crucified so that past and future sins could be forgiven and humans who believed would live forever? The archaic logic in this concept survives today in modern Christianity with the bloody sacrifice replaced by communion, confession and atonement.

Faith was defined by Paul in his letter to the Hebrews: "Faith is the assurance of things hoped for, the conviction of things not seen" (Hebrews 11:1). Religion glorifies faith, myth, and belief over science, reason and common sense.

Stenger, in *God and the Folly of Faith* (2012), defines faith as "belief in the absence of supportive evidence and even in the light of contrary evidence. Modern science finds no evidence to support revelation as a source of information, no sign of intelligent design, and no need for everything to have a cause. It is likely that the multiverse is eternal, with no beginning, no end, and no need of a creator."

Richard Dawkins, in *The God Delusion* (1997), reinforces this concept; "Human psychology has a near universal tendency to let belief be colored by desire."

The concept of cognitive dissonance focuses on the human quest for internal consistency. Belief in God, the central doctrine in Christianity, is a gift for some and an encumbrance for others. Due to the inability of the human mind to hold two opposing concepts at the same time, choices must be made between faith and reason.

In *Atheism: The Case Against God* (1989), George H. Smith illustrates this conflict.

> The conflict between reason and faith may be viewed as a struggle to control spheres *of influence* (italics in the original). Since reason and faith cannot simultaneously reside over any given sphere, the dominance of one requires the exclusion of the other. Once we see that a sphere for faith can be manufactured only at the expense of reason, we can appreciate why the 'unknowable' is a central tenet of theism and why Christianity has found it necessary to declare war on reason.

Wilfred Cantwell Smith believes a religious person lives the duality of two worlds: the mundane and the transcendent. Christian history has fluctuated between these two realms. The nature of the mundane world becomes increasingly known, but the transcendent world remains an enigma. Smith points out that although we are unable to readily observe a person's faith, we can observe the expressions of religious faith, deeds, rituals, morality and character.

Religion is not faith, nor is theology. Theology has a vagueness, an ephemeral quality that estranges it from science. Religion is a thing, an objective concept that can be described. Faith is an abstract and illusive concept, personalized by how each individual processes and imagines the universe in their own configuration of brain cells.

Although faith, when defined as belief in God, is central to the practice of Christianity, Christians cannot agree on whether faith alone is sufficient to be rewarded with salvation. Catholics believe the path to salvation involves faith *and* "works." Matthew reinforces this position, "For I was hungry, and you gave me food: I was thirsty and you gave me drink: I was a stranger, and you made me welcome, lacking clothes, and you clothed me, sick and you visited me, in prison and you came to see me" (25:35-36). Protestants think that faith alone, *sola scriptura*, is sufficient for attaining salvation.

Both factions agree that salvation is not something to be gained on our own but received as a gift from God: "For by grace are ye saved through faith; and that not of yourselves; it is the gift of God" (Ephesians 2:8). A different stance was taken by Pelagius (354-420), a British monk who believed that Original Sin did not flow down to Adam's descendants and that humans could lead a sinless life and gain salvation on their own. Pelagianism has been condemned by the Catholic church.

I believe Pelagius was on to something.

Knowledge can be derived from revelation, i.e. the Bible and other holy scripts; or from science. Our "knowledge" of God usually comes from authority figures, such as parents, priests, clergymen or women. What we learned was based on the age and wisdom differential between us and the eminent figure dispensing the information. However, what one believes may not be knowledge. Faith is sometimes wrongly conflated with knowledge.

We have the option to choose between faith and reason. If you have faith in God, then you believe that you have some knowledge of God even though your *actual* knowledge of God is unprovable.

In *The God Debate* (2013), Gerald Benedict cites Terry Eagleton, writing in *Reason, Faith and Revolution* (2010),

> . . . the relationship between belief and knowledge is complex. Belief can be rational, and history is full of rationally held beliefs, once assumed to be knowledge, that have subsequently been proved to be false, such as believing that the earth to be flat and the Sun circled it because that what was what it appeared to be doing. In both these cases, belief was taken to be knowledge, a confusion that had a profound influence on attitudes and culture.

According to British philosopher A. C. Grayling in *The God Argument*, (2013),

> The cumulative case against religion shows it to be a hangover from the infancy of modern humanity, persistent and enduring because of the vested interests of religious organizations,

proselytization of children, complicity of temporal powers requiring the social and moral policing that religion offers, and human psychology itself. Yet even a cursory overview of history tells us that it is one of the most destructive forces plaguing humanity.

A stark reminder of the negative effect of religion has been voiced by Stenger in *The New Atheism: Taking a Stand for Science and Reason* (2009): "Science flies us to the moon. Religion flies us into buildings."

Over the years, Christianity has inspired many with its message of peace, love, and humility. It has inspired artists and musicians to create exquisite paintings, beautiful sculptures, and inspirational music. It has stimulated lay people and clergy to minister to the less fortunate. Many priests, bishops, ministers, vicars, and rabbis have devoted their lives to religion and tirelessly and unselfishly ministered to their congregations. Many followers have been comforted by the egalitarian religious message of peace and love.

But Christianity — and other faiths — has also incited and encouraged fanatics and overzealous partisans to commit barbaric acts, torturing and killing "infidels" in the name of their God. This dual effect of scripture on individuals sometimes resulting from contradictory interpretations of Bible verses poses difficulties when discussing the pros and cons of religion. On balance, I believe the pain, suffering, and carnage from atrocities committed in the name of religion far outweigh any benefits conferred on the faithful. There is no rational justification that excuses these acts of violence.

Religious literature and ecclesiastical tradition invented a consummately meaningless cliché to explain everything: "It's God's will." This is the classic, ubiquitous, apologetic response to unexplainable and perplexing events occurring in the world; a requisite component of the daily vernacular of religious followers. It expresses Providentialism, the doctrine that God's will is evident in all occurrences, but His plan can't be understood by mere humans.

This phrase is diabolically elegant. It is a panacea; an answer to everything, covering every conceivable situation. It's handy, difficult to refute, unassailable (God knows what God wants or thinks), and difficult to contradict. It is used and reused by clerics and laypersons alike, and it never wears out. It is a formidable answer to any "why" questions, and for the believer it explains everything

For the nonbeliever it explains nothing.

One's vision of the world has to be balanced between what we see, experience, and know, and what can be imagined. Desire and imagination produce religion; reason and science produce reality.

It's not much of a stretch to stereotype humans as more emotional than anayltical. Religion may owe its staying power to our emotional makeup. Emotions become actuated at fear, misfortune, paranormal events, superstitions and the stresses of daily life. We don't spend much time on robust analysis of any of these feelings. Our plethora of worries overpowers our logic and we depend on religion for consolataion and reassurance.

The Earth's biosphere, the world ecosystems — a dazzling, harmonious union of geological and biological phenomena — is staggeringly complex. It contains over eight million identified species: animals, plants, fungi, fish, insects, reptiles, birds, trees, flowers, protozoa, bacteria and humans. A Creator would have to be even more complex to create and synchronize this world. Where did this complex entity come from?

If we conduct a realistic assessment of historic contributions of science and religion to our world, it seems obvious that science had a greater impact on the way we live than religion. Living conditions in this 21st century are the result of science, technology and the creative thinking of our ancestors. When you reach into your refrigerator for a cold beverage, watch the news on TV, drive to the grocery store in your automatically shifting car, consult your cell phone — a hand held computer — enjoy the warmth of your house on a cold winter day, or fly to visit your grandchildren, you are experiencing just a few of the contributions of science and technology to our lives.

As the human species strives to survive and cope with nuclear weapons and natural catastrophes, it may be more advantageous to rely on science and technology than religion. In fact, science is absolutely necessary if we are to survive. We are living in an increasingly complex world and coming to

Reason and Science Versus Faith and Mystery

a crossroad where decisions on our future as a species will have to be made. Prayerful supplications to a deity requesting interventions into world affairs may be a popular approach for some, but historically it has not been effective.

Science is developing sustainable agriculture practices that will help crops withstand disease, fungi and insect infestations. Stabilizing our population is an important goal. Religion offers little help and much hindrance with this issue. Science may even be able to prevent meteors from crashing into earth and creating extinctions.

The future of humanity is dependent on a planet that sustains us and rational human activity. To avoid warp speed destruction of the biosphere, it is necessary to re-examine our political and belief structure and move to a science and technology model. Human knowledge, experience, science and technology may offer the tools and direction for a pathway for the future of humanity. Religion has little to offer.

ALL FISH HAVE BONES

CHAPTER THREE
THE DECLINE OF CHRISTIANITY AND RISE OF SECULARISM

> *The idea of God implies the abdication of human reason and justice;*
> *it is the most decisive negation of human liberty, and necessarily ends*
> *in the enslavement of mankind, both in theory and practice.*
> — *Emma Goldman*

Understanding and interpreting Christianity requires study and comprehension of the history and its context when it originated in the first century, CE. Reconstructing that period of history is difficult. As John Dominic Crossan explains in *The Historical Jesus* (1991):

> The first century of the common era is obscured from our contemporary view by three giant filters. The past is recorded almost exclusively in the voices of elites and males, in the viewpoints of the wealthy and the powerful, in the visions of

the literate and the educated. That already constricted report is available sometimes through the deliberate decision of later dominations but also sometimes through the vagaries of chance and luck, fate and accident. Either way, further constrictions. And our present looks back to the past, to that already filtered past, dependent, of course, on where one's present is located, but let us say in individualistic, democratic, urban, middle class America, often with ethnocentric presumptions it is not even aware of projecting.

It is also necessary to deal with the literacy, education, and superstitions of the people living in that era. In *Atheism and the Case Against Christ* (2012), Matthew S. McCormick characterizes the perspectives of the citizens of the first century.

> Generally, people living in an agrarian Iron Age society with very low levels of scientific knowledge, education, and literacy will have a low level of skepticism for what we would identify as supernatural, miraculous, or paranormal claims. We have good empirical evidence that as a person's education level increases, her belief in survival of the soul, miracles, heaven, the resurrection, the virgin birth, hell, the devil, ghosts, astrology, and reincarnation drops off dramatically.

The Scientific Revolution initiated the decline of Christianity and the rise of secularization. In *The Passion of the Western Mind* (1991), Richard Tarnas characterized that period in history.

> . . . up through Newton the weight of science had tended to support an argument for the existence of God based on evidence of design in the universe, after Darwin the weight of science was thrown against that argument. The evidence of natural history seemed more plausibly comprehended in terms of evolutionary principles of natural selection and random mutation than in terms of a transcendent Designer.

With the publication of *The Origin of Species* in 1859, Charles Darwin offered a viable alternative to supernatural design. Unbelief now had a

The Decline of Christianity and Rise of Secularism

scientific explanation. Martin Luther, born in 1483, confronted the Catholic church in 1517 with his 95 Theses challenging papal authority — particularly the selling of indulgences — but it would be the Age of Enlightenment and the Scientific Revolution that would begin the substitution of science for divine intervention in understanding the workings of the world.

Copernicus published his famous book, *The Revolutions of Celestial Spheres* in 1543, asserting that geocentrism — the belief that the earth was the center of the universe — was incorrect and that the earth actually revolved around the sun. The scriptures, however offered a different view, taught by the church, "You fixed the earth on its foundation, never to be moved" (Psalm 104:5). Galileo's later observations reinforced Copernicus' heliocentric theory, but angered the Catholic Church. In 1615, he was investigated by the Roman Inquisition and found to be in conflict with scripture. Galileo was placed under house arrest for the rest of his life and his publications were banned, but the authority and teachings of the Catholic Church had been questioned and the door was now open to further examine and challenge Christian doctrine.

Religion was a central, meaningful component in the historical and political culture that forged our nation. From our Anglo-Judeo-Christian heritage to the current diverse religious fabric in the U.S., religion has served a sometimes controversial, but always important role.

Contrary to popular belief though, the United States of America was not founded on Christian principles. The founding fathers had no such intention. The word "God" appears in neither the Bill of Rights nor the Constitution. Nor was it originally in the national motto or Pledge of Allegiance. Zuckerman, writes in *Living the Secular Life* (2014),

> The actual founding American motto, adopted by an act of Congress in 1782, was 'E Pluribus Unum' (Out of many, one) a decidedly secular motto if there ever was one. But in 1956, at the height of the Cold War, and in an effort to distinguish ourselves from those godless communists over in Russia, the motto was changed to 'In God We Trust.' And the words 'under God' were

also not in the original Pledge of Allegiance.; they were added in 1954.

Zuckerman further points out that the Treaty of Tripoli of 1797 contains the wording, "The government of the United States of America is not, in any sense, founded on the Christian religion."

The framers of the U.S. Constitution were intelligent students of history and avid readers of the concepts of the European Enlightenment of the 17th and 18th centuries. The framers had the wisdom and intellect to study the benefits and drawbacks to various forms of political arrangements. Our republic is a product of the distillation of the governmental concepts from the Enlightenment that placed individual rights over those of the government.

Thinkers of the Enlightenment — Spinoza, Locke, Hobbes, Hume, Descartes, Voltaire and Kant — questioned civil and church authority, championed the rights of individuals and believed in applying reason and analysis to human problems. Jefferson, Madison, John Adams, Benjamin Franklin and George Mason were familiar with the philosophies expressed by Enlightenment thinkers and incorporated those principles into the philosophy and documents of the new republic. They questioned traditional autocratic political authority and believed that individual liberty should be balanced with the requirements of democracy.

The framers of the U.S. Constitution were opposed to any form of state-sponsored religion and went to great lengths to word the Constitution so that government and religion would not be mixed. Kenneth C. Davis, in *Don't Know Much About History*, writes,

> Ultimately, what is far more important than what any of the so-called Founding Fathers personally believed, is the larger concept that most of them embraced passionately, the freedom to practice religion, as well as not to. And certainly, to a man, they emphatically opposed the idea of a government sponsored religion. Franklin shuddered at the intrusion of religion into politics. Washington denounced spiritual tyranny

and felt religion was a private matter and the government had no business meddling. For him, 'government existed to protect people's rights, not save their souls.' Thomas Jefferson, who founded the University of Virginia, stipulated that no chapel or church be built on University grounds and no course in theology would be taught.

The goal of our founding fathers was an emancipation of men and women from the subjugation of the past. They incorporated in our revolutionary documents respect for the individual, and an opportunity to act and think as individuals without interference from civic authorities. The dignity of the individual was paramount, as was his or her right to worship any way and any God they wanted. Colonists could explore the vast dimensions of human experience without fear of government intervention.

In *The Moral Foundations of the American Republic* (1986), Walter Berns writes, "One of the striking facts about the unamended Constitution, then, is the absence of any statement invoking the name of God or providing for the public worship of God or according special privileges or place to churchmen or stating it to be the duty of Congress to promote Christian education as part of a design to promote good citizenship." Berns notes that the Founders did not establish religion, but rather religious freedom based on the natural rights of man. According to Berns, the subordination of religion was necessary before free government could be successfully established in the U. S. This subordination of religion underlies the principle of freedom of religion.

Indifference toward religion in America is growing. The church-going demographic is shrinking and the nonbeliever community is growing and becoming more vocal and vibrant. A Pew survey, *Religion and Public Life*, (2007) reports that 16.1 percent of Americans say they are unaffiliated with any religion. One quarter of this group describe themselves as either atheists or agnostics. Among Americans ages 18-29, one in four say they are not currently affiliated with any religion. According to the Pew survey, the greatest growth in religious groups is the "unaffiliated" or "nones." More than half of this "unaffiliated" group describe their religion as "nothing in particular."

Catholicism has experienced the greatest net loss in members. According to Pew, "While nearly one-in-three Americans (31%) were raised in the Catholic faith, today fewer than one in four describe themselves as Catholic." Another opinion survey conducted by the University of Chicago reinforces this finding, pointing out that roughly 10 percent of all Americans are former Catholics.

A follow-up Pew survey, *Religion and Public Life* (2015), reinforces the data from the 2007 survey that the Christian population is declining and the unaffiliated "nones" are growing in all geographic areas of the U.S. The percentage of adults who describe themselves as Christians has dropped nearly eight percent since the survey in 2007. And the number of religiously unaffiliated, "nones" has risen more than six percent. Among adults who were raised Catholic, 41 percent no longer identify with Catholicism.

Wayne L. Trotta's review of *American Humanism: The Cultural Contours of Nonreligious Belief System* in *Free Inquiry*, (August/September, 2016), describes the United States as having more individuals who consider themselves non-religious than any other nation except China (according to a World Values Survey).

The trend toward secularism continues today, extensively in Europe, somewhat less in the United States. An interesting development in the U.S. is the appointment of atheist "chaplains" at Harvard and Stanford Universities and the University of Southern California to counsel non-believers.

The *Wall Street Journal* (*WSJ*) reported on January 3, 2015, that plunging church membership in Europe is creating empty churches that are now being sold. More than 2500 churches are now closed or will be within a decade. Closing churches is an emotional event notes the *Journal*; "Here people worshiped, felt grief and joy, and quested for a relationship with God." The Church of England closes about 20 churches a year; 200 Danish churches are nonviable or under-used; the German Roman Catholics have shuttered 515 churches in the past decade.

The Decline of Christianity and Rise of Secularism

Conditions in the Netherlands are the most egregious. Roman Catholic leaders there estimate that two thirds of 1600 churches will be closed in a decade and 700 Protestant churches will be closed within four years.

Scott Thumma, professor of the Sociology of Religion at Connecticut Hartford Seminary says, "America's churching population is graying and unless trends change, within another 30 years the situation in the U.S. will be as bad as what is currently existing in Europe." The *WSJ* reported on April 4, 2015, that the population of nuns in the U.S. has declined by more than 70 percent and the annual number of priestly ordinations by 50 percent. My own experience of going to Catholic Mass in Europe during the '80s and '90s was that only the very elderly were attending.

I believe we are experiencing a major stealth revolution in religion in the U.S. that has serious implications for growth and sustainability of the Christian community. This is not an organized shift in religious philosophy but a growing recognition by many adults that the world can be logically understood without need of a supernatural explanation.

The winds of change may not be blowing hard but a breeze is picking up. Churches are being shuttered, vocations to religious life are declining, and surveys show declining belief in God.

It's a stealth revolution because those who are eschewing religion are not publicly announcing their disbelief but quietly living their lives without the religious beliefs of their youth. People are uncomfortable acknowledging unbelief publicly, but a passive unbelief and lack of a public affiliation with organized religion is perfectly acceptable and essentially goes unnoticed.

The evidence for this phenomenon can be seen in the lack of young people in church pews on Sunday, a diminishing number of men and women accepting religious vocations, and closure of churches and religious schools.

America is undergoing a reframing of religious views from regular church attendance to self-reliance. Americans are becoming more secular and not relying on church leaders for guidance in their lives. Religion has less allure.

Human dreams and aspirations can be fulfilled without relying on Christian doctrine or organized religion. This is reinforced by activist atheist writers and public personalities who openly declare their opposition to religious activities.

ALL FISH HAVE BONES

Phil Zuckerman reports in *Living the Secular Life* (2014),

> Somewhere between nine percent and 21 percent of Americans are now atheist or agnostic — the highest rate of nonbelief ever seen in U. S. history. Twenty-seven percent of Americans currently claim not to practice any religion, with 22 percent specifically stating that religion is 'not a factor' in their lives. Rates of secularity are markedly stronger among younger Americans: 32 percent of Americans under age thirty are religiously unaffiliated.

Unbelief is a fairly recent phenomenon in human history. According to James Turner, *Without God, Without Creed* (1985), until the 16th century, God's pervasiveness in world culture made it extremely difficult to seriously question His existence.

Prior to the 16th century, belief in God was virtually universal; the world could not be satisfactorily explained without invoking God. In medieval culture, God was a necessary ingredient to prevent the perceived world from disintegrating. By the late 19th century, unbelief had become intellectually acceptable and the God axiom could be questioned.

According to Turner, history began to be questioned from a secular and not a theological framework. Turner writes that in the 16th century, the intellectual option of godlessness became available. According to Tarnas, the Renaissance, Reformation and Scientific Revolution essentially ended the hegemony of the Catholic Church in Europe and ushered in the secular spirit of the modern age. Science and the Christian Church began competing to explain natural events in the universe, pitting Christian revelation with scientific discovery. Tarnas points out that the metaphysical incongruity of the two outlooks created a schism both within individuals and the larger society. Religion slowly became less relevant.

The ascent of the secular movement has many underlying causes. Part is caused by the aging of "religious" populations and increased disinterest in religion by the young. Many Christians today face disillusionment with the intellectual and moral integrity of religious leadership, causing them to rethink commitment to their religion. This is exacerbated by Catholic

The Decline of Christianity and Rise of Secularism

Church pedophilia scandals and immoral behavior of TV evangelists and other clergy.

The pedophilia scandals of the Catholic Church were and are deeply disturbing for many Catholics. Having placed their spiritual life in the hands of allegedly holy priests, ordained as successors to Jesus, they learned that church authorities engaged in moral crimes, hypocrisy, complicity, deception, and criminal cover-up. The collegial alliances forged in the insular priesthood and the secrecy surrounding cloistered communities helped nurture the debacle and failed to promptly identify and punish responsible individuals. This shattered Catholics' illusions of the priest as the incarnation of Christ. Devout Catholics felt betrayed by their spiritual leadership and began to question the moral authority and spiritual integrity of the Church.

This moral failure of Catholic clergy was a cultural breakdown that weakened the institutional authority and moral principles preached by those same people. Previously seen as devout, trustworthy, and virtuous, Catholic priests involved in pedophilia and those who covered up the scandal are now regarded as corrupt, sinful, evil and untrustworthy.

The moral bankruptcy of certain clergy of the Catholic Church has also led to economic bankruptcies. Many dioceses have become insolvent after paying substantial court-awarded damages to victims of abuse.

Failure to address the moral and criminal implications of this scandal and punish offending priests diminished church authority and caused many Catholics to rethink their faith. Catholic authorities failed their leadership and moral obligation to protect their congregations. The scandalous activity of priests and their superiors has weakened the Catholic Church institutionally.

Catholics are expressing their sense of indignation by quitting the church. There is also a growing divide between the ordained and the laity over issues of divorce and remarriage, contraception, abortion, celibacy, and women priests. The ramparts of Vatican City may become more useful as the Church defends against criticism for the pedophilia scandal, the alleged laundering of money by the Vatican bank and failure to address modernity issues. The Vatican Curia, a mysterious, religious fiefdom, is insulated from reality by

Vatican walls and allegiance to an ancient theology. The Church is unable to arrive at a coherent and objective assessment of its problems because it is constrained by a primitive kinship and devotion to the orthodoxy of an ancient scriptural message.

Two other major contributors to secularization are strident opposition by evangelicals to acceptance of all individuals as equals and ultra-conservative views of evangelicals on modern social issues. The non-religious community is disenchanted with orthodox Christian values on homosexuality, divorce, birth control, sex, gay marriage, and the negative attitude toward the lesbian, gay, bi-sexual and transgender (LGBT) community. These issues underscore the disinterest in religion growing in the U.S. Each of these factors has contributed to the slow, but steady, secularization of Americans.

I suspect there are many "closet" atheists afraid to "come out" because of their fear of the opprobrium from family and friends that may result from their public disclosure of unbelief. However, the atheist community is becoming more vocal. Many authors are writing books explaining the atheist viewpoint. On Sunday, more people jog, swim, golf, boat, bike, hike, watch sports on TV or watch their kids play sports than go to church. Church is inconvenient and without attraction for the younger generation. Absence from church doesn't require a formal declaration of unbelief, but it is a tacit admission of a disinterest in religious activities.

The organizational structures of institutionalized religion are beginning to collapse; imploding as a result of internal scandal and leadership failures, and confronted from outside by people who find religious doctrine irrational. Growing disenchantment with religion, especially among young people, is partly because religion offers no tangibles, nothing currently useful; only a mysterious promise that something wonderful might happen after you die. The *Wall Street Journal* reported on January 16, 2015, that church construction in the U.S. has fallen 80 percent since 2002. Spending on religious buildings is at half the level of a decade ago. One factor contributing to this decline is the "waning of religious affiliation." A substantial numbers of people on the planet don't believe in the supernatural: atheists, agnostics, freethinkers and secular humanists. Are they all doomed?

The emergent reality of this stealth movement is that modern churches, to attract followers, may have to deemphasize the portrayal of humanity as depraved sinners on a journey to perdition and focus more on charitable enterprises churches perform to assist the less fortunate. The survival of Christianity may depend on its ability to reexamine ancient doctrine, determine its relevance to modernity, and reinterpret its meaning and application in the 21st century.

Deemphasizing Original Sin, softening the portrayal of a vengeful God and reinventing the Christian church as a sympathetic, caring, neighborhood institution may aid in its survival and in becoming a resource that actually contributes to the betterment of communities. Even as Christianity declines in the U.S. we still see churches proselytizing and trying to grow membership.

Perhaps this is good place to express my amazement at the recruiting practices of religions. What motivates Catholic, Mormon, Seventh Day Adventist and other missionaries to travel the world preaching their version of the gospel and seeking converts? Finances may be a factor, but I sense a zealotry that extends beyond that. I fail to understand the missionary zeal of churches to expand their membership. Religion should be a private matter and people should be left alone to tend to their own beliefs.

The new charismatic Catholic Pope, Francis, has enchanted and mesmerized the public and the media with his deviation from the behavior of his predecessors — particularly Pope Benedict — who worked diligently to impede advances in church doctrine proposed in the Second Vatican Council (Vatican II). His humility and folksy, informal manner, his move out of the traditional Papal apartment into more modest quarters, his preference for compact cars in lieu of the Popemobile, his eschewing of Papal regalia, and his liberal public comments on the potential direction of church teaching has endeared him to the modern wing of his flock and lured many into believing that modernization of the Catholic Church is imminent. His liberal platitudes in informal contacts with the press and formal speeches have been portrayed as a breath of fresh air in the Catholic Church. His friendly gestures and outreach to the liberal wing of the church is admirable. Noticeably missing from his speeches, however, are solutions to the problems he elaborates.

It remains to be seen if Pope Francis wants to — or can — modernize the church. Since beginning his Pontificate, his commentary has been appealing to liberals and appalling to conservatives. However, if you listen and read closely, you will notice that no central Catholic Church doctrine has been annulled, modified, or modernized in any way. His rhetoric only tinkers at the fringes of modernity. He flies around the world preaching liberal theology but still reminds Catholics to "stop screwing like rabbits!" These performances endear him to the media but do little to foster an affectionate connection to his followers.

There are at least five entropic forces currently plaguing the Catholic Church: The pedophilia scandal, the relevance of Church doctrine to modern Christians, declining membership in the Church, reduction in vocations to the priesthood and women's religious communities, and internal dissension between conservatives and liberals on the direction of church doctrine. There are many clergy and faithful who remain stubbornly oriented to pre-Vatican II doctrine and practice. Convincing theologians in the hermetically sealed Roman Catholic Curia to abandon centuries of entrenched orthodoxy and embrace modernization may be more than one Pope can do.

It is unlikely that the U.S. or any other country will ever become completely secular. Reality dictates that religion will continue to be part of the fabric of societies. Religion plays a prominent role in our American heritage and demands a degree of respect, even as some zealous non-believers work to eliminate it. However, recent history shows that modern science is becoming more acceptable in penetrating the human psyche with plausible explanations of historical Christian events.

Belief in a superior cosmic force is likely to continue to be an unsolvable enigma until God appears and explains Himself, but science can give modern earthlings answers to troubling existential questions. Christianity is entering a precarious time in its history. As its inception recedes further into the past, it receives more rigorous scrutiny, the promises are less compelling and the mythic stature of Jesus diminishes.

Scientific achievement, pragmatic reasoning by an increasingly enlightened population, and a recognition of the failure of religion to achieve promised objectives of peace, tranquility, and brotherhood will slowly erode belief in Christianity's metaphysical validity and the notion that the universe was created, continually monitored, and under the control of a supernatural entity. As scientific discoveries advance understanding of the world we live in and research in neuroscience provides greater insight into the function of the brain and its effect on human behavior, the human race will become more comfortable with unbelief and the role of organized religion will lose its influence in our lives.

However, I also believe it's premature to write the obituary of organized religion. Religious belief may be declining, but it is unlikely to disappear completely. Paul Kurtz points out the main function of religion is: "to overcome despair and hopelessness in response to human tragedy, adversity, and conflict—the brute, inexplicable, contingent, and fragile aspects of the human condition." These circumstances will continue to exist as long as humans inhabit the planet.

ALL FISH HAVE BONES

CHAPTER FOUR
FAITH IN A FANTASTY

Religion is about turning untested belief into unshakable truth through the power of institutions and the passage of time.
—*Richard Dawkins*

Since the dawn of human history, men and women have been transfixed and puzzled with questions of existence and the mysteries of life and sought strategies to make sense of reality: As we grew up there was the expectation that our questions about God and existence would have plausible answers. We are awed by the majesty of our surroundings, but confused about our role in the universe. We search for meaning in a complex world.

Why are we here?
How did we get here?
Why are we sentient?
Why do we inhabit Earth?

Attempting to answer the "why" questions transcends our understanding and stretches the capacity of human intellect. We are the curious in search of the unknowable! Pondering supernatural questions may exceed the human capacity to understand. Attempts at solving existential questions have been largely unsuccessful in finding satisfactory answers. We may never attain the grail of *Why?*

Steven Pinker, in his intriguing book, *How the Mind Works*, suggests *Homo sapiens* may lack the cognitive equipment to solve difficult philosophical questions; not because they are irreducible but because our minds have not evolved the capacity to answer these questions. It may be sensible and rational for mankind to learn to be comfortable living on the periphery of "Why?" and avoid becoming bogged down trying to answer ineffable questions. Not every problem in life has a solution. Existence may be one of those problems. It is painfully evident that not everything can be comprehended and explained.

Some form of religious belief has been with us since antiquity, and religion has insinuated itself into most of our lives. Spiritual faith in the invisible, unknown, and unknowable is one of the baffling attributes of the human species. Humans have perpetually looked to gods for answers to life problems, believing in some cosmic force beyond understanding that controls the universe and its inhabitants. Even though modern humans have tools for a better understanding of the functions of the universe, we still share our ancestors' world view of wonderment and perplexity.

Throughout history, nations rise and fall, wars are fought, societies evolve, scientific discoveries enlighten, social mores and beliefs are altered, and philosophical concepts are offered to explain our existence. Humans progressed from hunter-gatherers to farmers. The Industrial Revolution began to modernize mankind. During these many long years, belief in mysterious gods continued unabated, though there was scant evidence for the existence of any supernatural deities.

Our prehistoric ancestors believed that every natural phenomenon — plants, rocks, animals, streams, mountains, wind — had a spiritual essence, awareness and feelings and could communicate with humans (animism). This morphed into polytheism — belief in many gods — during the Bronze and Iron Ages (beginning around 3000 BC), and finally into monotheism, — belief in one God — with the advent of the Abrahamic religions.

Much of ancient mythology is in fact a legal contract in which humans promise everlasting devotion to the Gods in exchange for mastery over plants and animals—the first chapters in the book of Genesis are a prime example. For thousands of years after the Agricultural Revolution, religious liturgy consisted mainly of humans sacrificing lambs, wine and cakes to divine powers, who in exchange promised abundant harvests and fecund flocks (Harari).

Insatiable human curiosity has found some answers in religion, but there is an enormous gap between the promises of religion and observable results. Religion is an emotionally-fueled false belief, resistant to reason. It's an imaginary experience marketed as objective reality, nourished and sustained by hope for eternal life and anxiety over the potential for eternal punishment. In a quest for comfort and security in a chaotic world, human imagination created a pernicious, ideological crutch that has arguably caused more harm than good: God is responsible for everything — end of story. This is not a very compelling argument.

Modern humans have inherited religion from their ancestors; and a burden of guilt and obligation to worship an ineffable deity. Religion is difficult to define and even more difficult to explain. Why do modern, educated people believe that God has always existed; that one person has three distinct but interchangeable identities; that Jesus was both human and divine; that some dead bodies go to a place called Heaven where they are reconstituted while some are consigned to a place called Hell for eternal punishment; that the whispered prayers of a priest converts wine and bread into the body and blood of Jesus, who died 2,000 years ago; that newborn babies have a corrupt nature; and that women are inferior to men?

Sometime during evolution, the need of humans to understand their surroundings inspired religious concepts. Religion is a human response to uncertainty; an emotional expression of the human struggle to cope with and understand the universe and human existence. Religion acts as a portal from the reality of existence to the fantasy of imagination and helps avoid difficult existential questions. Modern Christians share a collective expectation that an ancient myth is real and we will experience another life after we die.

The essence of religion may be inadvertently depicted by two towns and a resort situated along a highway following the meandering path of the massive Clark Fork river, which drains most of Western Montana before running into Idaho. In Idaho, there is a town called Hope. Just east of there is a resort called Beyond Hope. Away up the river in Montana is a town called Paradise. This offers an opportunity to experience the Rapture without dying, just by driving from Hope to Paradise. I find it amusing that going to Paradise requires passing Beyond Hope! The sequential location of these towns mixes humor with pathos. The early settlers were obviously prescient.

Religion is an amalgam of revelation, tradition, scripture, superstition and imagination used to establish and experience a supernatural being — God— as responsible for the universe. Harvard biologist Edward O. Wilson believes *Homo sapiens* is essentially a dysfunctional species which even in the modern era continues to "remain in the thrall of tribal organized religion, led by men who claim supernatural power in order to compete for the obedience and resources of the faithful." Religion is obsessed with ancient traditions, practices and taboos inherited from antiquity. Religion is based on the concept of fear — of God and of eternal punishment — which is irrational and without substantiation.

It is also paradoxical to fear someone who allegedly loves you!

Examined closely, the Christian explanation of life appears neither rational nor logical. It begins and ends with fantasies; the Garden of Eden and the expectation of immortality. This is a good place to put the "fish" to work; question assumptions, examine the basis for religious dogma, and think critically. Religion demands diagnosis, not only for its doctrines but its promise of eternal life. Also, it's unnatural to spend your life consumed by the idea that you are an inferior human with a proclivity to commit sin.

Questions to ask of any ideology are: Are its claims valid? Are they pertinent? Do they contribute to the improvement of the human condition?

The difficulty in answering these questions lies in the metaphysical aspect of religion. We may have to conclude that answers we seek are not forthcoming and learn to live with the questions.

Believers tend to place too much value on revelation and too little on reason and science. Science discovers things that are there; in religion there is no there. Religions champion the anticipated, imaginary afterlife over the real, existent, tangible life we are experiencing. But life can be enjoyed free of constricting religious doctrines.

It seems a waste of the only life we're certain of to spend it waiting for the apocalyptic second coming of a savior. Though we're random creations without intrinsic purpose, we're not precluded from having goals and creating purpose, meaning and enjoyment in our individual lives. Each of us has the ability as we mature to refine characteristics that define us, develop a distinct identity that expresses individuality and distinguishes us from our fellow humans; to become our own authentic person.

Faith is a personal experience with a variety of expressions. Many people have strong religious beliefs, others are indifferent. Religion is a significant component of life for many people; maybe not everything, but something. Religion can be a home, an earthly abode, a comfortable sanctuary while awaiting a mansion in the sky.

Religion can be therapeutic. It assuages imaginary fears. It offers a solution to the trials and tribulations of everyday life. There is a seductive charm in the scriptural message of peace, love, harmony, enlightenment and peaceful co-existence among humankind. However, the message has been obscured by rigidity and dogma.

For many, religion is a highly charged emotional experience. I recall a man getting up from his pew during Mass in the Basilica of the National Shrine of the Immaculate Conception in Washington, D. C., and prostrating himself for several minutes on the aisle floor. In my own home church, I have witnessed the same behavior on several occasions. On Good Friday in the Philippine Islands, some men nail themselves to a cross in a reenactment of Jesus' crucifixion.

ALL FISH HAVE BONES

For believers with unequivocal trust and faith in a transcendental entity, religion offers a panacea, an answer for everything. With faith, all questions have acceptable answers — whether the answer is "Yes" or "No." God is the spiritual 7-11 Store; always available to answer our questions and calm our anxieties. God is a convenient answer to life's intractable questions.

"Religion" and "faith" are often used interchangeably but, in reality, they are distinct. Religion is an institutional framework; faith is a self-contained concept in the mind. Faith requires willingness to embrace a fantasy; a mystical association with a vague divine cosmic presence. Faith thrives on emotion and imagination while science is content with experimentation and factual outcomes.

The words used to describe religious belief — faith, hope, trust, supernatural, transcendental, miracle, spiritual, metaphysical, promise, expectation — all lack certitude yet stimulate the imagination. The Catholic Church regularly refers to the "mystical body of Christ" in prayers and sermons.

Nowhere has God described Himself or where He lives, yet throughout history, humans have erected cathedrals, mosques, temples, churches and synagogues in which to worship with little indication that any supernatural, benevolent, cosmic force is paying any attention. At some point in religious history, we seem to have reached the conclusion that there is a correlation between the magnificence of church architecture and the favorable disposition of God toward its members. The imposing grandeur of the edifice allegedly has a positive effect on the relationship between God and the faithful. Yet, except for the "drop in so we won't go to Hell" crowd on Sundays, these expensive structures remain empty most of the time.

Jacob Pandian eloquently describes the function of religious faith:
> Historically humans have created beliefs and practices associated with supernatural beings and supernatural powers, and these beliefs and practices have been used to construct sacred self and group identities and to formulate models or narratives of coherence and meaning to cope with feelings of helplessness,

encounters with suffering and injustice, realities of uncertainty, and fear and anxiety associated with sickness and death.

However, Christianity, by any objective criteria, has not significantly improved the lives of humans.

Three primary teachings of Christianity have failed to materialize: Christians believed they were created by a supernatural deity who would look after them on Earth, offer them an afterlife, and was the cause for natural phenomena in the universe. None of this has come to pass. Humans have evolved along with the rest of life on Earth and were not created as the result of a divine intervention. Tragedy continues to befall people in spite of prayer and supplication. Supernatural explanation has been supplanted by scientific explanations for natural events. And there is no evidence of an afterlife.

If God wanted to establish a spokesperson on Earth to reveal Himself, it seems strange that he chose an illiterate Jewish peasant living in a sparsely populated desert in a remote part of the world. Since the intentions of God are largely unknown, we rely on religious personnel to interpret His goals and purpose for us. So, Christians believe Jesus was divine, went to heaven when he died, and will return in glory.

He wasn't, he didn't, and he hasn't, yet religion continues to prosper even without a supernatural spokesman!

The cornerstone of religion is precariously based on fables, folklore, and fantasies. It reflects the zeitgeist of preliterate people attempting to make sense of their world of superstition, curses, miraculous events and myths. This amalgam of ancient beliefs and practices constituted the organic material the Church Fathers and subsequent clerical authorities fashioned into Catholicism. The concept of a supreme, invisible deity who created and watches over the universe has little or no evidence outside the scriptural writings of an ancient, superstitious people.

Group think is a psychological phenomenon in which members of a group begin to think alike, seek harmony, stifle dissent, and isolate themselves from outside interference. Individual thought is lost. Loyalty to the group is paramount and individual creativity is discouraged. Decisions made in this environment are often illogical and ineffective. Religion is "group think" on steroids, imposing a uniformity of beliefs and behaviors on its disciples.

Religion is essentially delusional expectation, belief in a false concept, even though ample contrary evidence is available. Practice good behavior while you live on planet Earth and when you die you'll be rewarded with a pleasant afterlife. A simple equation: good now equals good later. But there is no emphatic, unequivocal, empirical evidence that this ever happened or is happening now. How many people do you know of who came back from being dead?

In Catholic school, nuns and priests continually reminded us that we had a "soul" and our soul set us apart from the rest of nature. In fact, the exact words used were "immortal soul." The soul almost has to be immortal. The idea of soul without immortality has little traction. A primary argument of anti-abortionists is that the fetus has a soul and therefore, is already a human being. Dominican friar Thomas Aquinas reminds us that the soul is the link between God and men, and the concept of an immortal soul provides consolation in the face of death. Yet, theologians can't amass sufficient evidence to convince non-believers that humans have a soul.

For that matter, neither can science disprove the existence of a soul.

Religions have paradoxical features. As Christians, we are automatically born into Original Sin. Simultaneously, we are offered a path to salvation through contrition, repentance, and participation in some form of atonement exercise.

I believe the primary attraction of religion is the promise of a hereafter — Heaven. Religion preys on the insatiable human desire to avoid death and a yearning for continuous life. Conspicuous characteristics of Christianity are the universal awareness of death and a dread of Hell. This is countered by the promise of immortality.

Everlasting life is the *raison d'être* of religion: It is the focus, product, belief, and sustaining component. The divine promise of immortality and admission into God's Kingdom is seductive and irresistible. Without the essential fabric of immortality, there would be no need for religion.

Religion is a faith-based view of the future, an eschatological concept of reward in the hereafter for righteous living during time on earth. Religion portrays life on earth as temporary and miserable, which may have been true 2,000 years ago. Today, life is fairly enjoyable for most people living in the West, yet we are constantly reminded that the afterlife is what's important. We are encouraged by religion to believe that pain and suffering are *beneficial* to atone for sin and that death is temporary.

Without the promise of a serene, supernatural life after earthly death, it seems to me that religion has nothing to offer. This heavenly expectation is unrealistic and there is little evidence that heaven is actually a real place where the righteous are gathered after death. Unfortunately, the religion experience can be described as a continuum between hope and fear.

Modern humans, blinded by the arrogance of perceived superiority in nature, are fertile receptacles for the promise of continued life after death. Christianity has institutionalized the concept of "going home," that there is another life in a chalet in the sky and time on Earth is shaky and transitory. However, there is much more evidence regarding our "shaky" earthly existence than a promised hereafter lifestyle. Just maybe we *are* "home."

For Catholics, the Nicene and Apostles' Creeds are the two professions of faith that establish belief in an afterlife. The Nicene Creed states, "We look for . . . the life of the world to come." The Apostles' Creed is similar, "I believe in . . . the life everlasting." Religion is not concerned with the quality of present life nor the pursuit of happiness. Religion, with its emphasis on sin and the corrupt nature of man, extinguishes love, romance, passion and the enjoyment of life. We have replaced the pursuit of joy with a surrender to anxiety. The assumption of an afterlife is the primary focus. Life and suffering here on earth are a necessary prelude to entering the Kingdom of Heaven. Promising an enchanting reward after death allows religions to control their minions.

The pragmatic practice of religion is a repetitious, somnambulant ritual resulting in predictable, disappointing, unsatisfactory results. Catholic Mass provides a good example of the repetitive ritual. Mass is a weekly public expression of faith and an attempt to communicate with God. It is presented as a "sacrifice," an attempt to appease God for misbehavior. It binds a religious community together; a repetitive performance of a static ceremony without visible or positive results.

The vast majority of Catholics have only a superficial knowledge of the theological constructs of their faith and are only passively connected with their religion. They occupy pews in the church on Sunday and are what I call, "mushroom Catholics." The Catholic Church has never encouraged reading the Bible and Sunday homilies seldom confront major theological issues or thorny intellectual questions of faith. Homilies are monologues delivered by the presiding priest. Opposing viewpoints, discussion, and dialog are not part of the protocol. Priests and preachers seem comfortable selecting non-controversial phrases from scripture as themes for their homilies. These sermons are "tweeners," filling between unspoken fractious doctrinal issues of faith and pragmatic issues of interest to the laity, such as abortion, divorce, women as priests, clerical celibacy and birth control.

Every week, at the designated hour, believers pour into churches like an incoming ocean tide. An hour or so later, depending on the length of the homily, the tide recedes and parishioners exit through expensive, exquisitely carved, ornate doors, no more informed than when they entered. The parking lot quickly empties and the congregation returns to their normal routines. The Church hierarchy appears comfortable dispensing this facile version of religion and parishioners seem content with their passive and dependent role.

As humans we have come to believe in a cause equaling an effect; religion fails to fulfill that expectation. Attendance at regularly occurring religious services is an exercise in futility.

Christianity, for an archaic ideology, has a remarkable history. It is a philosophical concept that began with a charismatic Jewish prophet and morphed into an organized religion. Will Durant's epic survey of world history, succinctly describes Christianity in the volume *Caesar and Christ* (1944).

> Christianity arose out of Jewish apocalyptic—esoteric revelations of the coming Kingdom; it derived its impetus from

the personality and vision of Christ; it gained strength from the belief in his resurrection, and the promise of eternal life; it received doctrinal form in the theology of Paul; it grew by the absorption of pagan faith and ritual; it became a triumphant Church by inheriting the organizing patterns and genius of Rome.

Shrouded in mystery with little empirical evidence for the existence of any of its asserted doctrines, Christianity has still managed to capture the hearts and minds of millions of people for over 2,000 years and become a guiding force in their lives. With its misogynistic, gloomy and despairing message, it has managed to survive centuries, hanging by the mythical thread of a promised afterlife. By any measure, it is a highly improbable success story. This success is predicated on mankind's awe of the majestic complexity of the universe, and difficulty in believing it is just accidental. Add an inability to accept death as an inevitable event; and an insatiable quest for immortality. The breathtaking beauty and diversity of earth's flora and fauna also underlie a belief by many that this splendid world can only have resulted from a planned design by a superior being.

Like astronomers, humankind continues to scan the universe for sign of some supernatural cosmic force but without success. A casual observation of nature would suggest that God — or the gods —have little interest in their creations or happenings on earth. The Holocaust, the Eurasian pandemic Black Plague of the 14th century, the Irish famine of 1740-1741 and the AIDS epidemic are estimated to have killed 232 million people. It is hard to discern benevolence in a God that would allow human tragedies of this magnitude to happen. It's not difficult to conclude that God is either nonexistent or non-caring. If non-caring, does our definition of God still fit?

Karl Marx called religion "the opiate of the people." Religion offers a respite and balm from reality; a magical interpretation for existence, an antidote to suffering, a tenuous explanation for the unknown and the promise of a happy afterlife. It assuages our fears and offers solace. Religion homogenizes people; rich and poor, educated and non-educated, men and women, children and adults, "red and yellow, black and white." Yet, each religion, formed by culture, myth and history, has its idiosyncratic spiritual version of God, the hereafter, and the proper behavior to attain that goal. The proliferation of sects, splinter groups, factions, and cults gives credence to the conclusion that man created God, not the other way around.

Historically, religion has been useful to explain naturally occurring phenomena to an uneducated, superstitious people. In preliterate societies, religion was a compelling, effective, and expedient abstraction. Gods were used as instruments to help people understand the complex world they lived in. Primitive tribes and advanced civilizations found illustrative solutions to baffling mysteries of the universe in religious beliefs. Religion prospered because it offered a plausible explanation for the workings of the universe to an illiterate and uniformed people as well as promise of an idyllic life extension after an arduous existence. Early Christians were misguided into believing that adherence to a creedal set of rules would lead to salvation and eternal life.

Maintenance of a religious identity requires some form of commitment to a religious body. Identity as a Catholic, Lutheran, Jehovah Witness or Baptist necessitates a continuous relationship with those respective communities. Religions often have a dogmatic intolerance for anyone who has another version of faith. Straying from the group jeopardizes religious commitment by exposure to viewpoints of others, which may disrupt one's belief system.

Because of this, —fear that a significant other has potential to adversely affect the views of a Catholic — the Catholic Church opposed "mixed marriages," of which my parents were an example; Catholic and Lutheran. Because of this *mixture* they were not allowed to be married at the Catholic Church altar but instead were married "outside" the altar. In spite of this slight from the Church, they remained happily married for 51 years — until my dad died.

In *Nature's God* (2014), Matthew Stewart offers an eloquent discourse on how religion is viewed in modern times.

> According to a widely accepted view today, religion is an eminently useful thing. Religious belief gives meaning to

our suffering, teaches respect for the moral law, transmits the wisdom of experience from generation to generation, inspires great art, and unites communities with bonds of shared trust and so enhances their prospects for survival.... Indeed, religion is so useful, some theorists today argue, that natural selection has seen fit to endow all human beings with a religious instinct that predisposes them to believe in what they don't understand.

Religion touches our lives in profound ways and cannot easily be ignored. The universe is complex and mystifying and religion is the panacea for our bewilderment, offering plausible explanations for our existence and the promise of a continued life in another world better than the one we are experiencing. The elegance of religion is reliance on an invisible, powerful, cosmic force that we cannot see, comprehend, understand, or challenge.

Nostalgia for the past may impede future change. Organized religion has its antecedents in primitive beliefs, superstitions and stories passed down through generations. Spinoza believed superstition was engendered, preserved and fostered by fear. Superstitious and preliterate societies used multiple Gods as tropes to explain naturally occurring phenomena.

Religion is an addictive imperfection in the spiritual psyche of humankind. As much as we might wish, hope, pray and seek some form of communication with a putative benefactor, it always fails. We have had little luck communicating with an ethereal God.

People are born. People die. Some lead happy lives; some have lives filled with tragedy. In this yin and yang of life, there is no indication of any caring supernatural force. Those marketing religion use fear and anxiety as the attractant and salvation as the product. However, commitment to religious belief and pledging fealty to a transcendent deity is not without risk to one's psyche and can be a one-sided exchange.

Religion elevates subjectivity over objectivity. Becoming a Christian entails relinquishing one's individual autonomy and ceding superiority to another, an outsourcing of one's beliefs. Religion requires admitting one's inferiority, subservience to an invisible being, giving thanks for life, bearing suffering stoically and hoping for a better life after death. Religion is a celestial bargain with God. One has to admit to imperfect behavior, promise atonement, express humility, beg for forgiveness and worship a transcendent being. In return, one hopes to trade eternal damnation in the fires of Hell for continued life in heavenly bliss. Making a covenant with an unknown, invisible being requires substantial faith and not a little imagination.

Religion claims to recognize the dignity of humans, but when critically examined, it does the opposite. Religion impoverishes the individual. Religion has some characteristics of captivity; your freedoms and activities are regulated and restricted. It discourages personal perspectives on life and the expression of opposing views; and deprives one of pride, self-esteem and the freedom of independent thought by substituting an ecclesiastical creed in the place of individual expression.

If religion were a color, it would be ashen grey. Religion fosters a melancholy, gloomy, pessimistic, dispirited and morbid view of life here on earth. Conspicuously absent from Christian dogma are references to romance, licit pleasure, enjoyment and fun. More often we're exposed to Thomas Hobbes description of life on earth; "solitary, poor, nasty, brutish and short." Religion has seized this pessimistic view of life and elevated sin to be the centerpiece.

Christianity devalues life on earth in favor of an afterlife. The human condition is characterized as unimportant, unworthy and sinful. We offend the Creator. We are taught that it is normal to live in despair and fatalism while awaiting salvation and eternal happiness. Religion has an obsession with death. In Ecclesiastes 7:1, we learn that the day of death is better than the day of birth!

Matthew Fox, a former Catholic priest, believes religion has failed the West because it has been silent about pleasure and allowed a culture of death as a substitute. Religion offers a bleak outlook on life with no beneficial results until passing. Religion has intruded on the enjoyment of life and driven a wedge between misery and happiness. Belief in a deity creates a genuine conflict between enjoyment of life and the anxiety and fear that are prominent features of religion.

Early Christianity espoused two distinctly differing views of spirituality: one perspective was God's love for humanity; the other embodied a stern and ruthless God. It is difficult to comprehend the allure of a philosophy whose disciples mix pious devotion with fear of a deity.

The major attributes of religion are: fear of eternal punishment, suffering characterized as beneficial, personal guilt, dominating religious authorities, an unknown leader, a subservient role for women, humans characterized as humble servants, no known benefits during one's lifetime on earth, a dubious promise of eternal bliss after you're dead and strict rules for living. This is a depressing and unappealing description of a lifestyle.

One of the pernicious affects of religion is *control over followers*. Religious organizations and their leaders tend to dominate their followers with extensive decrees and instructions on how to live, what to do and what not to do. Controlling societal behavior has long been a major concern of political leaders and religion has been used to attain that goal, appearing to act on the assumption that humans are incapable of maneuvering through the minefield of moral turpitude without divine intervention. Navigating life's journey is nearly impossible without input from others, but maintaining control over the decision making process is essential if you want to preserve your own perspective. Life is shared with family, friends, acquaintances, and colleagues, but you are an independent entity responsible for your own actions, thoughts, and life choices.

The Catholic Church greatly influenced political life in Europe during the Middle Ages, allying and collaborating with political leaders. Religious leaders conspired with the secular to maintain control over their constituents and prey on their credulity, with the Church focused more on preserving political influence than saving souls. The Middle Ages are replete with examples of political intrigue and collusion between Popes and kings; struggles over authority and power between the Church and the monarchs were continuous.

Western societies have a culture of guilt built on a mythological religious platform. The guilt culture espoused by Christianity was instrumental in the stable behavior of societies in Europe. Guilt cultures thrive on individual judgment. Guilt is the voice of an internal conscience. Guilt cultures emphasize atonement, repentance, punishment and forgiveness as methods to maintain moral order.

In honor and shame cultures, more prominent in the Middle and Far East, actions are judged by the community. Honor is judged as a person's standing in the community and shame a reaction to a transgression after it happens and how the misbehavior appears to others. In shame cultures, loss of face and humiliation are prominent features.

One who completely embraces religion truly has their life planned out for them in detail. In that case, religion is the GPS (Global Positioning System) of one's life: it recognizes where you are, knows your destination, and outlines a detailed map for your journey toward that destination, neither expecting nor tolerating any deviation or input from you. It expects that you will follow without question the prescribed route. Accepting religion into your life moves decision making on many important life questions from you to a third party.

Religion is both commanding and demanding. You are given detailed rules and regulations that influence your sex life, your financial affairs, your leisure time and your eating habits. You are instructed on the purpose of sex (procreation); what is permissible and what is not; the share of your income you should tithe to the Church; the amount of time you should commit to church activities; when to attend church services; how to behave in your work environment and in public; and when, how much and what you should eat and drink during certain church seasons.

Religious GPS is programmed to instruct you without your input. One of life's greatest regrets might be to discover at the conclusion that you had abrogated major decisions on your views of existence to authoritarian figures who made all your life decisions without any of your input.

Democratic governments rule by consent of the people. Religious organizations grant divine rights to a supreme, absolute, mysterious, invisible "higher" authority and leave no options for their adherents to question dogma. Religion requires fealty to proclamations of dead prophets and their living successors; a major exercise in self-abnegation that can result in a paralyzing dependency. Religion is an intellectual cul-de-sac. You cede ability to think for yourself in matters of faith, knowledge, holiness, sanctity, intelligence and morals to clerics who act as surrogates for an unknowable deity. You promise fealty and conformity to an abstract set of beliefs only superficially understood.

Religion forces you to substitute invisibility for visibility, unknown for known, metaphysical for rational experience, and mystery for reality. In most commitments, the other participant is expected to offer something in return. Since the second party to this accord is unknown and invisible, the alleged participation on his or her part will have to come principally from your own creative thinking. Your imagination will have to suffice as the basis of faith and belief in a metaphysical world.

Religions teach a theology of guilt, mercy, and reward. Generally, the expectations of religious conformity are forgiveness of sin, salvation, and an idyllic afterlife. There is little empirical evidence for this. Today we have more and more affirmation of ancient religious dogma and less and less justification, explanation, and clarification of the benefits of religion and the role it could or should play in our lives. Theologians use pure sophistry to confuse rather than inform or enlighten the faithful.

Religion suggests that we suppress or neglect our basic passions. Instead we are encouraged to seek a higher meaning in life. Every Sunday we are reminded from church pulpits of our failure to achieve this goal. Much oratory has been dispensed from pulpits on the proper way to live, but it is seldom accompanied by logical explanations or practical applications.

The Catholic Church remains firmly opposed to modernity, pledges instead obeisance to ancient dogma and texts. Theological mumbo jumbo is substituted for common sense. There are no mechanisms in place nor is there interest by high Church authority to institute debate or question religious orthodoxy. We are continually reminded that earthly existence is a prelude to celestial bliss and we should take comfort that life is short but eternity is forever. An astonishing thing about the appeal of religion and devotion to an unknown God is that it is an untested, unproven and unsubstantiated hypothesis, since it deals with imaginary things.

The tyranny of religion devalues existence in the only life we know, substituting an unknown postmortem promised land in its place. Religion requires us to view our earthly existence as temporary, a passageway to another life in paradise. Religion and happiness are incompatible. Religion teaches us that our purpose in this life is to endure its meaninglessness and concentrate on an eternity attainable only by dying where we are given two choices, a celestial paradise or the unquenched fires of hell.

Enduring the anxieties of belief and the uncertainty of salvation is unpleasant and counterproductive. Christianity demands that we spend our lives waiting for the Rapture and wondering whether our destiny is Paradise or Hell. This seems like a silly endeavor when there is scant possibility that either exists. One wonders why God didn't just create heaven to start with and skip the earth part.

This approach to earthly existence hardly reinforces the notion of a benevolent and loving deity. Blind faith may enchant some but one wonders if there isn't a more rational guide to life. It seems irrational to ignore the certainties of the life we have, and concentrate on an uncertain life that may not even exist.

Edward O. Wilson, in *The Meaning of Human Existence* (2014), eloquently describes our species with remarkable optimism:

> We were created not by a supernatural intelligence but by chance and necessity as one species out of millions of species in Earth's biosphere. Hope and wish for otherwise as we will, there is no evidence of an eternal grace shining down on us, no demonstrable destiny or purpose assigned us, no second life vouched us for the end of the present one. We are, it seems, completely alone. And that in my opinion is a very good thing. It means we are completely free. As a result, we can more easily diagnose the etiology of the irrational beliefs that so unjustifiably divide us. Laid before us are new options scarcely dreamed of in earlier ages. They empower us to address with more confidence the greatest goal of all time, the unity of the human race.

History is replete with misuses of religion: persecutions, wars, pogroms (massacres), jihads and crusades. One tragedy of the 21st century is continued pernicious use of religion as justification for atrocities committed against humanity to attain political goals. Religious fanaticism continues rampant in the modern world, yet it hardly occupies the moral high ground. In fact, the carnage, devastation and suffering that exists today dwarfs previous religious exercises in cruelty.

Religion offers motives for bad behavior and empowers believers to express themselves in malevolent ways. In the current world, it's impossible to pick up a newspaper or magazine or turn on the TV without encountering sectarian strife and faith-based violence. Driven by animus toward those who think differently, operating under a banner of righteousness, encouraged by misguided clerics, blinded by zealotry, inspired by "holy books" and the "promise" of God's approval, militants seek political, geographical, and religious goals through use of force.

Historically, corroboration between religious and civil authorities has generated many violent conflicts with outcomes benefiting both participants. Human history includes a chilling chronicle of hostilities motivated by religious ideology and political expediency. The Papacy has been involved with numerous unsavory regimes involving a long and sordid history of conquests and persecutions.

Religion was originally an attempt to make sense of the world and explain natural phenomena. It has disintegrated into monolithic platforms for justifying power and political motivations. Harnessing and exploiting religious fervor in pursuit of personal and political gain is inimical to the putative peaceful intentions of religion.

The Crusades are a quintessential example of abuse of religion. These barbaric, organized pogroms lasted over 200 years, were sanctioned by two Catholic Popes and caused the loss of thousands of lives on both sides. The Crusades were essentially acts of genocide, undertaken in the name of God and the furtherance of Christianity. They were examples of extravagant carnage and the use of violence to further church objectives.

A good Crusader was considered a good Christian. Recruits were promised a Plenary Indulgence, unconditional forgiveness of sin.

In 1095, Pope Urban II initiated the First Crusade to take back the Holy Land from the Turks. In 1202, Pope Innocent III proclaimed the Fourth Crusade. There were six major Crusades and several minor ones, finally ending in 1291. They were all essentially military and financial failures.

Pope Innocent III was also responsible for another famous use of force by the Church: the Inquisition, begun to safeguard orthodoxy. "Heretics" were examined during judicial hearings in which the burden was on them to prove their innocence. Many of the "guilty" were burned at the stake.

In 1252, Pope Innocent IV authorized torture to extract confessions from suspected heretics. John C. Dwyer, writing in *Church History* (1985), depicts the Inquisition as . . . "beyond a doubt the greatest scandal that ever disfigured the life of the Church, and attempts to explain it by pointing out that men of the day could not make a clear distinction between heresy and revolution really miss the point."

The paradoxical consequence of the Inquisition was it failed to suppress apostasy and eliminate infidels, apostates, witches, and nonbelievers; but the response to its barbaric nature caused the Church, over time, to reposition itself to a more liberal view of religion where it now, not only accepts the right of individuals to worship any way they please, but also acknowledges the rights of nonbelievers.

Another example of Catholic violence in furtherance of religion: the St. Bartholomew Day massacre of 1572. French Catholic mobs attacked and killed an estimated 5,000 to 30,000 Calvinists Protestants (Huguenots) in the name of their King and their God. Pope Gregory XIII ordered a hymn to be sung in thanksgiving and had a medal struck to celebrate the event!

Celebrating killing fellow Christians by the hierarchy of the Church is a shameless exhibition of power and authority and reinforces the prevalent stereotype of the Church as cruel, arrogant, elitist and willing to be ruthless in establishing and maintaining spiritual and political dominance.

In modern times, we are vividly reminded on a daily basis of the misuse of religion by countries to wage war on those who have different beliefs from their own. A cursory review of human history and survey of the state of the modern world strongly suggests that religious ideologies have a unique divisive characteristic, separating individuals, groups and nations while arguably causing considerable violence and misfortune; and sabotaging potential for a tranquil world.

Christianity is a monolithic philosophy firmly anchored in ancient superstition; unable — or unwilling — to incorporate contemporary scholarship to address primitive concepts and beliefs. The cultural differences between the time of Jesus and now is enormous, yet modern religious doctrine appears indistinguishable from the ancient and apparently no effort is underway to differentiate the two. Technology and science proceed at warp speed, supplying increased understanding of our universe, yet religious leaders employ first century ideas for a 21st century audience. Modern religions are not modern.

Religions are inextricably connected to their irrational beginnings, an obsolete cosmology reflecting worldviews of long ago. Zealous Christian clerics act as defenders of the faith, guarding against apostasy and any modern philosophical intrusion that would weaken their doctrine. And, modern humanistic developments tend to weaken church doctrine.

Christian history reveals two conspicuous, recurring themes that explain the success, prosperous growth, and seemingly endless lifespan of Christianity; one pragmatic, the other theological. The pragmatic theme is one of social control, the role of the divine in enforcing morality, enabling humans to live in harmony in social groups. The theological theme is the concept of immortality, a scripture-based expectation that after death our bodies will be reconstituted in some form in another world where we will experience a beatific state and spiritual ecstasy — or eternal pain. These beliefs, driven by human imagination and antipodal human emotions of hope and fear, help explain the captivating nature of Christianity and the triumph of hope over reason.

Christian leaders seem incapable of adjusting to modern knowledge, and obstinately continue to regurgitate 2,000-year-old superstitious myths. Contemporary clerics appear to be morally and intellectually stranded in a medieval theology. Theologians maintain their fidelity to ancient Christian doctrines and conveniently vault over the enlightenment years, landing comfortably in modernity securely clutching their ancient beliefs.

ALL FISH HAVE BONES

Gods were a plausible explanation for natural phenomena in the ancient world, but we now have scientific explanations that are more reasonable. The expanded corpus of knowledge that explains how the world works in the 21st century has passed by Rome unnoticed, unappreciated, and unread. Biblical Jesus has increasing non-relevance to modern humans, yet Christian clerics continue to wrap their archaic message in parchment and deliver it as indubitable truth

Even though Christianity is recognized as one of the three Abrahamic religions, it has divided numerous times to appeal to different groups and individuals. The primary bifurcation was Catholic and Protestant, with many further divisions among the Protestant line. Within these major groups of theological thought, individuals have developed "designer religions," a set of doctrines tailored to our artisan sense of religious beliefs. We live in a fractured religious landscape, many of us constructing our own personalized religion. We review accepted organizational doctrines, traditions, writings, and rubrics of a specific religion, ignore the imperfections, and choose those theological constructs that appeal and reject the rest. This selection process allows congregations to apparently function under the umbrella of one set of religious beliefs while, in reality, each individual practices his or her own personalized religion within their own comfort level.

This process creates thousands of "mini" religions individually calibrated to appeal to the sensitivities of each individual. One could argue there are seven billion religions on earth. This personal "editing" of church doctrine facilitates continued membership in a church of choice without commitment to the entire religious creed.

Many modern religious adherents treat God as a "Sunday God;" with a once-a-week excursion to their church of choice. Listen to the homily, drop a modest offering in the collection plate, visit with friends over coffee and donuts, and then return to the secular world.

Recently, religion has become industrialized, or more appropriately, an extortion racket, promising God's favor in exchange for monetary donations. Television turned religion into a career calling for evangelists. Disingenuous

Faith in a Fantasy

TV hucksters have seduced many naïve Americans into believing that God's benevolence is dispensed in quantifiable amounts, depending on your cash contribution! TV preachers have convinced a gullible public that currying favor with the Almighty is possible by simply writing a check! The TV God seems to be obsessed with money.

Recently, I watched an outwardly sincere TV evangelist implore listeners to contribute $500 to his ministry. According to him, 200 people would receive God's blessing if they sent a check for $500, a plea for $100,000! Apparently God likes round numbers.

These TV preachers link the listeners' health, happiness, and salvation to a financial contribution. They dispense salvation in graduated units; the larger the contribution, the smoother the path to salvation. Watching these hucksters provokes emotions from sadness to rage; sadness because of the susceptibility of the television listeners and rage because these fakers are using religion to pay for their lifestyle.

Christianity appears to be in a holding pattern. Dogma seems flash frozen in medieval times and shows no sign of thawing. Belief in God today requires a suspension of a belief in reality and an acceptance of magical explanations for our existence. Faith demands that we await the world to come, a promised world of bliss and immortality that will replace the misery and harsh realities of life we endure here on earth. We have jettisoned our rational experiences and intellectual integrity for the speculative covenant of an everlasting, blissful life in a kingdom somewhere else.

Early Christians apparently believed that Christ would soon reappear on earth and establish the Kingdom of God. We read in Matthew 16:28 that "some standing here will not taste death before they see the Son of Man coming in his kingdom." 1st Peter 4:70 states, "The end of all things is at hand." In 1st John 2:18, John writes "Thus we know this is the last hour." None of these predictions have come to pass in 2,000-plus years.

A fundamental imperfection of Christianity is the failure of Jesus to leave a sustaining structure — writing, organizational precepts or intellectual guidance — for his followers. This created a vulnerability to manipulation, allowing the early Christian "fathers" to impart their own interpretation to

ALL FISH HAVE BONES

Jesus' teachings and reconcile them with their vision of Christianity. What we have then, is not a Christ-preached belief system, but an expropriated and distorted version of the original preaching of Jesus.

I believe religion has continued to grow and prosper, in spite of its mystical doctrines, because of three unique human attributes: awareness of death, fear of punishment for bad behavior and hope for a reward for good behavior. These features of human temperament constitute a philosophical frame of fear and hope explaining the attraction of religious doctrines.

CHAPTER FIVE
SIN, SEX, SUFFERING AND SALVATION

Work out your own salvation. Do not depend on others.
— *Buddha*

Religion cultivates a pessimistic, dispirited, and somber view of life. The apocalyptic theology of sin and spiritual doom and gloom taught in Christianity is a primary contributor to religious anxiety. The concept of sinfulness and the threat of eternal punishment diminishes the enjoyment of life and nurtures a sense of anxiety and despair. Religion teaches us that disappointments in life, health issues, misery, pain, anxiety, worry and suffering are normal, temporary, and should be embraced as atonement for our sins. We should accept the vagaries of life as part of punishment for bad behavior and concentrate on an invisible hereafter. We are encouraged to have blind faith in a future shrouded in mystery and not become distracted by existing daily reality.

ALL FISH HAVE BONES

This fervent, obsessive focus on the melancholy aspects of life seems a bizarre way to approach the only life we may ever experience. Apparently, joy and happiness on Earth are found only in worshipping God and not in secular pursuits. According to Christian doctrine, happiness, lustful pleasure, contentment and gratification are sinful and not appropriate earthly goals.

Sin is an artificial, manmade construct. It only has relevance if there is a God. You may punch an unruly neighbor in the face and get arrested for assault and battery, but that is a violation of societal laws, not a sin. It only becomes a sin if it is a behavior that displeases God.

According to Rodney Stark, professor of sociology and religion at Baylor University, the concept of sin arose during the sixth century BC when many new religions were founded simultaneously. Zarathustra, Buddha, Confucius and the Hebrew prophets of Israel all appeared about the same time. Sin did not originate with Jesus.

The concept of sin is diabolically clever. According to Catholic Church doctrine, we are born with an imperfection — Original Sin — over which we have no control. Its removal can only be obtained by salvation — through Jesus — which makes religion necessary. Scripture teaches us that sinfulness is inherited and accompanies us throughout our lives. After years of being told you're a sinner, you begin to believe that maybe you do have a corrupt nature.

I don't believe humans are intrinsically sinful. Our lives should not be defined by sinfulness. We should vigorously reject any such notion by clerics that preach otherwise.

According to Catholic doctrine, sex is intrinsically sinful. In the Church vocabulary, sin and sex are synonyms. The foundation of this distorted belief is found by studying certain ancient societies, which were misogynistic, male dominated and inhibited in sexual matters. Mary as the virgin mother of Jesus set the tone for the Catholic Church stance on sex and established in early Christianity that sex was unnecessary. If you accept that *sex is sinful*, the natural reproductive system of the human species is essentially a sinful mechanism! Non-reproductive — recreational — sex is frowned upon.

Sin, Sex, Suffering and Salvation

If you believe in literal interpretation of the Bible, virginity is the lifestyle choice for an assured path toward salvation and a celestial reward.

Foundational roots for Christian teachings on sex were established by two architects of early Christianity, St. Paul and St. Augustine, both male chauvinists with ascetic dispositions and obsessive, distorted views of sex. St. Jerome, one of the most prolific writers in early Christianity, was an arch-misogynist who also contributed to the aberrant sexual doctrine of the early Church with his extensive anti-feminine writings. Jerome detested marriage and found second marriage particularly abhorrent (Barr, 1990). Augustine, Bishop of Hippo, one of the great Catholic theologians, believed that concupiscence — sexual desire — corrupted human nature and affected all that we do, thereby making all human activity sinful. Augustine codified the idea of Original Sin and believed it was transmitted from generation to generation through sexual intercourse!

The humanitarian teachings of Jesus were hijacked by Paul and Augustine and injected with a repressive sexual message, hatred of body and self and harsh punishment for those who strayed. They installed sexual sin as the centerpiece of their version of Christianity, where today it continues as a prominent fixture in Christian religion. Intolerant and delusional sexual doctrines continue to be defining characteristic of Roman Catholicism.

Paul and Augustine essentially invented a new religion based on their obsessive focus on sexual issues. They believed the proper path to salvation was the single, celibate life, which conflicts with God's message to "be fruitful and multiply." The dubious sexual doctrine of the Catholic Church remains unchanged from the opinions of three religious zealots from the first and fourth centuries. Jesus, the Good Shepherd and Prince of Peace, got lost in the audacious reinvention of Christianity by Paul, Augustine and Jerome.

John C. Dwyer, in *Church History: Twenty Centuries of Catholic Christianity* (1985) writes,

> . . . the question has been frequently raised of whether Paul distorted the simple message of Jesus – the message of the fatherhood of God and the brotherhood of man – and warped it into the theory of the atonement of an angry and vengeful God by means of a bloody sacrifice. Paul has been accused of exaggerating

man's guilt and despair beyond all bounds and of stripping the human being of all self-respect. His references to purity, to sexual sins, and his contrast of flesh and spirit, have led some theologians to find in him the source of that perverse hostility to the body which characterizes so much of what Augustine and the fathers of the eastern church wrote.

A significant portion of the New Testament — almost one quarter — is epistles to followers written by Paul or ascribed to him. Paul pivoted away from the compassionate message of Jesus and introduced a dark and melancholy theology to Christianity. The authenticity of some of Paul's epistles is debated by Biblical scholars and beyond the scope of this book.

Threats of punishments for nonbelievers are commonplace in the New Testament. One example: "Whoever believes in the Son has eternal life, but whoever disobeys the Son will not see life, but the wrath of God remains upon him" (John 3:36). It is insufficient after committing sin to confess and be sorry. Atonement requires punishment.

The Bible portrays suffering on Earth as a necessary prelude for entering into paradise. We are taught that suffering has a redemptive quality. Tell that to a stage IV cancer patient.

The crucifixion of Jesus as atonement for humanity's sins is held as an extraordinary example of extreme suffering. We are continually reminded of the sacrifice of Jesus by ubiquitous renderings depicting ghoulish images of Jesus on the cross bleeding from a crown of thorns, and nail and spear wounds. This macabre effigy is found on the walls of churches, schools, and homes as a reminder that we are "washed in the blood of Christ" (Revelation 1:5). This somber, iconic depiction of a bleeding, dying man nailed to a cross is so universal in our culture that its ghastly image no longer offends our sensibilities. The cross is a popular piece of jewelry for both men and women. Glorified suffering as a means to salvation is not a requirement of any God I want to be associated with.

The purported primary function of Western Christianity is salvation, an institutional quest to save souls. The authority for the Christian doctrine of immortality is found in scripture, John 3:16, "For God so loved the world that he gave his only son, so that everyone who believes in Him may not perish but may have eternal life." We are led to believe there is another world, outside the one we know, that is essentially a return to the Garden of Eden, minus the snake.

The redemptive teaching of the Christian church is that even though mankind is sinful, salvation is possible because of God's love for His creations. Yet, one of the sad but defining characteristics of Christianity is the contradictory message of salvation for those who believe and misery and punishment for those who do not believe. In Mark 16:16, we are told that you can only be saved if you believe in Jesus. If you don't believe, you are condemned. It's difficult to detect benevolence in that dichotomous choice.

The spiritual goal of Christians is attaining salvation; reconciliation with God, forgiveness of sin, redemption, and avoidance of eternal damnation. Christian salvation can be attained through baptism — remove the stain of Original Sin — obedience to Christian theological constructs, comporting yourself in a respectable and honorable manner, confessing improprieties, and dying in a state of grace! The path to a celestial reward for the Christian is complicated, particularly if the human soul has been preordained by God for salvation or punishment.

Even the righteous may not be guaranteed salvation. Predestination, St. Augustine's notion that God chooses people for salvation or damnation at the beginning of time, is complicated and contradicts the concept of free will. The complexity of the issue consigns it to arcane theological debate.

ALL FISH HAVE BONES

CHAPTER SIX
DUBIOUS DOGMAS

Don't be trapped by dogma which is living the results of other people's thinking.

— *Steve Jobs*

Religion is a philosophical rabbit hole, a portal to an alternative wonderland where believers encounter a bewildering array of metaphysical dogmas contradicting real world experience. Many religious organizations publish ecclesiastical pronouncements that have tenuous connections to the Bible or the original teachings of Jesus. In addition to strict sexual mores and fixation on sin, most religious beliefs involve some sort of repressive prohibitions, proscriptions and constraints. Religion has a melancholy litany of taboos.

Every religion seems to feature at least one repressive gesture that sets them apart from others. Southern Baptists don't drink alcohol. Mormons abstain from alcohol, tobacco and caffeine and wear special underwear called "temple garments" as a reminder of promises made to God. Catholics fast and eat fish on Fridays during Lent (in the past, Catholics abstained from meat every Friday). Catholic women used to have to wear a hat or hair covering when in church —women's hair was considered seductive. Jehovah's Witnesses don't celebrate birthdays, Christmas, Easter or other life events they believe had pagan origins; Muslims and Jews don't eat pork; Christian Scientists avoid medical intervention when they are ill.

These often-bizarre practices seem to have no causal connection with salvation. They are ostensibly based on interpretations of scripture, but it's difficult to understand what these self-inflicted prohibitions have to do with worshiping God. Religions seem frozen in the past, unable to comprehend the differential between the historic and the present and unwilling to review the relevance of ancient dogma in the 21st century.

I had a memorable experience with one of these ill-conceived ordinances. When I was a child, the Catholic Church had rigorous rules relating to the receipt of Holy Communion. You were required to abstain from food and water from midnight until you received communion. During a school event in which everyone went to Mass, we assembled in the school before marching to church. While waiting, I inadvertently took a drink from a water fountain. I had broken my fast and could not take communion with my classmates. I sat alone in the pew — isolated, embarrassed, humiliated and traumatized — imagining that everyone in the church wondered what grievous sin I had committed.

This nonsensical regulation has since been abandoned, but my recollection remains vivid. It is but one example of wacky rules that cloistered, celibate clergy can dream up that has nothing whatsoever to do with Jesus, God, salvation or common sense.

Progress in any field is based on a free exchange of ideas and recognition of advancements in the sciences. Religion, with its insular nature, fails to engage in substantive dialog with its constituency to determine relevance of ancient doctrine to modern times. Much of Catholic Church dogma employs theological sophistry, unsupported by tangible evidence, to argue the rationality of dubious religious doctrines and convince the faithful of their truthfulness. The following are some examples of those doctrines.

Dubious Dogmas

Transubstantiation. The Eucharist — Sacrament of Holy Communion — is a reenactment of the Last Supper and a central teaching of the Catholic Church. Transubtantiation is the concept that the wine and bread used in Holy Communion are converted into the body and blood of Jesus by whispered prayers of the priest. This conversion — predicated on the words of Jesus at the Last Supper — violates all known natural laws of chemistry and physics. This doctrine was established at the Fourth Lateran Council in 1215, and reaffirmed at the Council of Trent in 1551.

Resurrection of Jesus. Jesus rising from the dead is the cornerstone of Christianity and an extraordinary assertion. Scripture is the only evidence for this miracle, and there are major discrepancies in the four gospel renditions of the events surrounding the death of Jesus.

Matthew 27:51-53 describes an unbelievable occurrence: "And behold, the veil of the sanctuary was torn in two from top to bottom. The earth quaked, rocks were split, tombs were opened, and the bodies of many saints who had fallen asleep were raised. And coming forth from their tombs after his resurrection, they entered the holy city and appeared to many." This fantastic event has never, to my knowledge, been recorded anywhere else.

John Dominic Crossan (b. 1934) a former Catholic priest and scholar of early Christianity and Jesus, writes in his book, *Jesus: A Revolutionary Biography* (1994), "Crucifixion as a penalty was remarkably widespread in antiquity... among the Romans it was inflicted above all on the lower classes, i.e. slaves, violent criminals, and the unruly elements in rebellious provinces, not least in Judaea.... In general, however, if one had influence, one was not crucified, and if one was crucified, one would not have influence enough to obtain burial."

Crossan continues,

> Roman crucifixion was state terrorism; (and) its function was to deter resistance or revolt, especially among the lower classes; and ... the body was usually left on the cross to be consumed eventually by the wild beasts. It would have been impossible, without influence or bribery, to obtain a crucified corpse. And

it might also be very dangerous to request it, lest even familial association with a condemned criminal be judged as part of the problem and handled accordingly. With regard to the body of Jesus, by Easter Sunday morning, those who cared did not know where it was, and those who knew did not care.

John Shelby Spong, a former Episcopal bishop, writes in *The Sins of Scripture* (2005), "Of course stories of cosmic ascensions are mythological. Dead bodies do not walk out of tombs three days after execution. Angels do not descend out of the sky, earthquakes do not announce earthly events, soldiers are not reduced to a state of stupor by angelic power, stones are not rolled away from tombs to let the dead out . . ."

Virgin birth of Jesus. There are many figures in mythology that were born of virgins. It was common to attribute virgin births to illustrious figures of the time. There is little evidence for immaculate conception by the Holy Spirit. Many Biblical scholars attribute the concept of the virgin birth of Jesus to an erroneous translation of the Hebrew word *alma* which simply means "young woman" and not "virgin." There is substantial evidence in the Bible that Jesus had brothers and sisters (Matthew 13:55-56; Mark 6:3; Galatians 1:19; Acts 1:14). Mark and John make no mention of a virgin birth. Even Paul indicates in his writings that there was no virgin birth (Romans 1:3, Galatians 4:4).

Meier, in *A Marginal Jew* (1991), concludes, ". . . prescinding from faith and later Church teaching, the historian or exegete is asked to render a judgment on the NT and patristic texts we have examined, viewed simply as historical sources, the most probable opinion is that the brothers and sisters of Jesus were true siblings."

Father Raymond Brown, a Catholic theologian, in his book *The Virginal Conception and Bodily Resurrection of Jesus* (1973), writes that the infancy material in the gospels of Luke and Matthew are "virtually irreconcilable." "They agree in so few details that we may say with certainty that they cannot both be historical *in toto*." Acceptance or rejection of this doctrine will depend on an individual's faith and Biblical interpretation.

Dubious Dogmas

Incarnation. The doctrine that Jesus, the second person of the Trinity, had two natures, divine and human. He "became flesh" when he was miraculously conceived in the womb of the Virgin Mary and his divine nature became united with human nature. This doctrine is based on John 1:14, "And the word was made flesh." This concept — difficult to grasp —gave rise to three heresies, Gnostic (Jesus only appeared to be a man), Arian (Jesus was less than God), and Nestorian (Jesus and God shared the same body but retained two separate personhoods). Confusing? You bet. It took the Council of Ephesus in 431 and the Council of Chalcedon in 451 to officially declare that Jesus was truly God and truly man at the same time, "hypostatically" united into one person! This doctrine is a theological quagmire!

Mary's Immaculate Conception and Assumption. These two dogmas of the Catholic Church teach that Mary was conceived and born without Original Sin and also ascended body and soul into heaven. Pope Pius IX warned those who might doubt this dogma, ". . . let them clearly know that they stand condemned by their own judgment, that they have made shipwreck of their faith and fallen from the unity of the Church."

In 1950, Pope Pius XII, using the mantel of Papal infallibility, dogmatically affirmed that Mary was assumed body and soul into heaven, Pius XII issued a similarly severe warning about the dogma of the Assumption. ". . . let him (that doesn't believe) know that he certainly has abandoned the divine and Catholic faith." He left open the question whether Mary died before her assumption. It might be noted here that Orthodox Catholics (i.e. the Eastern rite) do not accept these dogmas.

Trinity. This idea is central to the teaching of the Christian Church: there is one God, but He is triune, exisiting as three persons — Father, Son, and Holy Spirit — who are distinct but equal. The concept is not mentioned in the Bible, but was developed later by church theologians. The Catholic Church notes that the Trinity is "an *absolute mystery*" (italics in the original) in the sense that we do not understand it even after it has been revealed" (*Catholicism*, 1981).

That is theologian-speak for, *We don't have the foggiest idea what this means.*

Birth Control. In the Catholic Church, the issue is one of contraception, not birth control, *per se*. What is forbidden is use of obstacles to procreation.

In 1960, a birth control pill was approved by the Food and Drug Administration (FDA). "The pill" — for use by women to prevent pregnancy — was a long-awaited opportunity for the sexual emancipation of women, but not Catholic women. "The pill" was banned by the Church since it artificially interrupted the generative process. The only methods of birth planning sanctioned by the Catholic Church are abstinence and rhythm (the avoidance of sex during fertile periods).

Sex and procreation are indivisible in the eyes of the Catholic church. The fecundity of the conjugal act is primary and any act that frustrates the capacity to procreate is forbidden by church dogma. Augustine believed the only purpose of marriage was to produce children and even lust in marriage was sinful (*On Christian Doctrine*, Part III, Chapter 18). The Church is unable to decouple sex from reproduction and unwilling to distinguish the biological component of sex from the social conception of sex as an expression of love, affection, commitment and bonding. This has resulted in Catholic culture being symbolized by large families! This antiquated church doctrine is a legacy from early Christianity when the attitude toward sex was developed and forged by dogmatic, male chauvinist church "fathers." Catholic Church policy essentially deprives women of the right to make their own reproductive choices.

Pope Pius XI wrote these harsh words in his encyclical, *Casti Connubii* (1930), "Since the conjugal act is destined primarily by nature for the begetting of children, those who in exercising it deliberately frustrate its natural power and purpose sin against nature and commit a deed which is shameful and intrinsically vicious. . . . Any attempt to deliberately frustrate the act. . . . is an offense against the law of God and of nature and those who indulge in such are branded with the guilt of grave sin. . ."

There is no such thing as a sin against nature. Nature cannot be offended. Nature is spiritually and morally neutral. Whatever can be done in nature is perfectly acceptable.

This 1930 encyclical reinforced a Catholic doctrine that traces its origin to the "sin of O'nan" who "spilled his seed" rather than impregnate his brother's wife. The Lord was unhappy and killed O'nan (Genesis 38:9-10). This doctrine has been reinforced by Popes throughout history; Pope Gregory IX (1148-1241), Sixus V (1521-1590), and Pius IX (1792-1878) also voiced opposition to any "non-natural" form of birth control.

Birth control has always been a wedge issue between the clergy and the laity. The clergy view birth control as sinful. The laity see it as a rational approach to women's health, sanity, sex and control of family size. A celibate clergy has little empathy for the laity position. The obstinacy of the Vatican was met by the tenacity of a laity who no longer accepted the Pope as the arbitrator of sexual activity. In the 1960s and 1970s, the Catholic Church experienced a ground swell of disobedience of birth control doctrine. In a sociological study (1986), Greeley found that in 1963 half of American Catholics accepted the Church's teaching on birth control. Ten years later, this had declined to less than 15 percent. Frustration with sexual teachings of the Church is immeasurable. Legions of women (and men) have agonized and been tormented while trying to adhere to this illogical doctrine.

Catholics often use humor to explain the church's interference with sexual activity. Birth control is described as "love by the calendar," and "Vatican Roulette." The "rhythm" method of birth control requires bedside thermometers to track menstrual cycles; all to adhere to a flawed sexual doctrine that is disassociated from reality.

My wife and I had two babies 16 months apart, disproving the theory that nursing mothers couldn't get pregnant. After our second child was born we quickly abandoned Catholic teachings on birth control!

With the world population exploding, the scriptural command to "go forth and multiply" is no longer relevant and needs to be reinterpreted in light of 21st century realities. The human population on the planet is increasing at a rate that threatens sustainability and the AIDS epidemic has decimated entire communities. Yet a succession of imperious Catholic Popes, demonstrating a complete misunderstanding of biology and modern life, has continued to regurgitate ancient boilerplate doctrine on sex and procreation;

subordinating the improvement of the human condition and the health and prosperity of the human race to an outdated mythical dogma.

The Church's dogged refusal to sanction condom use to slow the spread of AIDS is inexplicable by any criteria. This absurd ecclesiastical fiat ignores the reproductive health of women and the carrying capacity of the planet. In the 1980s and 1990s, death from AIDS was viewed by Catholics as the result of the wages of sin!

Catholic policy on birth control has caused untold misery — infant mortality, malnutrition among children and mothers dying in childbirth. It is unethical medicine, faulty logic, immoral Christian doctrine, and inhumane; a classic example of a religious ideology leading to disastrous public policy.

Flagrant disregard for the health of women and the planet in light of the scientific knowledge of the 21st century is bad science and dreadful church doctrine. John Shelby Spong writes in *The Sins of Scripture* (2005), "The time has come for the Christian church in all its forms to recognize that its traditional negativity toward birth control has itself become immoral and that limiting births has become the new virtue."

He goes on: "The day has arrived when people no longer believe that God commands them to be 'fruitful and multiply.' This 'terrible text,' this sin of scripture, has become a dated expression of an ancient survival fear and the literal understanding of the Bible that gave this verse its power must now be jettisoned."

For everyone on the planet to indiscriminately produce a maximum number of progeny is a measure of insanity. Is a woman's only role to function as a birthing machine; is motherhood their only purpose? To be led down this path by celibate men is pathological.

As recently as January 2015, Pope Francis — during a visit to the Philippines, one of the most Catholic countries in the world — reiterated the core message on birth control set forth in *Humanae Vitae*, an encyclical written by Paul VI in 1968. In a sermon during his Mass, he denounced "a society which is tempted by confusing presentations of sexuality, marriage, and the family." In one of his homilies he suggested that it's not true that to be a good Catholic you have to be like rabbits!

Dubious Dogmas

    This illustrates that the Pope has a shaky grasp on the role of sex in relationships and that the Catholic Church will continue its conservative stance on birth control. This is a classic example of theological insouciance, a Vatican Curia (Catholic Church bureaucracy) blissfully unaware of the role of sex in human behavior. Ignoring scientific discoveries, advances in medicine and biology, and warnings of eco-system destruction, the Vatican continues to unapologetically promulgate and reinforce a 2000-year-old church doctrine on sex and marriage, confirming that the role of sex in human relationships is totally misunderstood by Catholic church hierarchy. Catholic Church teachings on gender, sexuality, marriage, and contraception are oppressive, inflexible and mired in a medieval mentality.

    The reproductive policy of the Church fails to recognize that sex is a dominant force among living organisms and procreation is only one of many values in the act of sex. Without family planning and contraception, the planet will eventually be unable to produce sufficient food and commodities for an exploding population. There seems to be no consideration or commitment to a policy of healthy human sexuality. This doctrine is enforced by celibate men who appear openly dismissive of their audience and continue to mimic the platitudes of their predecessors.

    Catholic Church heirarchy seems to have a detached indifference toward this issue and show little interest in re-interpreting ancient church doctrine in light of modern knowledge. The Catholic Church's belligerence and intransigence toward modern contraceptive practice is unacceptable in the 21st century and exposes a Luddite mentality and ignorance of the sustainable health of the planet and the individual rights and health of women.

    The church continues to be unresponsive to the entreaties of Catholics for a sane and realistic sexual doctrine. Interfering with a woman's right to make her own reproductive choices is inhumane and based on flawed scriptural interpretation. Catholic doctrine on birth control is smug, sanctimonious, and unrealistic. A logical, humane birth control policy could liberate women and ease the pressure of over-population on planet Earth.

Indulgences. The Catholic Church requires some form of atonement or penance for sin, even after it has been forgiven. An indulgence is a partial or full remission of the penalties for the sin committed. "It was not enough to be sorry for one's sins; that only removed the *guilt* of sin. One also has to pay the *penalty* of sin," *Catholicism* (1981).

Indulgences were a conceptual vehicle purported to reduce the time spent in Purgatory before entering the Kingdom of God. Indulgences were a pragmatic approach to salvation. They can be traced to the third century. The concept of indulgences has been abused; they were bought and sold, quantified in terms of days and years, and promised the petitioner less time in purgatory before going to heaven. The Church outlawed the sale of indulgences in 1567, but the original concept continues today. When I was young, obtaining indulgences was encouraged. They were available for good works, prayers, and visits to holy places. Their prominance has diminished in modern times.

Money received from the sale of indulgences was used to fund the activities of the Catholic Church. During the crusades, indulgences were used as a recruitment tool; kill a few Jews, Muslims or fellow Christians and gain free admission to Heaven. Criticism of indulgences by Martin Luther led to the Protestant reformation.

Heaven, Hell, Purgatory, and Limbo. Eschatology is the theological study of the end of life. Scriptures tell us that those who believe will have "eternal life." This has been interpreted to mean that life will continue after death and eventually our bodies and souls will be reunited.

Belief in an afterlife is a mixture of hope and doubt; hope that there is an afterlife and doubt that one exists. The afterlife is essentially unknowable. If an afterlife is a certainty, why do we see so much grief at funerals?

In the Catholic Church, there are four destinations for humans when they die. Heaven and Hell are universal Christian doctrines, but Purgatory and Limbo are specific inventions of the Catholic Church. Where you end up depends on your earthly behavior.

In school we were taught that Purgatory is a "fiery" but temporary place where salvageable souls go to achieve atonement for committed sins insufficiently egregious to warrant condemnation to Hell. Although penal

Dubious Dogmas

and painful, it has an expiatory characteristic. According to McBrien, there is no biblical basis for the doctrine of purgatory, yet Catholics believe that praying for the dead in Purgatory will hasten their journey to Heaven.

Limbo is a speculative place Catholics believe infants go if they die unbaptized. They are too young to have committed personal sins, but they haven't had the stain of Original Sin removed through Baptism. It is a perplexing doctrine that assumes babies and young children are innately sinful due to Original Sin and thus are unworthy to view the "Beatific Vision" of God. These babies don't suffer but are denied the companionship of God. For this reason, the Catholic Church recommends baptizing babies as soon as they are born. Limbo was given formal recognition by Pope Innocent III in the 13th century.

The concepts of Purgatory and Limbo are slowly becoming more inconspicuous in Catholic teaching.

"Heaven" and "religion" should be synonymous. Without Heaven, religion has nothing to offer. It is the centerpiece of Christianity and the ultimate goal of all believers. Yet Heaven is a celestial mystery, a paradox; the most discussed topic in religion and the least understood. Heaven is an enigma. It has never been divinely described. No one has ever been to Heaven and come back to describe the conditions. All we have are descriptions by people with vivid imaginations.

Is it an ethereal place where dead people go or established on earth when God returns in the Second Coming? Are the souls of the departed faithful embodied or disembodied?

Heaven is a recondite concept yet it remains central to religious doctrine and the primary attraction of religion — and not just Christianity. Heaven is the reward promised to the faithful where they will enjoy celestial bliss, dwell in a state of perfect peace and harmony with God and all of their deceased relatives and friends.

Belief in Heaven is faith that life continues after earthly death. Yet evidence for Heaven is nonexistent. Even Jesus, who allegedly came from Heaven, never described it. Jesus is supposed to have uttered "Why have you forsaken me?" as he was dying on the cross. One would not expect this expression from a divine person returning to the Kingdom of God.

ALL FISH HAVE BONES

Theologians specialize in incoherent rhetoric. Catholic Heaven is described as where "the souls of the faithful, provided they are in no need of purification, will immediately see the divine essence." *Catholicism* (1981). There seems to be no mention of golf courses, fishing streams, continuous happy hour, or virgins and somehow staring at God for all eternity has little appeal. I can hardly wait to get there.

The Mormon Church has an interesting vision of Heaven in three levels: Telestrial, Terrestrial, and Celestial. William Taylor, a Catholic priest who came from a Mormon family, describes Mormon Heaven in his book, *A Tale of Two Cities: Mormons-Catholics* (1980). The first two levels are for non-Mormons and lukewarm Mormons. Fervent and devout Mormons will attain the Celestial level, where they will achieve an "exalted state," become gods and be ministered to by the less holy!

I was taught that in Heaven everyone was on an equal footing, but God evidently contrived a goodness scale for judging Mormons. The very righteous will occupy orchestra seats with waiters, the almost good will be on the main floor, and the not quite so good consigned to the Mezzanine. Imagine the irony of finally getting into heaven and finding yourself a servant to the neighbor you didn't like.

Heaven is a puzzling doctrine. The concept of eternal life tends to crumble when closely examined. Try to process the notion of billions and billions of people reincarnated in some metaphysical condition, somewhere in the universe, doing nothing and never ever, ever, *ever* dying.

Religion thrives on the hope of Heaven and the horror of Hell — the fear of eternal punishment. This fear is a delusion based on myth and superstition. With the concept of Hell, Christianity introduced a pandemic paranoia to the world. The inferno of Hellfire is a cruel and barbaric concept to foist on children or adults.

Since it appears that Hell is eternal and has no corrective or rehabilitative function, it must exist solely for vengeance, which tarnishes the benevolent attributes of a Christian God. The Bible appears to ignore the idea of proportional punishment — inflicting eternal punishment for all transgressions.

I believe there are few human behaviors that merit eternal punishment (for me, exceptions would be child molesters and con artists scamming life savings from the elderly).

Many people forgo pleasurable activities during their lifetime for fear their behavior will result in damnation to Hell. The anxiety and guilt commensurate with these beliefs are unnecessary and inhumane.

English philosopher John Stuart Mill (1806-1873) wrote that his father told him he had difficulty in conceiving of a being who would create the human race and Hell at the same time, knowing that many of His creations would be consigned to horrible and everlasting torment. Harvard religion professor Wilfred Cantwell Smith illustrates a unique perspective of Heaven and Hell: "For a believer, Heaven and Hell are parts of the universe, to an outside observer they are parts of a religion, simply items in the believers' mind." It should be noted that the fires of Hell also violate the laws of nature since they burn continually, yet do not consume!

Beatific Vision. This is the face-to-face encounter with God that occurs when we die and go to Heaven. According to *Catholicism*, quoting a papal bull (letter) of Pope Benedict XII written in 1336 (*Benedictus Deus*), the faithful will see "the divine essence with an intuitive vision and even face to face, without the mediation of any creature by way of object of vision; rather the divine essence immediately manifests itself to them, plainly, clearly and openly, and in this vision they enjoy the divine essence."

The faithful will "see clearly God, one and three, as God is, though some more perfectly than others, according to the diversity of merits" (Council of Florence).

This concept, clearly a fuzzy theological construct, is not mentioned in the Old Testament and rarely mentioned in the New Testament. It is based on Matthew 5:8, "Blessed are the clean of heart, for they shall see God;" and 2nd Corinthians 1:18, "All of us, gazing with unveiled face on the glory of the Lord, are being transformed in the same image from glory to glory, as from the Lord who is the Spirit." Beatific Vision rests precariously on dubious scripture interpretation and the imagination of two writers who never saw God and did not even know Jesus.

Baptism. There is an intriguing and peculiar relationship between sin and baptism that informs the basic philosophy of Christianity. According to Augustine, infants are born with Original Sin and a corrupt nature. However, this stigma can be removed by pouring water on their heads, a bizarre Christian practice fitting the definition of fantasy.

The origin of infant baptism is cloudy. However, it seems unlikely that pouring water on a baby's head or dunking an adult in a lake or river will help much on the journey to Elysian fields or heavenly paradise.

Angels, Demons and Witches. Angels are another fundamental Christian belief. Described as supernatural intermediaries between God and man, they were employed as messengers of a transcendent deity. Angels appear prominently in scripture as a clever abstraction linking God with humanity. Many prominent figures in scripture received regular visits from angels. Angels appeared to Joseph, Mary, Moses, Abraham, the Apostles and at the tomb of Jesus. The angel Moroni appeared to Joseph Smith to begin the Mormon religion. Islamic writings (Hadith) are attributed to visits from the angel Gabriel to Muhammad.

Although angels are invisible and unprovable, belief in their existence remains prominent today. A Baylor University Institute for Study of Religion poll in 2008, reported in *Time* on September 18th, 2008, found that 55 percent of Americans believed they have been helped by a guardian angel. As a child, I was taught that I had my very own guardian angel whose only function was to look after me. I imagine she is retired by now.

Fear of the unknown generates superstitions. Early Christians believed in demons and witches. Jesus, Paul, and Augustine all believed in demons and witches. During the Inquisition, hysteria swept through Europe fueled by the paranoia that Christendom was threatened by heretics and witches. The Bible tells us: "Thou shalt not suffer a witch to live" (Exodus 22:18). This scriptural passage served as authorization for witch hunting in Christian history when many (mostly women) were tortured and burned at the stake for nothing more than being different.

Dubious Dogmas

The first sentence in *Malleus Maleficarum* (*The Hammer of Witches*, 1484) by Heinrich Godfrey Kramer, a Catholic priest, set the tone for the persecution of witches — primarily women. "Whether the belief that there are such beings as witches is so essential a part of the Catholic faith that obstinately to maintain the opposite opinion manifestly savors of heresy." The *Malleus* was essentially a handbook —written in chilling and lurid detail — on how to identify, imprison, torture and execute witches.

In 1484, Pope Innocent VIII issued a Papal Bull, *Summis Desiderantes Affectibus* (Desiring with Supreme Ardor) at the request of Kramer, giving approval for the Inquisition to identify and persecute witches. Women who were mentally ill were killed in God's name.

The *Malleus* received Papal approval when it was written, but the Holy See condemned it three years later. It is a disgusting treatise and a horrific attack on women in particular; offensive to humanity and demonstrating the pernicious effect religious zealotry can have on the human imagination.

Three chapters are devoted to describing *Incubi* and *Succubi*, male and female demons who have sex with humans. The Malleus is extrordinarly misogynistic and suggests it's not surprising that women should come under the spell of witchcraft

> ... since they are feebler (than men) both in mind and body....
> But the natural reason is that she is more carnal that a man, as it is clear from many carnal abominations. And it should be noted that there was a defect in the formation of the first woman, since she was formed from a bent rib, that is, a rib of the breast, which is bent as it were in a contrary direction to a man. And since through this defect she is an imperfect animal, she always deceives.

The *Malleus* is an example of atrocious and inhuman misogyny and the extreme cruelty and misfortune an overzealous segment of society can inflict on another under the banner of God and religious belief. It is a repugnant diatribe against women and heretics; a disturbingly ugly narrative that should never have been written, especially by a Catholic priest, ostensibly dedicated to God.

ALL FISH HAVE BONES

In the introduction to a 1927 reprint of *Malleus*, the translator Montague Summers — another Catholic priest — praises "this great work — admirable in spite of its trifling blemishes . . . is one of the most pregnant and most interesting books I know." He excuses misogynistic passages as "wholesome and needed antidote in this feministic age, when the sexes seem confounded."

Summers — in 1927! —praised the Inquisition, and excuses their "drastic and severe" methods. "There can be no doubt that had this most excellent tribunal continued to enjoy its full prerogative and the full exercise of its salutary powers, the world at large would be in a far happier and far more orderly position to-day."

That this litany of strange beliefs continues to be held is difficult to imagine. The inhabitants of the Byzantine labyrinth of the Vatican Curia seem unable or unwilling to address modern and pragmatic issues of the every-day life of the Catholic faithful. Documents containing unfathomable doctrine continue to be issued by the Holy See. Other Christian religions also take a glacial pace in addressing modernity issues. The philosophical dependency on ancient beliefs by modern churches continues to contribute to the secularization of believers.

CHAPTER SEVEN
DOES GOD EXIST?

The unexamined life is not worth living

— Socrates

At the beginning of the 21st century, imminent intellectual questions challenging the modern world are:

Can we overcome the primitive legacy of belief of our ancestors?

Will survival of the human race continue to be dependent on belief in an unknown, metaphysical, cosmic force that controls the universe or is mankind teetering at the edge of a historical transition to a fundamentally different worldview grounded in experience, science, and reason and independent from belief in a supernatural cosmic force?

Can humans — unfettered from the fear of an invisible, celestial essence — employ their intellects to forge a peaceful, contented, sustainable life on planet Earth?

ALL FISH HAVE BONES

There are indications this might be beginning to happen. For many, the answers to these questions is "no," but for a growing minority, the answer is "yes!" Let's consider and evaluate the available evidence for the existence of God.

The God hypothesis is hard to define and impossible to prove. The idea of God probably began sometime when hominids developed into modern humans and began questioning their existence and place in the universe. There are thousands of religious beliefs in the world, each with its own creation myth, notion of an afterlife, the number of gods or goddesses, and their attributes. According to Steven Mithen, archaeological evidence — images found in caves from the Upper Paleolithic Age (50,000 to 10,000 years ago) — can easily be interpreted as depicting supernatural beings and burial rituals that indicate a concept of death as a transition to a non-physical form. Anthropologist Pascal Boyer posits that humans have certain intellectual concerns; they want to understand events and processes. "These very general, indeed universal intellectual needs gave rise to religious concepts at some point during human cultural evolution . . . most of the accounts of the origin of religion emphasize one of the following suggestions: human minds demand explanation, human hearts seek comfort, human societies require order, human intellect is illusion-prone."

An intellectual question is, *Did humans discover or invent God?* Genesis tells us that God created man in his own image. Or did man create God in *his* own image?

The Socratic challenge in the epigraph at the beginning of the chapter is analogous to my fish metaphor, although more famous and more elegantly worded. However, the message is the same: examine life critically and determine for yourself if you are comfortable and satisfied with your beliefs. Are we going to base our earthly life beliefs on theological gymnastics, or subject our views to critical examination and rational evaluation?

Immanuel Kant (1724-1804) believed that neither the existence nor non-existence of God could be proven since there was no empirical evidence. The God concept, simultaneously wondrous and baffling, suffers from having no observable facts to examine. God is an anthropomorphic, ideological abstraction, unseen and unheard; a belief in a hope. The God of believers always was and always will be; is all-powerful, yet compassionate; knows everything; and has a plan that hasn't been revealed. This is a hard concept to grasp.

A frustration for Christian believers is that God has been described as incomprehensible! How can we come to understand a concept defined as beyond our grasp? Yet curious humans continue a vain attempt to identify the unimaginable. Some ideas, such as the triune God, are probably simply too bewildering and complex to understand given the current evolution of the human brain. Proving or disproving the existence of a supernatural deity falls into this category but this does not preclude using the human thought process to arrive at a reasoned conclusion. It should be obvious that belief or disbelief in a transcendent being is an idiosyncratic life experience.

Martin Luther thought God was, "utterly incomprehensible and inaccessible to human reason." Karl Barth (1886-1968), a Swiss theologian, believed God was hidden and unknowable, a divine mystery that cannot be approached by rational thought processes. Stephen Weinberg, a theoretical physicist and Nobel Laureate said: "Science doesn't make it impossible to believe in God. It just makes it possible to not believe in God." After eons of silence from God and no unambiguous evidence that a deity exists we still cling to a naïve expectation that the God of our imaginations is real.

Yet for some, God's existence is apparent in everyday life. I'm amazed that TV evangelists, preaching to large audiences, refer to God as if He was a close personal friend who lives in their neighborhood. They just had Him over for a beer and barbeque. They discuss in detail what He thinks, what He likes and dislikes, and what He knows. They usually begin their sermon with a fragment from scripture and expand and embellish it so it appears perfectly clear and understandable to the modern mind. The mesmerized audience dutifully nod their heads in unison as the preacher makes a salient point (The audience is obviously unaware of the fish metaphor!).

The phrase "absence of evidence is evidence of absence" is often used to describe the difficultly in detecting God. For some, the universe contains an unknowable organizing cosmic force, an agnostic approach somewhere between belief and non-belief. Some believe God is an impenetrable enigma concealed from human understanding. But, God's deafening silence, undetectable activity and inexplicable invisibility during the past 2,000 years alone reinforces the notion that there is really no one out there.

Emotionally we would all like God to exist. It is virtually impossible to segregate emotion from reality when discussing religion and comparing the supernatural with human experience. Scientifically, God's existence doesn't make much sense, philosophically His existence is hard to understand, and observationally there is not much evidence that God does exist. The God humans have imagined is both durable and fragile; durable because we want a God that is strong, forceful and everlasting, fragile because our unconscious speaks to us that the God we created is a God of our imagination and that image can fade as quickly as it was formed.

Richard Tarnas eloquently encapsulates the thinking of the modern intellect:

> . . . that an infinite eternal God would have suddenly become a particular human being in a specific historical time and place only to be ignominiously executed. That a single brief life taking place two millennia earlier in an obscure primitive nation, on a planet now known to be a relative insignificant piece of matter revolving about one star among billions in an inconceivably vast and impersonal universe — that such an undistinguished event should have an overwhelming cosmic or eternal meaning could no longer be a compelling belief for reasonable men.

I believe reason offers the only productive and realistic path to determine if God exists. Belief in God requires a leap of faith, but faith is not a reliable methodology to determine the truth of God's existence. Religious faith is an amalgam of hope, imagination, peer influence, dependence on authority, self-deception, and childhood upbringing. Religious truth is what religious authorities tell us it is, not facts presented for our analysis and judgment. Truth tends to be distorted by the user to approximate one's personal sense of belief. Faith in God is personal yet in an incomprehensible way. Faith is not an effective investigative tool to supplant reason.

As humans we are incapable of entertaining a thought that is beyond our sphere of experience. The God concept occurs outside any experiential frame of reference. Matthew Steward in *Natures God* (2014) uses Lucretius (99 BC-55 BC), a Roman philosopher, to help describe the universe: "In the universe as Lucretius found it, there is no heaven but the one we project on the stars overhead. There is no hell but what our imagination can conjure out of our fears of this world. And there is nothing at all outside of experience that can bring us any more happiness, misery, good, or evil than we can find within the limits of the world we inhabit."

Here are two variations of belief in a God. Some simply believe in a God who created everything in the universe and then left it to function by itself. This is the disinterested God version. Others believe that God not only created man and the universe, but continues to show an interest, and like the Good Shepherd, periodically tends to His flock. This God is also available to intervene in worldly affairs in response to prayer and supplication. However, there is no evidence that God hears prayers or intervenes in any way in human affairs.

Here are three possible pathways to belief in God or the supernatural: the sin and atonement model, the creation model, and the awe model. The sin and atonement model assumes our misbehavior offends God, so we must apologize, beg forgiveness, do penance and receive forgiveness. Due to human frailty, this cycle of sin and forgiveness might be repeated an infinite number of times — with the hope of dying during the forgiveness phase. The creation model posits that God created the world as we know it according to the explanation in Genesis. This includes two creation stories and the flood that wiped out most of mankind and the flora and fauna existent at the time. The awe model is the favorite of the Creationists. Because the world is so complex and complicated, it must have been created by a complex supernatural deity. All of these models suffer from a lack of evidence, illogical assumptions, and an ignorance of science and evolution.

Particularly exasperating is the unknowable, indefinable, invisible nature of God. We appear to have a created a deity to assuage our anxieties over our existence, yet cleverly disguised His existence so the illusion will never be discovered. Since God never describes Himself, we are left to struggle with a definition.

ALL FISH HAVE BONES

Additionally, whenever we begin a discussion of God, we are immediately presented with a taxonomy dilemma. How do we identify which and whose God we are discussing? Each of the three major Abrahamic faiths has its own concept of God. Although each faith advocates a monotheistic divine entity, closer examination reveals a polytheistic variety of gods. By my count, there are at least five versions of the Redeemer: the punishing Old Testament Jewish God (Yahweh or HaShem); the New Testament God, a more humanitarian God; the Catholic God, one who responds to both faith and works; the Protestant God, one who is satisfied with just faith; and the God of Islam, Allah.

God has been described as invisible, transcendent, genderless, unknown, unknowable, outside time and space, incorporeal, a cosmic force, and a spirit. Let's make a bold assumption: an invisible, transcendent, unknown and unknowable spirit is incomprehensible to the human mind. Try imaging a non-gendered, powerful entity that created what we know as the universe.

This is the difficulty when we try to imagine God: the software of our imaginations, however exotic, is limited by our perceptions and understanding. Human ignorance limits our ability to describe God. He is incomprehensible even to theologians using tortuous reasoning and linguistic gimmicks.

In an effort to identify God — try to imagine an invisible power that created the earth, the universe and every living thing — you may find yourself using the Bible, church experiences, paintings, books you have read, stories you have heard and poetry you have read. Contemplate for a moment and see if your imagination brings any image into focus.

Each of us with our idiosyncratic imagination has devised our own personal vision of God, a God that fits our notion of a supernatural being. Think about this creator: what is God, who is God, where is God located, and what does God look like? Is God masculine, feminine or a non-gender entity — whatever that is?

Christianity is a worldwide religion of over one billion followers with an incomprehensible abstraction as the leader!

The concept of an invisible God is not the problem *per se*. Many things in our universe are invisible but *detectable*. We can't see atoms, protons, neutrons and many other invisible components of the universe but scientists can look for, discover, and measure them. God, on the other hand, is both invisible and undetectable.

The Abrahamic God is a clever and imaginative conception in the mind of man. We have invented a concept of God but are constricted by the limits of human cognition. We are incapable of accurately describing something outside our experience. Many have suggested that man invented God; not the other way around.

So the God we designed is a product of our experience and imagination. We manufactured our God, made Him male, festooned Him with attributes we thought were appropriate for a God; wisdom, justness, mercy, power, compassion, goodness, impartiality and insight. This is a complex mixture of attributes, even for a deity, and they are not always on display. We attributed familiar human characteristics to God because we had no idea what supernatural characteristics might be. Ludwig Feuerbach (1804-1872) a German philosopher and anthropologist, believed God's traits to be human in construction, a projection of some feature or need of human nature; God's appeal lies in the human traits we have given him.

God is viewed as a mythical, anthropomorphic construct living in the sky. We have imputed to him omnipotence, omniscience and benevolence. And then, in a stroke of genius, we declared Him to be incomprehensible, cleverly concealed behind a cloak of invisibility, thus foreclosing any opportunity to comprehend the very God we invented.

The paradox of man's creation is that the anthropomorphic God we constructed may be conceptually flawed. If we critically read the Bible we discover a substantially different God. Scriptural God is fickle, jealous, vengeful, unjust, cruel and a polar opposite from the God we manufactured. The God we invented is a *good* God, a kind, gentle "God of nice." However, if we observe the evil, suffering, pain, anxiety and misfortune in the world, there is sufficient evidence, I believe, to argue for a *bad* God, an unkind, merciless, ungracious "God of nasty." One could be called God of our wishes and the other, God of reality, nothing like we imagined. Now we have to reconcile these two Gods and determine who is in charge.

We could have multiple Gods, competing for supremacy. Western theology seems to have settled on the benevolent, omnipotent version of God, but there are other options. We could have a disinterested God who shows no concern for His creation. This God is plausible if we view the chaos in the world today. How do we think our God is omnipotent? Looking around the world, there are many things that need fixing.

God is an uncaused cause, a contradiction, and a logical impossibility. Our God is infinitely smart, good, knowledgeable, empathetic, and powerful. Buried among these attributes are logical contradictions. Why create a world with problems if God is perfectly happy? If God is perfectly happy, why send His son to be crucified? Why would a good and powerful God create a less than perfect planet and populate it with imperfect humans? Carl Sagan's wife, Ann Druyan, pointed out that an immortal God is a cruel God because He never has to face death, yet He created creatures that do.

Before God created the world, the universe must have been empty and without problems. After creation, humanity came into existence in varying degrees of stress, suffering, and misery. A perfectly empathetic and benevolent God should have difficulty in damning sinners to eternal punishment in the fires of Hell. An infinitely powerful God should be able to clone Himself, but then He would no longer be the most powerful person in the universe!

How can a perfectly good God allow evil?

Dan Barker, in his book *Godless* (2008), asserts that, "Omnipotence contradicts omniscience. To be omniscient means that all future facts are known to the person who is all-knowing. This means that the set of knowable facts is fixed and unchangeable. If facts cannot be changed, then this limits the power of God. If God knows what will happen tomorrow, then he is impotent to change it. If he changes it anyway, then he was not omniscient."

Everyone who ever attended a Catholic school or university was required to take "apologetics." It sounds like a course in apologies but it is a discipline in which believers of a faith attempt to present a rational basis for their beliefs and argue the reasonableness of their faith. It is difficult to compile probative evidence for a transcendental being. God's attributes are unable to be tested or disproved. Many of the arguments for the existence of God are merely semantic musings of ancient philosophers. Arguments for the existence of God are attempts to rationally justify something we hope is true. This is not unexpected.

Richard Dawkins believes that a supernatural entity would have to be at least as complex as our world. Where did this complex entity come from?

Four major arguments are offered for the existence of God: ontological, first cause, moral and design. Once again we rely on those pesky philosophers with tortured semantics and tautological arguments to help us understand the way we think about the universe.

The **ontological argument** begins with the conception of existence and was first purposed by St. Anselm in the 11th century. If a person can conceive of a being that which nothing greater can be conceived — a perfect being — then this being must exist. If it exists in the mind, then it must exist in reality. This perfect being is God. This argument has been largely refuted, partially on the grounds that it doesn't make any sense.

The **first cause argument** for God was postulated by Thomas Aquinas, stating that everything must be caused by something else. This requires an endless regression until reaching the "cause which has no cause." Aquinas called this uncaused cause "God." The refutation of this proof is very easy. Aquinas arbitrarily decided that the uncaused cause was God and argued that God needed no cause.

The **moral argument** for the existence of God is simple: because humans are generally moral there must be a God responsible for this condition. This argument assumes that humans are incapable of developing a moral code of behavior as a product of social interaction and evolution. Scripture is often cited as the basis for Christian morality but the Bible is morally inconsistent.

A divine concept of morality is not the only explanation for respectful and honorable treatment of fellow human beings. Religious organizations may believe human intellect is so infantile that it is incapable of navigating the challenges of moral turpitude in life without divine assistance, but this assertion fails to recognize the peaceful coexistence among thousands of men and women who don't believe in God or primitive tribes that have never heard of God. They have learned cooperation and respectful treatment of others in a society without divine facilitation.

Morality doesn't depend on divine imperative. The Golden Rule, or ethic of reciprocity, has been around since antiquity. The guiding principle of the Golden Rule is to live in peace and harmony with your fellow humans. It has been incorporated in almost all religions, both Eastern and Western. Our remote ancestors learned that cooperation between individuals and among groups was superior to hostility. Being courteous to fellow human beings and treating them with respect is the foundation of man's sense of fairness and justice. Rather than being nice to people in an attempt to secure a celestial reward and avoid the wrath of a vengeful God, the position of the nonbeliever is that it is vastly superior to be nice to people because it's the appropriate thing to do.

Even our primate cousins, the bonobos, exhibit cooperative efforts and empathy for each other, and do this without religion. Frans De Waal, a Dutch primatologist and professor of Primate Behavior at Emory University, has found examples of sympathy, reciprocity and an ability to follow social rules in chimpanzees, bonobos, and other primate societies (*The Bonobo and the Atheist*, 2013).

After studying primates, his view of morality is, "The moral law is not imposed from above or derived from well-reasoned principles; rather, it arises from ingrained values that have been there since the beginning of time. The most fundamental one derives from the survival value of group life. The desire to belong, to get along, to love and be loved, prompts us to do everything in our power to stay on good terms with those on whom we depend."

For De Waal, "Morality is a system of rules concerning the H's of Helping or at least not Hurting fellow beings. It addresses the well-being of others and puts the community before the individual." He does not claim that apes are moral in the same sense as humans, but that they show compassion and community concern.

Does God Exist?

The design (or teleological) argument for the existence of a supernatural creator is that the world is too complex to have accidentally come into existence by itself so it must have had a designer who is God. Creationists and intelligent design advocates believe in a designed universe that requires a designer, that all living organisms had to be designed. This ignores evolution as the explanation of how organisms develop over long periods of time with incremental variations.

An additional argument occasionally used to explain the existence of God and the arrangement of the universe is the Anthropic Principle: since we are able to observe the world in which we live; it must have been created for us. Since the universe has the necessary conditions and the constants among the planets are so fine-tuned to bring about life on earth, it has to be the result of a creator, not an accident of the universe. Dennett says of the Anthropic Principle: "According to the Anthropic Principle, we are entitled to infer facts about the universe and its laws from the undisputed fact that we are here to do the inferring and observing."

Some Christian apologists cite miracles as proof of the existence of God. To my knowledge, we have not had a scientifically verifiable miracle where it could be proven that natural laws were reversed or suspended. We turn to Hume (1711-1776), a Scottish philosopher who believed that miracles were a violation of natural law and impossible. Hume argued that, ". . . no testimony is sufficient to establish a miracle, unless the testimony be of such a kind that its falsehood would be more miraculous than the fact which it endeavors to establish."

Miracles may be pious fiction or a misunderstanding of natural events in the world. Miracles mentioned in the Bible probably never happened but were included to establish and enhance the divinity of Jesus, and it is unlikely "miracles" that occurred 2,000 years ago will ever be completely understood or empirically verified.

Sam Treiman (1925-1999) was an American theoretical physicist known for Treiman's Theorem: "Impossible things usually don't happen." Crossan asserts that, "To claim a miracle is to make an interpretation of faith, not just a statement of fact." Karen Armstrong, in *The Case for God*, writes, ". . . in the ancient world, 'miracles' were quite commonplace and however remarkable and significant, were not thought to indicate that the miracle worker was in any way superhuman." She points out that many prophets and "healers" performed "miracles" in the distant past and none of them were thought to be divine.

The "proofs" cited above are highly unsatisfactory and underscore the difficulty in describing an invisible being shrouded in mystery. They are unlikely to persuade anyone who is not already a believer. "Proving" God has been an elusive pursuit by philosophers and theologians. No overarching thesis has ever been discovered. Atheists point out that the competing arguments are philosophical and employ semantic manipulation of words devoid of any empirical content.

Bertrand Russell (1872-1970), a British philosopher, social critic and Nobel Laureate, was once asked what he would say when God asked on Judgment Day, "Why didn't you believe in Me?" Russell replied, "Not enough evidence."

Once you begin to really think about the belief that God takes a personal interest in your day-to-day activities and those of everyone else on the planet, the logic of His existence begins to unravel. If God really exists and possesses the traits of benevolence and love, why can't He manifest himself in some public, unequivocal way; demonstrate that He does exist; and explain indiscriminate catastrophic acts of nature, the pain, suffering, life-threatening illnesses of children, and the endemic evil in the world.

We need a performance event to assure us of God's existence. What would convince me, and I imagine most others, would be a TV appearance or press conference by God simultaneously on all stations in every country where He explains himself, where He comes from, and what He has planned; and then takes a few questions from reporters!

A spectacular miracle would also work!

Since God is remote, inaccessible and ineffable, prayer is commonly recommended in attempts to communicate with Him. The basis for prayer is found in Matthew 6:5-6, where we are admonished to pray in secret but our rewards will be visible. Prayer is a central component and distinguishing ritual of religion and an integrating force for religious groups. Conceived of as an attempted dialog between earthlings and their God in the heavens, prayer is highly recommended for the laity and mandated by cannon law for Roman Catholic clergy. Prayer also functions as atonement. The penance for sins admitted in Catholic confessionals is usually some form of prayer.

John 14:13-14 states, "And I will do whatever you ask for in my name, so that the Father's glory will be shown through the Son. If you ask me for anything in my name, I will do it." This is a pretty unambiguous statement by Jesus on the power of prayer. In Matthew 17:20 and 21:21, Jesus tells his followers if they want to move a mountain they can! However, for most people, positive results of prayer are seldom encountered.

Prayer is a unifying force in religion and obligatory if one wishes to attain salvation. It is promoted as a chance to personally talk with God. Prayer can also be directed to saints and deceased family members who are presumably in Heaven. For believers, prayer is the primary form of religious activity; the only communications channel for conversation with God. Some cloistered religious groups, in convents and monasteries, spend much of the day for their entire lives in prayer.

Every Sunday, Catholic Mass begins with the congregation expressing aloud their guilt by praying the Confiteor. This prayer is also used at the beginning of Lutheran services.

> *I confess to almighty God and to you, my brothers and sisters,*
> *that I have greatly sinned in my thoughts and in my words,*
> *in what I have done and what I have failed to do,*
> *through my fault, through my fault, through my most grievous fault;*
> *therefore, I ask blessed Mary, ever Virgin, all the Angels and Saints,*
> *and you, my brothers and sisters, to pray for me to the Lord our God.*

The Confiteor is ingenious in construction. It epitomizes the perfect prayer. It incorporates all the elements of Christianity: sin, remorse, repentance, forgiveness, and a plea for salvation. It assumes everyone is a sinner and guilty of something. It holds you accountable not only for your commissions but your omissions, stuff you did and stuff you didn't do. That pretty much covers everything. *You have greatly sinned and are grievously at fault.* You ask everyone to intercede to God on your behalf. All in all, it's a great way to begin a worship service commonly promoted as an uplifting experience!

The concept and practice of prayer has many elaborate, complex protocols, architectures, nomenclatures and structures. There are many inventive "how to" guides for prayer. Suggested body postures are prostrate, kneeling, standing, walking, hands folded, hands unfolded, eyes open, eyes closed, head bowed, head not bowed, head stationary, head bobbing, body swaying — and breast beating. Does God really care about particular body configurations when you talk to Him? Is a supplicant's posture critical to a favorable response?

There are liturgical time allocations and periods of the day when prayer is suggested: *lauds* in the morning and *vespers* at night. Canon law requires priests in the Catholic faith to recite their breviary every day.

Does God have a preference for prayer in a specific language? Greek and Latin are the historical languages for Christianity, but modern church services are conducted in the vernacular of many countries.

Prayer supposedly functions as a communications network for conversing with God, but the difficulty with prayer is reciprocity — getting a response.

Does God listen when we pray? Apparently He listens to some. The U.S. Religious Landscape Survey, conducted by the Pew Research Center on June 1st, 2008, found a significant minority of Americans (31 percent) reported that prayer resulted in a definitive and specific answer from God once a month and 19 percent heard from God once a week! A problem with the conclusions of these surveys is that answered prayers have an inherent ambiguity – was the prayer actually answered by God or was the outcome a coincidence?

Christian Scientists believe prayer is superior to medical intervention when one of their members is ill. Numerous health studies have been conducted to determine if there is a positive effect of prayer on the sick. None of these studies have detected a measurable difference between a prayer group and a control group.

TV evangelists link monetary contributions with prayer and exhort their listeners to give as much as possible to receive the full benefits of the TV preacher's prayer. One of the disparaging descriptions of religion is, "pray, pay, and obey." Most studies of the efficacy of prayer report no effect or they are inconclusive.

Very sick people pray and most die. Infertile couples pray for babies and then adopt. Farmers pray and droughts continue. The lottery continues to be awarded to someone else, even though we fervently prayed. There is little evidence that prayer works.

When I was in high school, our team would march into the vestibule of our church in full uniform before every home football game with the sound of cleats on tile floors reverberating and intruding on the serenity of the church. We would pray to win and not be injured. We performed this ritual even when playing another Catholic school, which must have created a dilemma for God! It appears God is silent and indifferent to his followers and also silent to their entreaties.

In 1952, U.S. President Harry S. Truman enacted a National Day of Prayer to take place on May 7th. Humanist groups launched a National Day of Reason to occur on the same day. A 2010 USA/Gallup poll reported that 57 percent of Americans said they favored a National Day of Prayer while only five percent opposed it and 38 percent said it didn't matter either way. A 2013 Pew Research Center survey found that 55 percent of Americans pray every day, 23 percent said they pray weekly or monthly, and 21 percent said they seldom or never pray.

If there is no God, does prayer have any purpose? I believe it has a practical value. The original concept of prayer was *vertical* communication between the supplicant and God; earthlings praying to a God in heaven. Though there is little evidence of the efficacy of this endeavor, I believe there is a beneficial *horizontal* aspect to prayer. When congregations pray

ALL FISH HAVE BONES

together, it alerts them to problems and can inform parishioners to the need for sympathy and support for the person(s) in need. If the Smith family is in need of help, praying for them in church on a Sunday alerts the congregation to the problem and sets in motion efforts to assist and support the family. Additionally, prayer has a psychological benefit for a petitioner who can self-analyze the problem during the prayer ritual.

The idea that God exists is conceptually flawed, implausible, unsupported by evidence, scientifically unprovable and unverifiable. I believe the following are rational, persuasive arguments against the existence of God.

In Matthew 16:28 and 16:34, Mark 9:1 and Luke 9:27, Jesus says, "I say to you, there are some standing here who will not taste death until they see the Son of Man coming in his Kingdom." In Matthew 5:17, Jesus preaches, "Repent, for the Kingdom of Heaven is at hand."

Two thousand years later, these prophecies have not been fulfilled. Like Charlie Brown in the "Peanuts" cartoon, waiting in vain for the appearance of the "Great Pumpkin," 21st century Christians also wait in vain for the appearance of the Kingdom of God.

Mike Davis, in his book, *The Atheist's Introduction to the New Testament*, claims Matthew was for him the "smoking gun."

> It proved to me that Christianity could not possibly be true. End of story. Case closed. It's the verse where Jesus tells his listeners that the judgment day will come before the generation he's speaking to passes away – meaning that some of them would still be alive when the sun went dark, the stars fell from the sky, and Jesus came riding down from heaven on clouds of glory. It's been nearly 2,000 years now since that generation passed away, and the sun is still shining, the stars still twinkle in the sky, and clouds arrive with no passenger from heaven, glorious or otherwise. For me this sealed the issue. Jesus was wrong. Therefore, he could not have been divine, but just a guy, preaching what he believed in, and no more deserving of our belief than any other guy.

We will never know, with ontological certitude, the true story of Jesus, what he really did during his short life or what he personally believed. He will forever remain a person we don't know but wish we did.

The first chapter of Genesis describes how God created the heavens, the earth, and all its inhabitants. Genesis 1:31 says God looked at everything he had made and he found it *very good* (my italics). Assuming benevolence and a desire to fabricate a perfect environment for creatures created in His own image and likeness, planet Earth fails the test. We live in a tectonically unstable world, wonderfully beautiful, yet lethally dangerous.

We would expect a perfectly good God to create a perfectly good world! That's not what we have. What we have is a planet barely hospitable to life. We have a poorly designed, fragile planet of shoddy construction. Planet Earth is a contingent world, dependent on the sun as a life giving energy source. Cosmologists tell us the scenario for the end of the earth is our sun burning out and everything alive suffering a chilly demise.

The supercontinent Pangea formed about 300 million years ago. One hundred million years ago, it began to break into the current configuration of the continents. Earth's surface is 71 percent non-potable salt water with the land masses resting on seven major tectonic plates that drift and subduct, creating earthquakes and tsunamis. Additionally, there are two uninhabitable ice caps and a vast temperate zone only habitable by humans with man-made structures. Almost none of Earth is habitable by humans without structures to protect them from the elements.

In addition to earthquakes and tsunamis, nature produces hurricanes, tornadoes, freezing rain, flash floods, icebergs, volcanic eruptions, mud slides, snow storms, avalanches, droughts, famine, forest fires, giant rogue ocean waves, dust storms, hail storms, sand storms, waterspouts, asteroid strikes, and monsoons. Evidence suggests that an asteroid strike in the Yucatan peninsula caused the extinction of dinosaurs.

Seldom does a week go by without some planetary catastrophe. These natural disasters are unpredictable, kill thousands of people, cause pain and suffering for many more, produce significant property damage, disrupt commerce and destroy communities. We witness erosion of ocean shorelines, flooding of low-lying towns, and fires destroying forests. Humans are powerless to prevent these disasters. It is difficult to reconcile these violent tragedies with a loving God who looked at his creation and deemed it "very good."

Earth has abundant design flaws. The surface of our planet is a movable crust with unpredictable fits and starts that cause destruction and loss of life. In five billion years our sun will run out of hydrogen and cease to radiate heat and light, resulting in the death of planet Earth. We'll never know!

One would think that given God's immense powers, Earth might occupy a more prestigious zip code in the universe, but we are a speck located way out on a spiral arm of the Milky Way, one of millions of galaxies. The Milky Way is only the second largest galaxy in a group of galaxies that lies on the edge of the Virgo Super Cluster, which contains thousands of other galaxies.

Bellah (2011) puts it in perspective: "So we learn that not only is our sun a minor star in a not very interesting galaxy nowhere near the center of anything, but that our species, of which we are so justly proud, is far from the center of the biological universe, though a considerable danger to the survival of much of that universe — bacteria, however, being relatively safe from our depredations."

Humans have to deal with a significant number of pathogens, infectious viruses, fungi and bacteria. Suggesting that God inflicts us with these to test us is preposterous. As conducive to life as earth appears to be at this stage in its life, it can easily be described as a very dangerous planet. Five major extinctions — elimination of 50 percent of all animal species — have occurred in Earth's history, the first 440 million years ago and the most recent 65 million years ago (Bellah, 2011). More than 99 percent of all species that have lived on earth are extinct! Ninety-five percent were unable to compete for resources or failed to adapt to the environment.

We who have adapted are one asteroid strike away from joining the dinosaurs. Humans have discovered that the world is not friendly. Natural laws govern all living organisms and it matters not to nature that humans are fragile creatures.

People living in the western U.S. (as I do) have reason to be concerned with natural catastrophe. A recent reminder of the unpredictability of and the devastation that can be caused by nature's random events is the volcanic eruption of Mount St. Helens on May 18th, 1980. Located between the major West Coast cities of Portland, Oregon, and Seattle, Washington, its eruption was the single most powerful natural disaster in American history. The memory of this explosion and the potential for a similar catastrophe is very real for people living along the West Coast and the Inland Northwest.

According to the U.S. Geological Survey there have been 500 volcanic eruptions during recorded history. The volcano that formed Mount Rainier outside of Seattle and the Yellowstone caldera in Wyoming both have the potential to alter the landscape of the U.S. with global consequences. The San Andreas fault extends along the West Coast from Canada to Southern California. The Cascadia Subduction Zone (CSZ), a "megathrust" fault, begins in Canada and extends 800 miles south to Northern California. Both have potential for a catastrophic realignment of the entire coastline of the western U.S. The death, injuries and destruction that could occur is incalculable. An occurrence of this magnitude might be the tipping point for believers who worship a caring and benevolent God.

Volcanism, plate tectonics, earthquakes, tsunamis and global warming and cooling continue to randomly sculpt the topography of the planet and affect all living organisms, without any discernable goal and apparently with complete disregard for human life. God appears to be a disinterested bystander. God's handiwork as a planet builder was an underachievement and exposed an imperfection in his omnipotence. To date, there is no compelling evidence that God has any interest or intervenes anywhere in the universe.

Physicists have so far identified a number of particles that are the basis for everything, including electrons, protons, neutrons, quarks, leptons, muons, tauons, gluons, and photons. A creator would have to be very complex to make these particles and then understand their interaction to provide a somewhat stable universe. A more sensible creator might have been more parsimonious, using only one or two particles. Science continues to discover ghost-like particles with unfathomably short life spans. It seems less likely they were deliberate creations from the mind of a deity and more likely the result of the continuing interaction of the fundamental forces in nature.

Earth is a dangerous place to live. Asteroids crash, volcanoes erupt, tsunamis flood, and earthquakes rattle the Earth's mantle. We live on a planet that shakes, explodes and floods; hardly what one would expect from a benevolent creator. Planet Earth is hardly a masterpiece of creation for God's chosen creatures.

I would give God an F on planet design and a solid D minus on planet construction. Maybe it was his first planet or a practice planet or the "Big Bang" got out of control. Possibly other planets in parallel universes will fare better. It is difficult to believe that a benevolent creator would subject his followers to these natural disasters and human suffering. Nature's indiscriminate destructive force is inconsistent with a loving God.

One philosophy posits that in the universe there might be nothing, that our earth is ostensibly a cosmic possibility in the mind of God. However, one would expect from a perfect God an elegantly designed planet that is pleasant and comfortable; a combination of tropical gardens, temperate forest and lake ensembles, savannas and deserts. This would accommodate everyone's taste for residency. A more desirable planet might have freshwater oceans without sharks, forested mountains without grizzly bears and swamps without alligators and crocodiles. I don't see the goodness, the benefit to society, or the ecology of the planet from impulsive critters that eat humans.

Why did God create us in the first place? A perfect being, by definition, should be perfectly happy. It is difficult to become more than perfectly happy! Why does a perfect deity need to create and populate a planet with imperfect beings? The humans He allegedly created are another example of His less-than-benevolent nature. The Catholic Baltimore Catechism assures us that "man" is a creature composed of body and soul and made in the image and likeness of God! The following are samples of human conditions that are sufficient evidence we are not the products of a benevolent creator.

Dementia
Dwarfism
Down's Syndrome
Children born with ambiguous genitalia
Turrets Syndrome
The need for pediatric neurosurgeons and oncologists
Autism
Cerebral Palsy
Polio
Tetra-Amelia (born without arms and legs)
Anophthalmia (born without eyeballs)
Anencephaly (born without a brain)
Type I Diabetes
Cancer
Painful childbirth
Alzheimer's disease
Conjoined twins

I am skeptical of a supernatural deity — God the Father, looking down on a world He created — who allegedly has the capability and capacity for continuous monitoring and recording of the diurnal and nocturnal activities of seven billion earth inhabitants. According to Matthew 10:30 and Luke 12:7, "Even all the hairs of your head are counted" (Of course, in my case that would not be a difficult task!). God even knows when a sparrow falls to the ground (Matthew 10:29). These are prodigious feats, even for a deity!

People do stuff every day. Some stuff is beneficial and some malevolent; some will benefit the doer and society and some of it is injurious to others and society as a whole. The number of personal human events, good and evil, that happen every minute of every day is incalculable. Are these acts non-events, routine, prosaic functions of everyday life or an immoral, criminal behavior? It's impossible to consider all the nuances that define the totality of human activities. These normal functions are the stuff of human existence and happen all the time throughout the life of every person on the planet. A truly kind and benevolent God should have to have an impeccable judicial process for the 150,000 individuals who die every day and face determination of reward or punishment.

An illustrative experiment may aid in grasping the high improbability of such a prodigious capability of a supernatural deity. The next time you are in an airplane flying over a city, note the thousands of houses and apartment buildings in your field of vision, extending in an infinite succession of rows. Now try to imagine what each person in each house or apartment is doing at that very minute. Now multiply by 60 (to get one hour), then by 24 (to get one day), and then by 365 (to get one year). Here the math gets a little tricky because we lack the life span in years of each person in those houses, and then we have one last multiplier — seven billion — the number of humans on the planet. God now has a database.

These data have to be gathered, monitored, stored, retrieved, processed, and identified with the proper person, so when they die it can be judged if their behavior was good or bad, moral or immoral, offensive, harmful, or injurious to others. All the subtleties and the context of when each act was committed have to be considered. These data then have to be interpreted in a fair and just manner during the end-of-life judgment proceedings. This imagery is difficult to comprehend and mentally digest, and seems highly unlikely to me. I believe this is incontrovertible evidence and the single most powerful argument for the non-existence of a supernatural deity.

I am confident that the arguments that God *does not exist* are more logical, plausible, and compelling than the arguments that God *does exist*.

Baron d'Holbach (1723-1789), a French/German philosopher, writer and prominent atheist, is quoted in Mitchell Stevens' *Imagine There's No Heaven* (2014). D'Holbach wrote this amusing reflection on the attributes of God and his relationship with man:

> If their gods are infinitely good, wherefore should we dread them? If they are omniscient, wherefore inform them of our wants, why fatigue them with our requests? If they are omnipresent, of what use can it be to erect temples to them? If they are lords of all, why make sacrifices to them; why bring them offerings of what already belongs to them? If they are just, upon what foundation

believe that they will punish those creatures whom they have filled with imbecility? ... If they are omnipotent, how can they be offended; how can we resist them? If they are rational, how can they enrage themselves against blind mortals, to whom they have left the liberty of acting irrationally? If they are inconceivable, wherefore should we occupy ourselves with them?

ALL FISH HAVE BONES

CHAPTER EIGHT
WOMEN IN CHRISTIANITY:
THE THEOLOGY OF EXCLUSION

For man did not come from woman, but woman from man;
nor was man created for woman but woman for man.
— *1st Corinthians 11:8-9*

Since the inception of Christianity, women have been marginalized, disparaged, misrepresented, unappreciated, ignored and psychologically abused by male-biased Christian dogma, doctrine and policy. They have been maligned and excluded from full participation in the Christian church based solely on their gender. The 21-word sentence above, from an epistle of Paul, established the status of women in the Christian church.

The Pauline writings express a remarkable antipathy toward women. In 1st Timothy 2:9-12, he expresses his aberrant opinion of women: they should be silent, wear no jewelry, not braid their hair, be subject to man and not teach. In 1st Corinthians 14:34-35, he states: "women should keep silent in the churches, for they are not allowed to speak, but should be subordinate, as even the law says. But if they want to learn anything, they should ask their husbands at home. For it is improper for a woman to speak in church."

Paul's edict that women should be silent in church had the unintended and unfortunate consequence of depriving church choirs of female voices. So, beginning in the 16th century, the Catholic Church, never at a loss for innovative ways of maintaining church tradition, had young boys castrated, insuring a plentiful supply of soprano voices to substitute for women, who had to remain silent and could not sing. The "Castrati," who suffered cruel and barbaric mutilation, maintained their soprano voices into adulthood and were trained and distributed to church choirs throughout Italy. This perverted, ungodly, wrong-headed practice by Catholic Church authorities can only be described as insanity. Shameful exploitation of defenseless children is morally wrong and difficult to reconcile with a putative religious organization. Justifying this practice by claiming that singing in church is a form of praise to God is faulty logic and defective theology.

In 1st Corinthians 11:5-9, Paul further defines the subjugation of women to men: "... any woman who prays or prophesies with her head unveiled brings shame upon her head, for it is one and the same thing as if she had her head shaved. A man, on the other hand, should not cover his head, because he is the image and glory of God." Women wearing hats in church were common in my youth. We would often see a handkerchief used as a substitute when women forgot their hats. Women had cameo roles in the Bible, relegated to the fringes of events and activities.

Paul, considered the "second founder of Christianity," viewed women as inferior to men. His writings and theological orientation had considerable influence on nascent Christianity. A case can be made that Christianity should be called Paulinity. The corpus of his views can be found in the 14 epistles that occupy more than half of New Testament writings. His opinion of women, later reinforced by Augustine, has its roots in Genesis when God declared that he will "intensify the pangs of childbirth and children will be born in pain."

Women in Christianity: The Theology of Exclusion

Sadly, the Christian belief that women were inferior to men was one of the classical views inherited from Greek philosophers who believed sexual desire should be sublimated in favor of intellectual pursuits. Aristotle believed females were a mistake, branding them "mutilated males."

Female subordination was rampant in the Bible and Biblical times; stoning for transgressions was widespread. The demeaning of women is prominent in scripture. Women were declared "unclean" after childbirth and during menstrual periods — normal female human functions. Scriptural writers evidently had no understanding of the function of the endometrium (the lining of the uterus) and its role in human reproduction.

Paul's theology presents us with an eccentric, distorted view of half the world's population, yet his attitude toward women provided the major justification for the subordinate roles for women in the Catholic Church.

St. Jerome was another major contributor to early Christian sexual ethics and the concept of monasticism as an exemplary way of life for devout Christians. According to Wills in *Papal Sin* (2000), Jerome believed the laity should refrain from sexual activity on the eve of receiving the Eucharist.

J. N. D. Kelly (1909-1997), a prominent member of the theological faculty at Oxford University, in his book, *Jerome*, writes, "At the heart of his teaching lay the conviction that chastity was the quintessence of the gospel message, and that its supreme exemplification and proof was Mary, the virgin mother of the virgin Savior. This complex of beliefs was to remain a central bastion of Catholic spirituality in the West, and Jerome was one of its chief architects."

Jerome believed virginity was God's preferred state for humans, with marriage in second place. He championed absence from intercourse even in marriage! He believed sex to be intrinsically evil and that second marriages demonstrated carnal weakness. According to Jerome, sexual intercourse only occurred after "the Fall" in the Garden of Eden. Much of the misogynistic material written by Jerome is contained in *Against Jovinianus* (393 AD), a response to a treatise by a little known monk, Jovinian, criticizing the orthodox celibacy, virginity, and the asceticism of the Church. Jerome's polemical response exposed his male chauvinism, declaring, "…. wives stand on the border line of good and evil."

Kelly further describes the influence of Jerome on the early church. "Jerome's treatment [of celibacy, the virginity of Mary and marriage] enormously helped to shape both the Mariology of the Latin Church and the Christian sexual ethic that was to dominate Western civilization until the Renaissance at least." Kelly notes that Jerome was instrumental in establishing the Catholic orthodoxy celebrating celibacy as the noblest state. Marriage was tolerated as a 'remedy against sin,' to be used only for the propagation of children and not for pleasure. Jerome extols the virtues of virginity in *Against Jovinianus* (1:120): "And therefore Christ loves virgins more than others, because they willingly give what was not commanded them".

Thomas Aquinas (1225-1274), one of the great thinkers of the early Church, had similar attitudes toward women. "As regards the individual nature, woman is defective and misbegotten, for the active force in the male seed tends to the production of a perfect likeness in the masculine sex; while the production of woman comes from a defect in the active force or from some material indisposition, or even from some external influence" (*Summa Theologica*). According to Mclaughlin (1974), Aquinas "follows Aristotle in his view that the male is ordered to the more noble activity, intellectual knowledge, whereas the female, although possessing a rational soul, was created solely for with respect to her sexuality, her body, as an aid in reproduction for the preservation of the species." The whole attitude toward sex in late antiquity— pagan and Jewish as well as Christian— was marred by misogyny, fear of body and the lure of false spiritualism (Wills, 2000).

Augustine, another important early Christian "father" was also anti-feminine. His writings express hostility toward sex, pleasure and marriage; and favor stoic avoidance of worldly pleasures in favor of spiritual commitment to God. His views on sexuality influenced early Church doctrine and were incorporated into Church theology. The Catholic Church has historically considered sex and sexuality as profoundly evil, requiring oversight and ecclesiastical supervision.

John C. Dwyer, in *Church History: Twenty Centuries of Catholic Christianity* (1985), depicts the sexual attitudes of Augustine: "Augustine regarded sexual activity even in marriage as basically shameful, and argued that it could be excused only if both partners had the intention of procreating a child." Augustine's defense of the superiority of sexual abstinence seems disingenuous based on stories of his promiscuous youth.

In the *Case for God* (2009), Karen Armstrong accurately describes one consequence of Augustine theology: "Born in grief and fear, this doctrine (Original Sin) has left Western Christians with a difficult legacy that linked sexuality indissolubly with sin and helped to alienate men and women from their humanity."

Conspicuously absent from Christian writings and doctrine is any sign of feminine influence. Instead we find a culture characterized by pretentious machismo. The idea of a sexually autonomous woman is threatening to male-dominated Christianity. Pope Leo XIII's 1891 encyclical, *Rerum Novarum*, is one of the foundational documents of modern Catholic teaching, yet it portrays women as suited only for work in the home and raising a family. For me, this negative attitude toward women is one of the significant cultural defects in the Christian tradition.

Any meaningful analysis of Christianity has to begin with its maleness. The chauvinistic masculine bias began at the dawn of Christianity with the proclamations of a male prophet and his twelve male companions. Christianity was founded, nurtured, practiced, and administered by men. The history of Christianity is told through the voice of a male. The androcentric bias in history is strikingly evident in the word itself; his-story, not her-story! Paul's theology became the foundation for Catholic Church doctrine and Augustine augmented it, giving structure and cohesion to Paul's doctrine.

Catholic seminaries and many other religious training venues have exclusionary entrance requirements; not unlike the signs on doors of tree houses built by young boys, *No Girls Allowed*. Greek philosophers, Catholic theologians, Enlightenment scholars, and Age of Reason Scientists were all male and their philosophy and science was conceived with a male bias. This superiority of the male finds its origin in the Genesis story in which the female is created from the rib of a man.

ALL FISH HAVE BONES

Christianity is a patriarchal ideology masquerading as an inclusive, tolerant theology; hypocritically teaching benevolence and compassion toward mankind, while subordinating women to men. This theology of exclusion was developed through scriptural interpretations of the role of women as subservient.

Biblical descriptions of women are hardly flattering. In Ecclesiastes 7:26, we find an appalling portrait of women: "More bitter than death I find the woman who is a hunter's trap, whose heart is a snare and whose hands are prison bonds. He who is pleasing to God will escape her, but the sinner will be entrapped by her." Many Bible passages portray women as ignorant, self-centered and sexually tempting.

The albatross of sexual guilt was imposed on women by men who dominated early Christian writing. It is both distressing and regrettable that Christianity and religion in general have exhibited androcentric prejudice. We now have a masculine Church with an anti-feminine theology.

Patristics, a special branch of theology which derives its name from the Latin *"pater,"* or "father," concentrates on the study of Christian Fathers of the first six centuries, AD. Studying the anti-feminine writings of the Patristic Fathers is enlightening and facilitates a better understanding of the aberrant sexual doctrines of the modern church. Viewed organizationally, Christianity (and most other religions) could be considered a private men's club in which women are allowed to attend meetings but prohibited from meaningful membership.

Scripture was written and interpreted by men. It is a story about men. Later, church *Fathers* interpreted and codified rules and regulations regarding doctrine.

Describing the plight of women in *Not in God's Image, Women in History from the Greeks to the Victorians (1973)*, O'Faolain and Martines profile another of the Patristic Fathers, Tertullian. Tertullian (155-240 AD) was a prolific early Christian writer who expressed the common bias against women in his writings. "You are the devil's gateway; you are she who first violated the forbidden tree and broke the law of God . . . Because of the death you merited, the Son of God had to die."

Tertullian blamed Eve for the "curse" on mankind. Because of her sin, women were responsible for bringing evil into the world. He also believed

Women in Christianity: The Theology of Exclusion

all women were "ritually unclean" and unable to partake in religious activities during menstruation. The Patristic Fathers excelled at using intemperate language in their writings and establishing pernicious doctrines. It is difficult to overstate their malignant influence on Christianity.

Bernard P. Prusak, a professor of religion at Villanova University, points out that early Christian writers wrote in a period of patriarchal culture when women were excluded from public roles and that they created myths displaying their prejudices. Some of the myths may have faded but the prejudices still exist today. Constance F. Parvey, a consultant for the Lutheran Church of America, summarizes the plight of women in Christianity: "Throughout the history of the Church this (subordination of women) has led to complex and confused theological arguments, with consequent social distortions, the sum of which is that men belong to this world and do the work of the Church, while women belong to the next world and act in the Church only as hidden helpers and servants to men."

Christianity — with a few minor exceptions — is still today a male bastion, ruled by male priests, pastors, deacons, elders, monks, popes, friars, bishops, archbishops, cardinals and ministers.

Catholic Church doctrine was formulated by a group of males, insecure in their own masculinity and fearful of female sexuality. Prevalent among Greek and Roman philosophers and authors was the belief that women were voracious in their sexual appetite (Wills). Bonnie J. Morris writes in *Women's History* that, "Early Church Fathers, however, grew increasingly obsessed with the female body as the cause of all trouble, so that the old emphasis on women's powerful fertility seen in ancient goddess statues (and in Judaism) was replaced by the values of virginity, celibacy, and shame."

Since sex was considered sinful, many males retreated to the safety of virginity and celibacy. Temptation could be avoided by purging sex, marriage and pleasure from life. J.N.D. Kelly refers to the practice of asceticism in the early church as a respectable tradition. "Ordinary Christians in the fourth century, like philosophical-minded pagans, were haunted by guilt-feelings about sexual enjoyment, and cherished an immense respect for self-control, even complete abstinence, in sex."

ALL FISH HAVE BONES

The Christian ideological spectrum has not expanded in 2,000 years. The guilt culture and quirky views of women and sex preached by Paul, Jerome, Augustine and Aquinas have survived and remains today deeply entrenched as a central theme of Christianity. Their perverse fixation on sex launched a Christian attitude toward gender that was not only endorsed at the time but continues today as a central precept in Christianity. It becomes obvious why the role of women in religion continues to be virtually nonexistent, based as it is on the culture of misogyny existing at the origination of Christian sexual doctrine.

I believe that the male sexism pervading Christianity gravely distorts any doctrine promulgated by ecclesiastical authorities. The absence of feminine influence is noticeable in both Christian doctrine and practice. Women's viewpoints need to be included in religious policy discussions.

In 1975, Pope Paul XI, in a letter to the Archbishop of Canterbury — who was contemplating allowing women to be ordained — disclosed that doctrine excluding women from the Catholic priesthood was in accordance with God's plan for His church. The primary defense for continuing a male-dominated Catholic priesthood is based on the notion that Jesus and his apostles were male and women are unworthy since they are tainted with the sin of Eve.

The Bible essentially portrays women as chattel. This callous disregard for the rights of women and their marginalization has survived to modern times. Many churches continue to rely on the twisted logic of fundamentalism to subordinate women and prevent them from serving in ecclesiastical positions of authority, relying on the tortuous argument that they are inferior and "unclean." The raw and denigrating portrayal and treatment of women by clerics is a sobering illustration of their status in religious settings. It is astonishing to me that modern church authorities continue to embrace the medieval cultural bias against women.

Catholic Church policy is offensive to women and an appalling failure to recognize the flawed cultural roots of this tradition. Women have been relegated by men to the sidelines of Catholicism due to a primitive understanding of women's physiology and sexuality, and a misguided belief that salvation is more easily attainable by avoiding women and devoting one's self to an ascetic lifestyle.

The influence of the Patristic Fathers on sexual doctrine had an enormous negative effect on Western Civilization. Any potential for liberation from the androcentrism and misogyny prominent in medieval times will have to address the theological pessimism concerning sexual love that originated with the Patristic Fathers. To preach inclusiveness yet fail to recognize the dignity and equality of women is a grave blunder of Christian leadership. Unfortunately, misogyny is a not only a prominent characteristic of Christianity, but also Orthodox Judaism and Islam.

The misrepresentation of women by early Christian writers was damaging and a moral injustice. It was also an affront to men who held more egalitarian views of humanity. Today, women are prime ministers and presidents of countries, CEOs of Fortune 500 companies, Nobel Laureates, and university presidents. It is a remarkable, though dubious achievement that Christianity, particularly Catholicism, has sustained a bias against women for 2,000 years. With the current enlightened attitudes toward women and their contribution to human development as scholars, scientists, doctors, engineers, political leaders as well as nurturing mothers and family stabilizers, it's puzzling that their status in religious organizations remains subordinate and insignificant. Women should be respected and recognized for their talents and welcomed as equal participants in Christian organizations.

Failure to recognize the humanity and rights of women in the 21st century stigmatizes Christianity as a moribund philosophy. The dismissive indifference exhibited by many Christian churches toward women and the Church's steadfast refusal to embrace change reflects a continued adherence to ancient cultural bias, and as long as religion in the Christian tradition continues to be dominated by male clerics, the status of women will not change. Any expectation for a sane and rational sexual ethic and marriage policy from an insular, celibate, male Catholic clergy is probably hopeless unless the entrance requirements for ordination are changed.

ALL FISH HAVE BONES

The attitude toward sex in the first centuries of Christianity was flawed by misogyny and a hatred of the human body. A culture of asceticism was prominent. Early church fathers believed that renunciation of pleasures of the flesh was a preferred virtue in attaining eternal salvation.

It's difficult to comprehend that the sex and marriage doctrine and regulations of the Catholic Church were formulated centuries ago by unmarried men who disliked women and believed them inferior to men. That doctrine is now interpreted and promulgated in the 21st century by a celibate male clergy! How bizarre is that? Earnest, pious and devout as they might have been, Paul, Augustine, Aquinas, Jerome and others shaped anomalous sexual doctrine that triumphed over the humanitarian message of Jesus and continues to haunt humankind and confuse and mystify committed believers.

The anti-feminine culture of the Classical Era was appropriated by Christianity and assimilated into fundamental Christian doctrine and was then materially influenced by this handful of eccentric, intellectual writers who withdrew from worldly pleasures to focus on an ascetic life they believed was the proper path to salvation. Paul, Augustine, and Jerome displayed similar temperaments, exhibiting an unambiguous hostility toward sex and marriage, favoring virginity as a virtue and a holy and rewarding lifestyle. How much fun would that be? If that lifestyle became popular, the human race would diminish, leaving the planet to the bugs! The Shakers, who practiced celibacy in colonial America in the 18th century, have already shown us that path. Their legacy is furniture!

Catholicism continues to maintain a troubling undercurrent of misogyny that began in the first century. The nonconformity to normal human behavior of Paul, Augustine, and Jerome; their fatalistic view of humanity; their emphasis on virginity as a lifestyle pleasing to God; their ascetic dispositions and obsession with suffering as a suitable lifestyle; and their opposition to marriage and subordination of females created an artificial reality that significantly distorted the message of love and compassion preached by Jesus. Their idealization of virginity, antagonism toward sex, and contemptuous view of marriage was instrumental in creating a culture of anxiety and a guilt in the Catholic Church that remains a central tenet in Catholicism. The Church has conveniently forgotten the pleasures associated with the strong evolutionary drive to reproduce.

Women in Christianity: The Theology of Exclusion

The Patristic Fathers feared women's sexuality; for them, women were irresistible, insatiable, lustful beings capable of extended sexual activities, i.e. serious impediments to living chaste lives. Augustine, believed that spiritual inspiration and enlightenment, in the quest to worship and please God, could only be experienced if one lived a chaste life without distractions. Women and marriage were distractions. In early Christianity, women were considered temptresses, leading men to sin and away from God. Evidently, the female body projected a carnal image that was disruptive to the God-centric, contemplative lifestyle.

To combat temptation, these men sought refuge in chastity, virginity, and celibacy. Their aversive obsession with sexuality had its origins in the story of the Garden of Eden where Eve was blamed for causing the downfall of mankind. "Because of Eve's sin, women were thought to be carnal and deceitful, easily susceptible to pride, loquacious, and the source of the world's problems" (Hofmann, 2007).

Anti-feminist rhetoric insinuated itself into the fabric of early Christian doctrine where it remains today. "Throughout centuries of literary culture, the demonization of women's traits, combined with the promotion of other anti-feminist assumptions, helped men gain and hold advantages over women ... and the Catholic Church, with its male hierarchy, played a prominent role in this gender-based hegemony" (Martin).

Eleanor Commo McLaughlin, a Harvard Divinity School professor, points out that female insufficiency makes them ineligible for the priesthood. "... ordination confers a superiority of rank that cannot be received by one who is by the order of creation in a state of subjection. Thus the woman, like the slave, may not validly receive Holy Orders." The residue of this ancient bias continues to be expressed today by the Church policy of celibate priests and nuns and a failure to recognize the humanity of women.

Christianity was born in a crucible of male sovereignty and female subjugation. Clara Maria Henning, an expert in Catholic Canon Law, describes the Church's attitude toward women:

> The law of the Church is designed to elevate one group at the expense of another: women are sacrificed as human beings to elevate priests to the status of sanctified beings. The law was written over the centuries by men for men, and by men who regarded sex as quite undesirable. In that men wrote for men, and then celibates for celibates, women were written out of the organization of the Church and out of the sanctuary. As far as the spirit of canon law is concerned, the Church seems to assume that it can do very well without women.

Apparently, only men can communicate with God. Eliminating the deep-seated prejudice expressed by the Patristic Fathers toward women will be a formidable challenge to Christian doctrine.

It seems inappropriate for modern Christian congregations, half of whom are women, to be ruled by an all-male ecclesiastical hierarchy who derive their authority from 2,000-year-old tribal traditions and social mores. Yet, the unenlightened, misguided, and calcified intellects that occupy the Vatican Curia have been unable to forsake first century roles of women as inferior, submissive and subordinate. They appear incapable of modern recognition of women's worth and equality.

In recent years, considerable disingenuous rhetoric concerning women's rights and status in the Church has been promulgated by the Vatican. It appears inclusive, but little or no visible progress toward equality has been forthcoming. Women remain excluded from major posts in the Church. The hermetically sealed Vatican world seems unaware that half of the human population are women! The misogynist fervor of the early Church Fathers shows no sign of abatement among the Vatican Curia who steadfastly refuse to reexamine the Church's doctrine on equality of women. The longevity of Christianity's anti-feminist bias staggers the imagination.

Women should be dignified, not marginalized, yet branding women with the odious distinction of inferiority is an affliction that remains today as a distinguishing characteristic of religion. The pathos of religion is that this orthodoxy is the residue of an archaic belief that still goes unrecognized today by predominately male clerics. This remarkable antipathy toward women has survived and modern Christianity seems unable to liberate itself from this fairy tale. Catholicism continues to maintain a troubling undercurrent of misogyny that began in the first century.

The moral and sexual framework of Christianity, developed in the first century by a handful of misanthropes, is inappropriate and impractical for people living in the 21st century.

ALL FISH HAVE BONES

CHAPTER NINE
THE GOD ILLUSION

Thus we call a belief an illusion when a wish-fulfillment is a prominent factor in its motivation, and in doing so we disregard its relations to reality, just as the illusion itself sets no store by verification.
— Sigmund Freud

One of the great moral and philosophical issues of our time is the role of religion and belief in a supernatural being — God — in our society. The panorama of human history reveals that all civilizations have endeavored to understand their origins and predict their futures. Religion and belief in a supernatural creator have often filled that purpose. In primitive societies, gods and goddesses were consulted to furnish answers to the mysterious forces observed in the world.

Fueled by anxiety and fear, religion survived and prospered by appealing to and exploiting the human emotions of hope and fear. Surrounded by superstition, baffled by the violent behavior of nature, and frightened by the prospect of suffering, death and potential eternal punishment, people living in the first century were susceptible to persuasive exhortations of prophets that a caring cosmic force would assuage their fears. As De Waal says, "Superstition blurs the line between reality and imagination as does religion and a belief in God."

So why do modern humans continue to believe in God? They appear to be seduced by the promise of an afterlife and unable to process the reality that the life they are living may be the only one they will ever have. Humankind seems to possess an infinite tolerance for deception and a willingness to be deceived by religious authorities dispensing mysterious religious propaganda.

Christianity has prospered due to the inability of the human mind to grasp the notion of mortality, that all living organisms have finite life spans. The search for a comfortable ideology has led to mystical faith in a transcendent deity. Religion, however, does not provide clear and authoritative answers.

Christianity is an ideology infused with deception and illusion. Its claims defy logic. It fails as an explanatory mechanism for natural occurrences in the universe (we no longer have need for a supernatural explanation for natural catastrophes like tsunamis, hurricanes and earthquakes; in fact, they are counter indicators of a benevolent God). There is no evidence for any of its promises. It is an ineffectual agent for world peace. It disparages and excludes half the population of the planet — women. The Kingdom of God has never materialized as it was promised in the first century, and there is no evidence of a blissful afterlife.

Jesus preached that something good would happen soon, perhaps even in his listeners' lifetimes. Subsequent generations continued to believe this, yet, after 2,000 years, nothing has happened. One would expect, after 20-plus centuries, if a promised event has not occurred, there is a low probability that it will. The likelihood of the Kingdom of God coming to Earth diminishes as time passes.

My argument that God does not exist may be illustrated by a three-legged stool. Each leg corresponds to a body of evidence and the seat of the stool represents my concluding philosophy. The three legs are the **Bible** itself, which is *not* the inerrant word of God; **evolution**, the scientific explanation for life on Earth; and the **illogical claims of religions,** arguments for God's existence that don't make rational sense. This chapter will examine each of these three concepts in detail.

The Bible

Human history is chronicled in illustrious stories that help us make sense of the world. The Bible is full of these stories, epic accounts of early cultures that shaped our world. The Bible is, without doubt, the most famous and influential book in the history of Western civilization. It is allegedly the word of God. Its impact on individuals, nations, cultures, and religious organizations is incalculable.

That does not make its contents true.

Many believers consider the Bible to be the revealed truth of the universe. The book of Genesis explains how life began on our planet and establishes mankind's relationship with the rest of the universe. However, the Bible is also opaque, difficult and contradictory, and a reader can be easily confused by the implausible stories told by writers who lived in ancient times in a culture substantially different from ours.

There are tendentious interpretations of these stories by every religion. Nimble theologians, parsing every word, are unable to agree on common meanings. One page has a message of love, serenity, and harmony while another page speaks of hatred, vengeance, and ethnic cleansing. One passage extols family values while another advocates the supremacy of the individual. Some passages are silly and absurd. Others are disturbing and horrifying. Scripture exhibits a flair for drama, tragedy and poetic expressions of ancient culture. Nothing is mundane or routine. Blood, sex, killing, lust, passion, sin, death, and chaos are ever present. Many of the miracle stories contradict the laws of nature. After reading the Bible it becomes blindingly obvious that it is not the divinely inspired, infallible word of God but rather a hodgepodge of stories written by many people and altered many times.

In the Old Testament, God formed a covenant with his chosen people and communicated with them Himself from the clouds or through angels and prophets. In the New Testament, He used His son Jesus as the communication link. Unfortunately, due to the illiteracy of Jesus and his disciples, we have no direct written record of their life and times.

Modern scholars tell us that the Bible contains historical, non-historical and semi-historical information. It is neither true nor false but an allegorical, ambiguous, confusing, and contradictory collection of stories, legends, myths, and anecdotes. It is a reflection of culture in the period in history in which it was written.

We do not know who wrote it or precisely why it was written. The events portrayed are based on oral tradition and written many years after they occurred by second- or third-hand writers who were not eyewitnesses. Scripture was not written by historians, but believers in a religious movement. Scripture is dependent on what the writers chose to include or exclude, what they thought significant or what they felt was unimportant. That which was included, embellished, minimized and even left out form the bias of the Bible.

The Bible reflects the thought processes, superstitions and lack of education of people living in the first century. It is a collection of religious fables, stories about events that transcended human understanding at that time. There is no attestation to the actual occurrence of the events. It is a stunningly egregious distortion of reality. History is not always an accurate depiction of reality but takes on the hue and agenda of the storyteller. Those who insist that every word in the Bible was divinely inspired have a very strange God indeed.

The words of today's New Testament have had a long, treacherous journey and may bear little resemblance to their original meaning. They began their journey as orations in the deserts of Palestine. After the death of Jesus, his parables were kept alive by his followers in the oral tradition of an illiterate population. The language of Jesus and his followers was Aramaic, the *lingua franca* of their time. Only years later — during the last half of the first century — were they transcribed into Greek.

During the latter part of the fourth century, Pope Damasus commissioned St. Jerome to produce a Latin version of the Bible. According to Bart D.

Ehrman, in *How Jesus Became God* (2014), Jerome reviewed the available Latin and Greek versions and revised and translated them into the common language of the day; what is now known as the Latin Vulgate.

Jerome's translations have been criticized for his biased alterations of the original writing. According to J. N. D. Kelly, Jerome's "improved" version of the Gospels was met with a "howl of indignation" for "flouting tradition and tampering with the inspired words of the Gospels."

Jerome's writings display antipathy toward women. According to Jane Barr, in *The Influence of Saint Jerome on Medieval Attitudes to Women*, Jerome's work was influenced by anti-feminist prejudices, and they can be observed in some of his translations. His alteration of Genesis 3:16 changes God's admonition to Eve from "Your desire will be for your husband and he will rule over you." In Jerome's version the verse reads, "You will be under the power of your husband and he will rule over you." Another example Barr provides is Genesis 39:1-10, in which Potiphar's wife attempts to seduce Joseph. In the original Hebrew text, the woman says to Joseph, "Lie with me" and he "refused." In the Jerome version "refused" becomes "by no means agreeing to this wicked deed."

Jerome detested the appearance of pregnant women. A quote attributed to him is, "Women with child present a revolting spectacle."

The Bible was finally translated into English in 1611, an endeavor considered heresy by the Catholic hierarchy. It allowed ordinary people to read and interpret the Bible without relying on Church authorities. William Tyndale, who was responsible for much of the King James Version, was ruled a heretic by the Catholic Church, strangled and burned at the stake.

By November of 2012, the Bible has been translated into 518 languages (Wikipedia). The 106 English versions include King James Version, Revised Standard Version, New Revised Standard Version, Good News Version, Jewish Publication Society Version, New English Bible, Revised English Bible, Jerusalem Bible and New Jerusalem Bible. It is impossible to assert that each of these is an accurate representation of the original words of Jesus or revelations of God. Each has its own nuanced rendering of scripture.

Since its original transcription, the Bible has been copied, edited, revised and translated into the vernacular of hundreds of countries. The Bible has

ALL FISH HAVE BONES

obviously been altered by these copyists; redacted and forged by numerous editors. There is a misogynistic bias in the Bible that very probably alters the meaning of many of the stories in the Scriptures. The words were originally spoken by men, orally transmitted by men, transcribed by men and interpreted by men. There is virtually no chance that the spoken words of Jesus, their meaning, intention, or the cultural context in which they were expressed have been accurately preserved through 20 centuries of writing, revision, and translation.

In the 21st century we have investigative tools such as literary criticism, archeological inquiry and sociological analysis to help decipher the content and meaning of the Bible. Yet, with the numerous translations, editions and revisions, it is still difficult to determine the original wording, context, and meaning. Word meanings and their original intent in an ancient culture — like those preached by Jesus — may have a substantially different essence than the words we read in today's English Bible. Interpreting and accurately transcribing the Aramaic utterances of Jesus into Greek many years after he died, and then translating them into Latin for the Roman Empire was staggeringly complex. Translations of the original words of Jesus renders a Bible in the vernacular subject to the individual translators' interpretations, which may or may not accurately convey the original meaning. The Bible is essentially a Gordian knot theologians have been trying to unravel for more than 20 centuries.

The Bible should be read as a series of stories about how ancient people lived and believed. It is not the "Gospel" truth. An illustration of this phenomenon is stories you share with family and friends. As they go through numerous iterations, the original accuracy is usually lost.

Today, the Bible is treated by believers as a divinely-inspired, organized collection of books premeditated and designed to chronicle the development of early Judaism leading to Christianity. In reality, it is a collection of books arbitrarily cobbled together in "canons" by anonymous early Jewish and Christian clerics.

The Canon of the New Testament resulted from a gradual process during the first three centuries CE. There was a vast Christian literature extant at that time and Christian authorities selected those books that exhibited a common, generally-accepted message of Christianity and rejected books that conflicted with this message, labeling them unorthodox and apocryphal. The 27 books of the New Testament are those that are representative of God's revelations to early Christians.

The Bible presents us with incompatible perspectives and inconsistent interpretations by numerous writers and editors. The debate over the "truth" of the Bible is essentially about literal truth versus scientific, evolutionary explanations for events described in scripture. In spite of its perplexing story line, confusing construction, puzzling semantics, arbitrary assembly and questionable authenticity, "the Good Book" has had an epochal effect on generations. Understanding this phenomenon is our challenge.

The Bible can be interpreted literally, metaphorically, or allegorically, but the creation account in Genesis cannot, in any way, be reconciled with scientific evidence of the natural world. Though Bible scholarship has advanced considerably in the past few decades, I don't detect much difference in the homilies preached now from those when I was in high school. There appears to be a disconnect between theologians and parish clerics on current church doctrine. The Catholic Church has never encouraged in-depth study of scripture, resulting in a Biblically illiterate flock.

An example of the Bible's inconsistency can be found in the first seven chapters of Genesis, in which God creates the universe twice and then destroys it by flooding. In Chapter One, God creates the universe and then man and woman — in His own image. In Chapter Two, Adam is created first, then the rest of the world. Then Eve is created from the rib of Adam, which is often the scriptural citation justifying women's subservient role to man in Christianity. The simultaneous creation of both genders in Chapter One is conveniently ignored by Catholic theologians.

By Chapter Six, God has become disenchanted and angry and decides to drown everything He created. "I will wipe out from the earth the men I have created, and not only the men, but also the beasts and the creeping things and the birds of the air, for I am sorry that I made them" (Genesis 6:7).

He's angry and upset with humans but decides to kill every living thing? The beasts, birds, and creeping things had done nothing to incur His wrath.

It's difficult to find a coherent theme in the opening pages of the Bible. In Genesis 1:31, "God looked at everything he had made and he found it very good." A few pages later in Genesis 6:6, " . . . he regretted that he had made man on earth, and his heart was grieved." We have a very fickle God.

There are numerous contradictory stories in the Bible but one particularly illustrative is the putative origin of the Christian celebration of Christmas: the story of Jesus' birth. John and Mark make no references to Jesus' birth, and the nativity accounts in Luke 2:1-16 and Matthew 2:1-14 are significantly inconsistent. Joseph and Mary are residents of Nazareth in Luke and Bethlehem in Matthew. Jesus is born in a manger in Luke and a house in Matthew. Jesus' créche is visited by shepherds in Luke and wise men in Matthew. Angels and a heavenly host appear in Luke, yet a star guides the three wise men in Matthew. Luke has the holy family returning to Nazareth but Matthew has them fleeing to Egypt to avoid Herod, who slaughters the "innocents." There is no Herod in Luke.

The leitmotif of the New Testament is love: God loves us all and we should love each other. Psalm 103 represents God as "Merciful and gracious . . . , slow to anger, abounding in kindness." However, this is inconsistent with the God of both the Old and New Testaments. It is countered by the concept of retribution, violence, slavish adherence to rules and regulations and strict rubrics for the worship of God. The descriptions of the God in the Bible reflects a colossal contradiction in behavior and personality.

One scriptural message that has obstinately persisted and burdens mankind today is the potential of eternal punishment after death. The concept of everlasting punishment in Hell appears prominently in the Bible; "Where the worm dieth not, and the fire is not quenched" (Mark 9:48). The Bible is obsessed with sin and punishment.

Adam is held responsible for the first sin and the rest of us are guilty as the result of being born: "Wherefore, as by one man sin entered into the world, and death by sin; and so death passed upon all men, for that all have sinned" (Romans 5:12). The Bible contains many stories of brutal and irrational punishment for misbehavior and plentiful examples of human and divine retribution. The Bible explicitly demands that human transgressions be punished.

Death by stoning seemed to be the preferred method of punishment in the first century, and apparently there was little distinction among offenses. Cursing your father or mother was punishable by death (Leviticus 20:9) as was adultery with a neighbor's wife (Leviticus 20:10). One passage would be comical if not for the brutality. In Deuteronomy 21:18-21, the punishment for a "stubborn and unruly son who will not listen to his father or mother, and will not obey . . ." is stoning by his fellow citizens! Fortunetellers were also stoned to death (Leviticus 20:27).

Speaking ill of the Lord could also get you in trouble. The Lord told Moses to take a "blasphemer" out and have the community stone him to death (Leviticus 24:11-16). Woe to a woman who was discovered not to be a virgin on the night of her marriage; this was a "crime against Israel" and the Lord commanded her townsmen to stone her to death. Note that there is nothing in the Bible about males being virgins on their wedding night! Misbehaving in the first century was met with serious consequences.

Paul is explicit about what constitutes sin: ". . . neither fornicators nor idolaters nor adulterers nor boy prostitutes nor practicing homosexuals nor thieves nor the greedy nor drunkards nor slanderers nor robbers will inherit the kingdom of God" (1st Corinthians 6:9-10). "Now the works of the flesh are obvious: immorality, impurity, licentiousness, idolatry, sorcery, hatreds, rivalry, jealously, outbursts of fury, acts of selfishness, dissensions, factions, occasions of envy, drinking bouts, orgies, and the like" (Galatians 5:19-21).

Some passages in the Bible are amusing. In Deuteronomy 25:11-12, "When two men are fighting and the wife of one intervenes to save her husband from the blows of his opponent, if she seizes the latter by his private parts, you shall chop off her hand without pity." In Exodus 35:2-3, Moses tells the Israelites that the Lord commanded them not to work on the Sabbath. "Anyone who does work on that day shall be put to death. You shall not even light a fire in any of your dwellings on the Sabbath day." Evidently, God didn't care if you and your family were freezing in the winter on the Sabbath.

"When a man strikes his male or female slave with a rod so hard that the slave dies under his hand, he shall be punished. If, however, the slave survives for a day or two, he is not to be punished, since the slave is his own property" (Exodus 21:20-21). "You shall put twisted cords on the four corners of the cloak that you wrap around you" (Deuteronomy 22:12).

The lifespan of early figures in the Bible was particularly remarkable. According to Genesis, Adam lived 800 years, Noah lived 500 years and apparently living just short of 1,000 years was common!

Circumcision was mandatory under Mosaic Law and God's covenant with his followers required circumcision in order to be saved (Genesis 17:10, Acts of the Apostles 15:1). Having a foreskin was an impediment for going to heaven? If God didn't like foreskins, why did he create them?

You also needed your "stones and privy member" intact to enjoy the Lord's favor; if you are wounded in the stones or have your privy member cut off you cannot enter the congregation of the Lord (Deuteronomy 23:1). If heaven is a state of constant euphoria, I'm not sure of the value of one's stones and privy member there, except maybe for nostalgic reasons.

Let's examine some of the attributes of God and Jesus found in the Bible, but not commonly heard during Sunday homilies.

Wrath: "If you do not heed me and do not keep all these commandments, I will punish you with terrible woes" (Leviticus 12:19). "I trod them in my anger, and trampled them down in my wrath; their blood spurted on my garments; all my apparel I stained" (Isaiah 63:3).

Vengeance: "Beloved, do not look for revenge but leave room for the wrath; for it is written,'Vengeance is mine, I will repay, says the Lord'"(Romans 12:19).

Narcissism: "As I live, says the Lord, every knee shall bend before me, and every tongue shall give praise to God" (Romans 14:11). "You shall not have other gods besides me" (Exodus 20:3).

Brutality: The Biblical penalty for disobedience and many sexual and legal issues was death by stoning. A literal interpretation of the Bible reveals an inhumane God.

Alienation: "If anyone comes to me without hating his father and mother, wife and children, brothers and sisters, and even his own life, he cannot be my disciple" (Luke 14:26).

> Do you think I have come to establish peace on earth? No, I tell you but rather division. From now on a household of five will be divided, three against two and two against three; a father will be divided against his son and a son against his father, a mother against her daughter and daughter against her mother, a mother-in-law against her daughter-in-law and a daughter-in-law against her mother-in-law (Luke 12:51-53).

The Biblical God also played favorites. He states on numerous occasions that the Israelites were his chosen people.

Richard Tarnas writes in *The Passion of the Western Mind*. "... so much of the spirit and narrative of the Old Testament was dominated by the figure of a jealous God of stern justice and ruthless vengeance, arbitrarily punitive, obsessively self-referential, militantly nationalistic, patriarchal, moralistic ... that Gods' cherished compassionate qualities were often difficult to discern."

Punishment in the Old Testament was harsh and capricious. God was into killing people wholesale. Punishment for enemies of the Lord was brutal and universal; essentially ineffable acts of genocide. He started with the Flood, wiping out every living thing except Noah, his family and some animals. God had Moses execute 24,000 Midianites (Numbers 25:1-9) excepting female virgins (Numbers 31:9). He had Saul destroy the nation of Amelek: "... kill men and women, children and infants, oxen and sheep, camels and asses" (1st Samuel 15:1-3). He killed all firstborn male Egyptian children after the nine plagues failed to convince Pharaoh to release the Israelites (Exodus 11:4-5).

After the defeat of the Amorites, Moses was instructed to "... seize all his (Shion, King of the Amorites) cities and doom them all, with their men, women and children; we left no survivors" (Deuteronomy 2:34). The people of Jericho met the same fate. After an attack by Joshua, they "... put to the sword all living creatures in the city: men and women, young and old, as well as oxen, sheep and asses" (Joshua 6:21).

ALL FISH HAVE BONES

The behavior of religious zealots is inimical to the best interests of a peaceful society, yet devout partisans of all stripes have been killing people in the name of Yahweh, Jesus, or Allah for thousands of years without noticeable success and no end appears in sight.

In the New Testament, punishment got worse. With the arrival of Jesus on the scene, stoning was replaced by eternal damnation in hellfire and brimstone (the ancient name for sulfur). Hell was called by several names; Gehenna (Matthew 5:29), Netherworld (Luke 10:15), Hades (Revelation 20:14). The description of Hell was graphic and detailed.

"The angels will go out and separate the wicked from the righteous and throw them into the fiery furnace where there will be wailing and grinding of teeth every day" (Matthew 13:49-50). Revelation 14:10-11 describes hell as a place where people will be "tormented in burning sulfur...and the smoke of the fire that torments them will rise forever and ever and there will be no relief day or night...the two were thrown alive into the fire pool burning with sulfur" (Revelation 19:20). In Hell, there is no parole for good behavior.

According to Scripture, the acceptable punishment for sin is *everlasting* punishment (Mark 9:43-44). Throughout history, preachers have continued the Biblical obsession with damnation and instilled fear in the hearts of their followers by graphically describing Hell. One sermon noted for its vivid and appalling language was preached by Jonathan Edwards (1703-1758) in Enfield, Connecticut, in 1741.

Entitled *Sinners in the Hands of an Angry God*, Edwards' homily described Hell: "That world of misery, that lake of burning brimstone, is extended under you. There is the dreadful pit of glowing flames of the wrath of God; there is hell's wide gaping mouth open; and you have nothing between you and hell but the air; it is only the power and mere pleasure of God that holds you up. (*Words That Made American History*, 1962). Eternal damnation to Hell without potential for release is a frightening concept and runs contrary to any sense of compassion expressed by Jesus.

The dichotomy of God's "rewards" — eternal damnation in the miasma of hell, or euphoric bliss behind the "pearly gates" in Heaven enjoying what

Catholics call the "beatific vision" — seems unjust, arbitrary and just plain silly. The Catholic Church cleverly invented purgatory, a temporary version of hell, from which there is an eventual escape. Purgatory, a concept with no Biblical foundation, was designed as an intermediate expiatory realm where one atoned for sin. This arbitrary reward and punishment concept depicts a mercurial and capricious God. It should be noted here that Origen, one of the major theologians of early Christianity, believed in apokatastasis, or universal salvation. Everyone would be saved. This belief was condemned by the church.

The story of the Ten Commandments may be the quintessential example of the silliness of the Bible. Most of us are familiar with the story of Moses receiving the Ten Commandments from God (Exodus 20:1-17). The list has been reproduced thousands of times. However, I believe that very few of us know about the *three* sets of Commandments described in the Bible.

Dan Barker, the author of *Godless* (2008), describes in an engrossing and enlightening manner, the three versions of the Ten Commandments. According to Barker,

> When Moses took his first trip up the mountain, he came back down with no stone tablets at all. He simply spoke what God told him and that list of edicts in Exodus 20 is what made it into Jewish and Christian tradition. Moses went back up the mountain a second time, and this time he did come back with Ten Commandments, laws engraved by the finger of God, though not formally called the Ten Commandments. Moses smashed those tablets to pieces when he saw the children of Israel worshipping the golden calf. So, Moses went back up the mountain a third time to get a replacement, and what God told him would be identical to the previous list. . . .

Here is the list Moses got the third time around:

I. You shall not worship any other God.

II. You shall not make for yourselves any molten gods.

III. You shall keep the feast of Unleavened bread.

IV. To me belongs every first-born male that opens the womb among all your livestock whether in the herd or in the flock.

V. No one shall appear before me empty-handed. For six days you may work, but on the seventh day you shall rest.

VI. You shall keep the feast of Weeks with the first of the wheat harvest; likewise, the feast at the fruit harvest at the close of the year.

VII. Three times a year all your men shall appear before the Lord, the Lord God of Israel.

VIII. You shall not offer me the blood sacrifice with leavened bread, nor shall the sacrifice of the Passover feast be kept overnight for the next day.

IX. The choicest first fruits of your soil you shall bring to the house of the Lord your God.

X. You shall not boil a kid in its mother's milk.

This list is from Exodus 34:14-26. You don't see many monuments on courthouse lawns inscribed with these edicts!

Symbolic of Judaism, and thereby Christianity, is the concept of bloody sacrifice; from animal and bird sacrifices in the Old Testament to the crucifixion of Jesus in the New Testament. The Old Testament is replete with references to burnt sacrifices to appease the Lord, who appeared to be particularly fond of bloody sacrifices of birds and animals, and not just any bird or animal, but the best, "without blemish" (Leviticus 3:6).

"According to the law almost everything is purified by blood, and without the shedding of blood there is no forgiveness" (Hebrews 9:22). Leviticus 1 and 2 offer extensive rituals for animal sacrifice. Burnt offerings are routinely described as "sweet-smelling oblations" to the Lord (Exodus 29:18; Leviticus 23:13; Numbers 15:10, 28:17 and 28:6). Leviticus 17:60 describes one of the rituals: "The priest shall splash the blood on the altar of the Lord at the entrance to the meeting tent and there burn the fat for an *odor pleasing to the Lord.*" (my italics).

Reason would suggest that angry Gods exist only in our minds, yet throughout history we have seen bizarre and horrific ritual sacrifices performed to appease them. It is inestimable how many birds, animals and maidens have been sacrificed in an insane attempt to please and mollify an angry, invisible, cosmic force.

The God Illusion

In the Bible is Exodus, the story of the captivity and enslavement of the Israelites by the Egyptians and their subsequent release by the Pharaoh — but only after ten plagues unleashed by God. The Israelites, approximately 600,000 of them, wandered and camped in the desert for 40 years. Today, Jews recall the Exodus by celebrating Passover as one of their most significant holidays. The problem is that the Exodus never happened!

According to Israel Finkelstein and Neil Asher Silberman in their book, *The Bible Unearthed* (2001), "... repeated archaeological surveys in all regions of the peninsula, including the mountainous area around the traditional site of Mount Sinai...have yielded only negative evidence: not even a single shard, no structure, not a single house, no small trace of an ancient encampment." They continue, "The conclusion — that the Exodus did not happen at the time and in the manner described in the Bible —seems irrefutable when we examine the evidence at specific sites where the children of Israel were said to camp for extended periods during their wandering in the desert and where some archaeological indication — if present — would almost certainly be found."

Biblical passages are cited by believers for numerous outlandish and dangerous practices. There is a high attrition rate among Pentecostal preachers who partake in the ritual of snake handling. Quoting passages from the Gospels of Mark and Luke, they believe they are immune to the poison of snakes. Christians Science practitioners eschew modern medicine. They follow the writings of Mary Baker Eddy (1821-1910) who claimed that sickness is an illusion and can be overcome with prayer in the manner of Jesus. Amish sects reject modern technology, dress plainly and live in isolated communities.

The most appalling and damaging doctrine to be found in the Bible, far surpassing eternal damnation in Hell or Original Sin, is the concept of the superior status of mankind in nature. This sentiment, inspired by God's admonition in Genesis 1:28 to subdue the earth and establish dominion over all living things, demonstrates a colossal misunderstanding of the synergism between mankind and the flora, fauna and inorganic assets of the planet and has the effect of disengaging humans from nature. Continued belief in this idea has a potential of catastrophic consequences for the human race and the planet. This tragically misunderstood and misinterpreted passage rationalizes industrial depletion of natural resources to satisfy consumer demand.

We inhabit — and share — a majestic universe but have been taught by religious authorities that humans have an "immortal soul" which separates us from the rest of nature. Deluding humans into believing they are special creatures in the eyes of God and therefore enjoy some special privilege in nature is an underpinning for the whole concept of religion. The bifurcation of man from the natural world cultivates a misunderstanding of our true relationship with the planet and has haunted mankind since the writing of Genesis. Our goal has been to conquer the "wild" and use it for our benefit.

With the assistance of religion, we interpret our self-awareness and ability to communicate verbally with others of our species as distinguishing us from nature. This is instrumental in the assumption that we occupy a privileged position in the universe and are the pinnacle of existence. Genesis elevates the status of man to righteous master over all of nature. We have become enthralled with our status and anointed ourselves as rulers of the universe, viewing the world as a dualistic hierarchy, with us as dominant species. Embedded in this idea is the colossal error that nature exists only for our enjoyment and consumption.

We are not a "chosen" species nor is human life the purpose of creation.

When I hike in grizzly country in Idaho and Montana, I am extremely aware that I am not the dominant species. Quite the contrary. I pay rapt attention to my surroundings and do my best to avoid testing the concept that I am superior. Viewing the cosmos as human-centric is to ignore the obvious laws of nature. Observing subtle or violent expressions of the environment should be adequate evidence that we are not in control but merely along for the ride. Withers and Lovelock advise us that we do not enjoy elite status among the organisms that inhabit the earth, but are a component of nature, neither essential nor in charge.

The U.S. has only about five percent of the world population, yet we consume approximately one third of the world's resources. Americans have

The God Illusion

a dismal knowledge of ecological relationships. Our ego has relegated nature to a role of servitude. Instead of being humbled by nature we have binged on her resources, believing our activity is sanctioned by Scripture. Conspicuous consumption, aided by a booming human population, threatens to collapse entire biosystems. Today, as natural resources become increasingly scarce, and in some cases vanish, humans continue unabated to plunder, seemingly unaware of the consequences.

According to Harari, human intimacy with nature was fractured about 10,000 years ago with the beginning of the Agriculture Revolution which allowed human settlements to replace hunter-gather groups by manipulating a few plant and animal species.

Thomas Berry believes we have lost intimate contact with a meaningful universe, initiating our children into an insensitive, unfeeling and predatory attitude toward nature. Tom Hayden, former member of the California State Senate, argues in his book, *The Lost Gospel of the Earth* (2006), that our environmental crisis began when tribal systems of belief were replaced by formal religions. With the advent of monotheism, the nature worship and mysticism of tribal religions was replaced by human-centric theology and engagement with God. Our commitment to scriptural passages in lieu of respect and appreciation of nature alienates us from our origins. Embedded in this myopic and distorted view of the world are the seeds of our demise and the possibility that we will be the cause of our own extinction.

A cursory glance at the current state of nature indicates there is not a sympathetic, supernatural environmentalist in the sky. The planet already shows signs of abuse. Human cultures, in their haste to exploit nature, tend to ignore the long term value of nature and its critical role in the continuation of the species. The biosphere we live in has been significantly altered and degraded by human activity causing deforestation, atmospheric change, ocean pollution, ecosystem degradation, melting ice caps, rising sea levels, species extinction, and radioactive contamination. I'm afraid the environmental consequences of these actions may be leading us toward an irreversible planetary catastrophe. It might be prudent for humans to ignore delusional religious doctrine and assume responsibility for the planet. Continued reliance on ancient scripture as we confront 21st century ecological challenges is faulty theology and dismal science. It's time to replace our fixation on a transcendent deity with reverence and respect for our habitat.

If we are to survive as a species and leave a healthy planet for future generations, it is necessary to fundamentally alter the nature of humankind's interaction with the biosphere. The consequence of embracing the concept of superiority prevents man from living in harmonious relationship with nature. The doctrine of superiority impedes man's understanding of his place in the universe and leads to excessive exploitation of the resources needed for continued existence of our species. We have a right to prudently partake of nature's bounty and harvest plants and animals essential for our survival but not at the expense of harming entire ecosystems. We should remind ourselves that the planet supports us, not the other way around. Someone once said, "Humans, despite their artistic pretentions, their sophistication, and their many accomplishments—owe their existence to a six-inch layer of topsoil and the fact that it rains."

Failure to recognize the flaw in the Genesis mandate of dominion relegates humans to a corrupted relationship with nature, a false sense of supremacy and an unfortunate disengagement from fellow organisms on the planet that contribute to our well-being. One solution to the misguided concept of human superiority would be a redirection of our attention from monotheism to science and reason. If the goal of humankind is a sustainable civilization, we need to abandon the cult of unlimited growth. This will benefit both man and his habitat. There is no little irony in Biblical messages containing both tidings of the salvation of humanity and teachings that may contribute to its end.

If religions continue to proclaim that everything happening on earth is God's ineffable will, and that someday He will take care of the universe He created in His own way and on His own timeline, I have a profound concern that the viability of the planet is at stake. Religious leaders teach that God's fingerprint is on everything. A casual survey of nature contradicts an image of a caring cosmic force. There is an urgent need to recognize the destructive impact of man on nature and develop an intellectual and pragmatic program of reintegration of modern humanity with the community of nature.

Nature has the ability to regulate itself and reestablish equilibrium when imbalance occurs. Disruptions of nature by mankind, however, are rarely repaired by mankind. We *look* at nature but we don't *see* or understand it. We have lost our connection. We need to redirect our spiritual aspirations from illusionary religious goals to a realistic reconnection with nature.

We could regain some connection by learning from Native Americans, who had a reverence for the cosmos and a sense of kinship with nature.

> Every phenomenon and every aspect of creation within the Native American cosmos has a spiritual dimension, but the Earth, which is home to all living and growing things, is regarded as having special sanctity… This cosmos recognizes no separation between the spiritual and the material, between the real and the supernatural, or between the animate and inanimate, because everything and everyone is endowed with spirit power, or 'medicine.' *Mother Earth, Father Sky* (1977)

Failure to reject the Biblical vision of the universe and rediscover and embrace our oneness with nature has the potential to doom our planet.

We are squandering the health of the planet and its use by future generations via extravagant consumption. Affluence is insidious and addictive and can only be fueled by destruction and depletion of natural resources. Many scientists fear we are approaching an ecological tipping point and have coined a catchphrase to express it: Anthropocene Epoch (The Age of Humans). At some point in the near future we are going to have to reconcile our voracious appetite for resources with the future health of the planet. As the future unfolds, will we humbly accept a status as a member of the Earth community or remain defiant and continue to degrade our planet? Can our intellect save us or have we become too apathetic? The brainpower and knowledge is probably there but I'm not very confident the willpower is available. The paleontologist Richard Leakey calls this the "Sixth Extinction."

Biblical writings reflect the beliefs and thought processes of an ancient, uneducated and superstitious culture. Christianity has abandoned the bloody rituals, but their original intention is retained in the form of the sin-repentance-confession custom in the liturgy of the modern church. It is difficult to imagine that a rational, objective, educated person would conclude that the Bible is the inerrant word of God and should be literally interpreted and used as a guide for living.

The Bible has been used to predict an apocalypse. To date, these claims have all been wrong. However, we now have the capability to annihilate ourselves and our planet without the help of Biblical revelation. With the proliferation of nuclear weapons and man-caused climate change, we are capable of causing a cataclysm that would bring an end to life as we know it.

Questioning the authenticity of improbable events and passages in the Bible questions the veracity of the Bible itself and its value as a historical document. If, as some theologians argue, some passages are to be taken literally and others symbolically, the objectivity of the Bible crumbles. If some passages are dubious, ambiguous, unbelievable or blatantly false, it becomes difficult to conclude that the Bible is the inspired word of God, which renders it unsuitable as the causal authority for Christianity.

The Christian doctrine of today is a distillation of scripture by church fathers living in the first few centuries after the death of Jesus. Walter Lippmann (1889-1974), distinguished journalist and political commentator, writes, "The deposit of wisdom in the Bible and in the classic books does not contain a systematic and comprehensive statement of moral principles from which it is possible to deduce with clarity and certainty specific answers to concrete questions… The voluminous and very detailed corpus of Christian laws is the work of popes, bishops, councils, canonists, casuists, doctors and writer of textbooks."

The Bible remains an inscrutable document of appalling theology and sufficient discrepancies to make it unsuitable as basis for a religious belief such as Christianity. Using scripture to justify intolerance and violence diminishes and contradicts the humanitarian message contained in the Bible.

Scriptural passages that suggest humans should dominate nature, that we are all guilty of sin at birth, that women should be oppressed, and concluding with the idea of eternal punishment in a fiery place are sufficient evidence that the Bible should not be taken seriously.

The debate among academic Bible scholars is informative, furnishing provocative historical insight into the lives and culture of people living when it was written. In the analysis of Christianity, it is not particularly important what Scripture says or doesn't say but if what it professes really happened. There is little evidence, outside of the Bible itself, that many of the events it portrays actually occurred or occurred in the manner described.

Reading the Bible word for word, it becomes obvious that it's not the intellectual musings of a brilliant deity who inspired earthly scribes. It's more accurately described as the opinions of numerous individuals, each with their own agenda.

Evolution

The centrality of evolution in science, and by extension, in our lives, is undeniable. Daniel C. Dennett, in *Darwin's Dangerous Idea* (1995), describes the universe before life began: "Once upon a time, there was no mind, and no meaning, and no error, and no function, and no reasons, and no life." Darwin's thoughts on evolution were a revolutionary explanation of the development of living organisms and undermined the superior status of humans in nature. As a science-based explanation for the development of humans, evolution replaced thousands of myths.

Darwin's theory of evolution is fairly simple in explanation but complex in philosophical and spiritual consequences. Evolutionary science was a seismic phenomenon in the field of biology but a catastrophic problem for theology. It offered a plausible scientific explanation for human existence and development without any need of the supernatural. Prior to Darwin, God was the answer to universal design questions. Darwin's theory was a direct challenge to Genesis, asking which was a more plausible explanation for the origin of species: an omnipotent creator or random beneficial mutations of organisms over time. Evolution eviscerated the concept that divine intervention was a necessary ingredient for the development of life on Earth. Darwinism was subversive to religious doctrine.

In *Why Evolution is True* (2010), Jerry A. Coyne succinctly describes the theory of evolution: "It can be summarized in a single (albeit slightly long) sentence: Life on earth evolved gradually beginning with one primitive species—perhaps a self-replicating molecule—that lived more than 3.5 billion years ago; it then branched out over time, throwing off many new and diverse species; and the mechanism for most (but not all) of evolutionary is natural selection."

Evolutionary evidence is found in fossils: mineralized biological material found in sedimentary rock formations. More recently, the discovery of DNA has allowed molecular biologists to trace evolution at the molecular level. As just one part of nature, we share DNA with all living things. Science continues to reinforce the validity of the theory of evolution. On February 12th, 2015, the *Wall Street Journal* reported that scientists studying the same Galapagos Islands finches that intrigued Charles Darwin during his voyage on the *Beagle* discovered a gene influencing the shape of the bird's beaks.

Evolution was a wondrous discovery. It offered a plausible explanation for the staggering complexity of the universe by utilizing a few simple rules. The publication in 1859 of Darwin's seminal book, *The Origin of Species*, explained the mechanisms of random mutation and natural selection, which permit simple life forms to develop into complex organisms over billions of years. Evolutionary theory asserts that organisms change gradually over vast periods of time via random genetic mutations passed to offspring, allowing some to better adapt to their environment and pass on heritable traits. Random mutation, natural selection and vast periods of time are the mechanisms that explained the diversity of life on earth. Darwin called it "descent with modification." Mutations are unpredictable and most often have a negative effect on organisms. Beneficial mutations give individuals in a species a greater chance of survival in their environment. These traits are adaptive and reproductive and replicated in the next generation.

In *The Atheist's Guide to Reality* (2011), Alex Rosenberg points out that two of the extraordinary elements in Darwin's theory are passivity and lack of foresight. "Most important, in this process (evolution) there is absolutely no *foresight* (italics in the original) about what variants will be useful to their bearers in the future. The absence of foresight in nature is better captured by the label 'blind variation' than the more usual 'random variation.'"

In *The God Problem* (2012), Howard Bloom humorously describes the Darwinian mechanism of natural selection:

> Natural selection, nature's pickiness, nature's way of playing favorites, her way of putting her creatures through a game that gives procreation privileges to the winners, that will be Charles Darwin's contribution to a theory... Darwin will say that nature acts like a breeder of sheep, pigeons, or strawberries. She gives her prize winners the privilege of sex and reproduction. But she sidelines the lame and the halt. She turns the malformed and the crippled into sexual rejects. So the gorgeous will get to have kids. And the inglorious or the just plain homely will not get that privilege. Nor will those in the wild who just don't get it. Those who can't find a way to make a living in the woods, the meadows, and the mountain slopes won't get the girls. Wild sheep and red grouse who can't find enough food will not get sex. Ever.

Evolution and religion are incompatible because one is science-based, and the other relies on metaphysics. Theological assertions are incompatible with science since science is based on observable facts and theology is based on the mystery of the unknown. The Catholic Church teaches that it is permissible for Catholics to believe in the theory of evolution as long as somewhere in the process, God performs a divine infusion, giving humans "souls." Church dogma is equivocal on evolution but insists that the human soul is a spiritual substance created by God (*Encyclical Humani Generis*, 1950, Pius XII).

For the Church to accept evolutionary theory entirely will require substantial reworking of doctrine. In their book, *Theology of Evolution* (1972), Ervin Nemesszeghy and John Russell, two Jesuit philosophers, explain:

> ... the Church in her official teaching never condemned the theory of evolution as such and the cautious, and at times

perhaps hostile attitude, on the part of the Church towards evolution could be explained by her earnestness to safeguard two major dogmas of our faith: the spiritual nature of man, and original sin. Hence if evolution is accepted then a new theological understanding of these two basic dogmas is called for.

Writing in the magazine, *Free Inquiry* (Dec. 2009/Jan. 2010), British evolutionary biologist Richard Dawkins emphatically attempts to convince skeptics that evolution is accepted in the scientific community. "Evolution is a fact. Beyond reasonable doubt; beyond serious doubt; beyond sane, informed, intelligent doubt; beyond doubt evolution is a fact... It is the plain truth that we are cousins of chimpanzees, somewhat more distant cousins of monkeys, more distant cousins of aardvarks and manatees, yet more distant cousins of bananas and turnips."

The major themes in evolutionary theory — random mutation and natural selection — make it difficult to argue that organisms progressed with some intention and direction. Evolution also exhibits some strange adaptations which tend to obviate the idea of an intelligent designer, God. For example, whales have vestigial legs. They walked on land before they began living in the ocean.

Humans are an accidental consequence of a non-directional evolutionary process that has neither goals nor purpose. In *The Atheist's Guide to Reality* (2011), Alex Rosenberg writes: "Darwin's theory tells us that we, along with every other creature that roams the Earth, are at best *improbable* (italics in the original) outcomes of natural selection... sapient life of any kind is an improbable outcome. Indeed, the theory of natural selection suggests that complex life of any sort is an improbable outcome."

The late Stephen Jay Gould, famous Harvard paleontologist and evolutionary biologist, suggested in his book, *Wonderful Life: The Burgess Shale and the Nature of History* (1989), that if we rewound the evolutionary tape it is unlikely that humans would have been one of the results!

Evolution is an elegant and simple concept and a powerful tool to explain the development and diversity of life on earth. Yet, according to a 2013 Pew Research Center study, a third of the American population reject the idea of evolution, saying that "humans and other living things have existed in their present form since the beginning of time." It seems staggeringly difficult for some to comprehend that humans are the long-term result of cells oozing forth from the primordial soup, and that a fish crawling out of the ocean is one of our ancestors. But even each individual's existence is extremely improbable. Imagine the odds of one determined sperm out-swimming all of his millions of competitors to unite with an egg that resulted in the miracle that is each of us.

Eugenie C. Scott, in the second edition of *Evolution vs. Creationism* (2009), portrays the problem people have with accepting Darwinism.

> Why does Darwin still bother so many of us in the Western world? Is it because Darwin's ideas of evolution are so difficult to understand? Or is it the very *idea* (italics in the original) of evolution that is causing the problem. The answer, of course is the latter: the evolution of life through natural processes — and especially the recognition of our own species, *Homo sapiens*, is as inextricably linked to the rest of the living world as are redwood trees, mushrooms, sponges, and bacteria — still does not sit well with an awful lot of the citizenry of the United States and other Western countries. It is not that such skeptics are stupid—or even, at least in terms of their spokespersons, ill-informed. It's not, in other words, that creationists don't understand evolution: it's that they don't like it. Indeed, they revile it.

Creationism is the concept held by Biblical fundamentalists that the universe was created according to the stories in Genesis. Creationists and Intelligent Design (ID) advocates argue that life on earth is too complicated to have happened by accident and can only be explained by crediting the hand of an intelligent deity. Adherents to this belief also think the universe is just a few thousand years old.

The primary objection of Christians to Darwinism is its conflict with the creation story in Genesis. If the Bible is wrong about that, the remainder of the Bible is called into question and the basic doctrines of Christianity begin to crumble.

Teaching creation "science" in schools was declared unconstitutional, which gave rise to Intelligent Design (ID), a refurbished version of Creationism. ID retains the core concept of Creationism — the world was created by a supreme being as according to the Bible — but burnishes Creationism with acknowledgment of scientific facts; not unlike putting lipstick on a pig. ID argues that certain biological organisms are so "irreducibly complex" that they could not have evolved and thus required an intelligent creator. They ignore the core element of evolution, stating that complex systems evolve from simpler systems over immense periods of time. ID believers cite the human eye as an organ that could only have been designed by a deity. I would add that the inner ear fits this definition but believe that slow evolution makes more sense that a one-time creation of the finished products.

Intelligent Design challenges Darwinian evolution and suggests that the complexity of living systems requires a designer. ID disciples even constructed a $27-million creation museum in Petersburg, Kentucky in 2007, covering 60,000 square feet. This museum has dioramas portraying humans coexisting with dinosaurs. It depicts the earth as 6,000 years old and attempts to show that life did not evolve into its current forms.

Creationists offer only pedestrian insights to complex evolutionary concepts. "Creationists believe that the mind sprang suddenly into existence fully formed. In their view it is a product of Divine creation. They are wrong: the mind has a long evolutionary history and can be explained without recourse to supernatural powers" (Mithen, 1996).

In *The Meaning of Human Existence* (2014), world-renowned Harvard biologist Edward O. Wilson explains how we got here:

> Humanity, I argue, arose entirely on its own through an accumulated series of events through evolution. We are not predestined to reach any goal, nor are we answerable to any power but our own. Only wisdom based on self-understanding, not piety, will save us. There will be no redemption or second chance vouchsafed to us from above. We have only this one planet to inhabit and this one meaning to unfold.

The God Illusion

Wilson summarizes the view of the overwhelming majority of scientists toward Creationists:

> ...Creationists, they insist that God created humankind and the rest of life in one to several magical mega-strokes. Their minds are closed to the overwhelming mass of factual demonstrations of evolution which is increasingly interlocked across every level of biological organization from molecules to ecosystem and the geography of biodiversity. They ignore, or more precisely they call it a virtue to remain ignorant of, ongoing evolution observed in the field and even traced to the genes involved. Also looked past are new species created in the laboratory. To Creationists, evolution is at best just an unproved theory. They believe that the random processes outlined in orthodox Darwinism could not have produced the world as we know it. To a few, it is an idea invented by Satan and transmitted through Darwin and later scientists in order to mislead humanity.

The belief that evolution is "just a theory" reinforces ID's ignorance of science and what theories mean to scientists. Scientific theories are often misunderstood by the general public. American illiteracy of science is staggering. Theories are postulated ideas that spawn hypotheses that can be tested and shown to be or not to be viable explanations for phenomena. Theories cannot be "proven" true or false, but are considered accepted explanations for a phenomenon until falsified.

The controversy over teaching evolution will not go away. Creationists are adamant that their version of creation should be taught in high school biology classes along with Darwin's theory. This conflict is not new. The Scopes Monkey Trial in Tennessee in 1925 set back the teaching of evolution for many years. John Scopes, a high school teacher, was charged with teaching evolutionary theory, which was against the law in Tennessee. The verdict was overturned on a technicality, but not before he was found guilty and fined $100.

Humans certainly appear not to be designed by an intelligent "creator." Robert N. Bellah, in *Religion in Human Evolution* (2011), points out one of the major design flaws of humans, the post-birth experience. "Humans are an altricial species ... unlike precocial mammals, the young are born helpless, in a sense 'premature,' because developments that would have taken place in the womb are completed after birth in a state that needs constant parental care."

Male humans also have design defects: the urethra passes through the center of the prostate gland. The prostate gland can become inflamed, enlarged or cancerous, causing various health problems including surgery to remove the gland.

These design defects are only two of many that reinforce the concept that man evolved and was not intelligently designed.

Chimpanzees are the closest living relatives of humans, sharing nearly 99 percent of our DNA (*Scientific American*, May 2009). However, many people unfamiliar with basic evolution science believe popular reports that humans are descended from monkeys. Scott (2009) puts this misconception in perspective:

> Did man evolve from monkeys? No. The concept of biological evolution, that living things share common ancestry, implies that human beings did not descend from monkeys, but shared a common ancestor with them, and shared a common ancestor farther back in time with other mammals, and farther back in time with terapods, and farther back in time with fish, and farther back in time with worms, and farther back in time with petunias. We are not descended from petunias, worms, fish, or monkeys, but we share common ancestry with all of these creatures, and with some more recently than others.

Earth does not appear to have been designed with humans in mind — or any specific organism. Although Earth is a living planet — the mother deity Gaia of the Greeks — organisms thrive or die depending on their ability to adapt to their environment. Humans are along for the ride, as well. We exhibit a certain arrogance, assuming we are in control of our destiny, but that is folly.

We are temporary inhabitants of indeterminate life span subject to the same natural causes as other organisms that inhabit the earth. Anointing ourselves as the pinnacle of evolution leads to an inappropriate disregard for our fellow travelers on the planet. We are not exempt from natural relationships with other life forms. At one time, I imagine dinosaurs "thought" they had the upper hand but after 180 million years of existence they disappeared. It is estimated that 99 percent of all species that ever existed on Earth are now extinct!

There currently are many "endangered species," in danger of joining their extinct predecessors ranging from the ivory-billed woodpecker in the U.S. to the mountain gorilla in Africa. Lovelock (1988) puts humans on Earth in the proper perspective, "I see the world as a living organism of which we are a part; not the owner, nor the tenant, not even a passenger."

In *Learning to Listen to the Land* (1991), Bill Willers writes,

> A common misperception about Gaia ... is that in the manner of a good mother, it must have a fondness for us humans, and that it exists primarily to nurture our species. This may be a normal assumption for beings who have become as divorced from the natural world as we have become. But to hold such a view is to avoid the central point that Gaia's processes are directed toward maintaining the well-being of Gaia, and there is every indication that, were it necessary in order to maintain its own good health, Gaia would dispatch us as dispassionately as we might wipe out weeds in a garden. The realization that from the standpoint of Gaia we are co-equal with other resident species is a step we must take before it is possible to see clearly that we are parts of something rather that masters of something. The realization is both humbling and comforting. We enjoy, we use, we belong; we are not, however, at the helm.

Darwin's epic theory and the discoveries of Newton and Galileo are foundational explanations for phenomena observed in the universe and critical milestones in undermining the claims of religion that a supreme deity is responsible for the workings of the world. There is so much corroborating evidence for evolution that it would be amazing if it were not true. It is unnecessary to become a scientist to understand evolution, just to become an informed human.

Illogical Claims of Religion

In the history of human thought, there has never been a more destructive idea of man that has had a more pernicious influence on humanity than the belief that a supernatural force is responsible for and connected to human existence. This belief, morphed into organized religion, has been responsible for the torture and killing of innocent people, destruction of property, suffering, death, and pandemic anxiety. It began in antiquity and continues apace today, all the while the participants pledging allegiance — and shuffling responsibility — to an imaginary, unseen, supernatural spirit.

Faith in the unknown, invisible and unknowable is one of the baffling attributes of the human species. Religious people inhabit dual worlds; the real, observable, pragmatic world of every day experience and a mysterious, fabricated world of the imagination. Christianity teaches us we can be saved, transported from the real world to the imaginary. But saved from what and for what?

It's difficult to comprehend on any level the basic concept of Christianity: the salvation narrative. Sins are committed—God is offended – a bloody sacrifice is offered—sins are forgiven—salvation and a happy afterlife are attained. Ancient God appeared to react favorably to burnt offerings and bloody sacrifices. Modern God seems content with confession and contrition, a less barbaric and more refined expression of atonement, but the sin and salvation conflict continues to mystify us in modern times.

Reward and punishment are hallmarks of Christianity. An attractive afterlife is the reward for good behavior and misbehavior is punished. Sacrificial atonement for the sins of humanity is illogical, but without this tension between reward and punishment, the basic content of religion has been eviscerated. Irrational fear of a deity while harboring hope and expectation for a blissful afterlife create puzzling bookends to religion.

The idea of a benevolent God is difficult to comprehend, highly improbable and probably impossible. I wish it were true, but odds are it's not. Does God love us? Is He angry? Does He care? Why can't He give some indication that He exists? Two thousand years of silence is a compelling indicator that He doesn't exist.

The God Illusion

Normally, when something new is created, the creator has some obligation to monitor and oversee the creation. In the case of our universe, there is trifling evidence that our God is interested in His handiwork. Disinterest seems to characterize His involvement, which critically damages the notion of a benevolent creator.

Imagine a man standing on Main Street in your town, with an abundant beard, dressed in a long white robe, and holding a staff. He is shouting at passing cars, proclaiming that if you eat his body and drink his blood you will obtain eternal life. I think the majority of us would assume he was suffering from a mental disorder and ignore him. Yet Christians celebrate this ghoulish idea every Sunday!

Further confusion: the crucifixion of Jesus is claimed to atone for Original Sin as well as all past and future sins of mankind. The sin of two persons — Adam and Eve — affects the entire human race? And then God, unhappy with the behavior of a people he created, dispatched his son to earth to be ignominiously crucified so He would be able to forgive both past and future sins? This is a difficult concept to grasp. Crucifixion of a son seems an odd solution for disappointment at the bad outcome of creation.

Who was Jesus? Former Episcopal Bishop John Shelby Spong posits an alternative view of Jesus;

> It is quite possible, maybe even probable, that the Jesus served in most of the Christian churches of the world today is simply an idol created in a primitive time that is destined to die. The story of a theistic deity who assumes human form suggests as much. When this incarnate one is said to have entered history via the miracle of the virgin birth and to have departed via the miracle of the cosmic ascension, one's suspicions should be heightened. Trinitarian language likewise does not communicate in our world; neither does the image of the vicarious savior who absorbs on the cross the punishment due to us for our sinfulness so that God's righteousness can be fully served even as we are washed in the saving blood of the sacrificial Lamb of God.

Jesus of Nazareth, who the Jews initially believed was the Messiah, was a Jew whose mission was to save the Jews. His apostles were all Jewish. Sam Harris, in his book, *The End of Faith* (2004) points out that: "There is no evidence whatsoever, apart from the tendentious writings of the later church, that Jesus ever conceived of himself as anything other than a Jew among Jews seeking the fulfillment of Judaism — and, likely the return of Jewish sovereignty in a Roman world."

Bart D. Ehrman, writing in *How Jesus Became God* (2014), describes Jesus as a Jewish apocalyptist, who preached a

> ...proclamation of coming destruction and salvation: he declared that the Son of Man would be coming on the clouds of heaven, very soon, in judgment on the earth, and people needed to prepare for this cataclysmic break in history, as a new kingdom would arrive in which the righteous would be vindicated and rewarded for remaining true to God and doing what God wanted them to do, even if it led to suffering.

Former Catholic priest Dominic Crossan describes Jesus as "an illiterate peasant, but with an oral brilliance that few of those trained in literate and scribal disciplines can ever attain." I believe Jesus was a charismatic, delusional Jewish countryman who preached a populist message of love, hope, and reward to a rustic population living in a world characterized by poverty and misery. I presume he believed in the message he preached, but there is little evidence he was divine.

Considering the remarkable claims made for Jesus in Christian writings, the silence of historians of that era is instructive. If the extraordinary feats attributed to Jesus in the Bible are true, there should have been reporting of his activities by numerous sources. There were approximately 40 historians writing during the time of Jesus, yet there are only two fragmentary mentions of him by non-Christian writers of the time. In one of these writings, the *Testimonium Flavianum*, Jewish historian Flavius Josephus wrote: "Now, there was about this time, Jesus, a wise man . . ." This is the only known historical Jewish reference to the existence of Jesus. It also appears out of context in the *Testimonium* and is suspected of being inserted by someone other than Josephus. A Roman witness, Cornelius Tacitus, writes about the death of Christus, sentenced by Pontius Pilatus.

Crossan writes, "In my opinion, apart from the texts of Josephus we have already seen, this vast Roman literature contains no independent reference to or information about Jesus of Nazareth." Crossan reminds us, "Jesus was a marginal Jew leading a marginal movement in a marginal province of a vast Roman Empire."

The centerpiece of Christianity and Paul's mystifying interpretation of Jesus's message is the concept of atonement. The Pauline model of atonement is penal substitution (Romans 3:19-31 and 5:1-11). According to the Bible, sin entered the world through Adam (and Eve) with his (and her) transgressions in the Garden of Eden (Romans 5:12-14). Death is equated with sin and since all men have sinned, all would die. With the "fall" of Adam we all inherited the mantle of wickedness.

Attaining salvation required reconciliation with God for forgiveness of our sins. This atonement could be only accomplished by the shedding of blood, the fundamental means of expiation in Biblical times. Jesus's death on the cross was the answer; a substitutionary sacrifice for the sins of mankind. This sacrifice satisfied the righteous wrath of God (Romans 5:9-11). "Jesus death on the cross satisfied God's judgment on sin" (Mathers, 2012).

Christianity tends to instill in its disciples a sense of unworthiness and guilt. According to scripture, frail humanity lives in a carnal world unable to avoid sin and repeatedly succumbs to weaknesses of the flesh. Early Christian clergy and scholars seem preoccupied with sex, sin, and guilt.

Adam and Eve corrupted human nature with their "sin." According to French theologian John Calvin (1509-1564), the sin of Adam and Eve caused moral corruption in the human race and an enslavement to sin. He called it "total depravity."

Permeating Christian belief is the notion of ever-present need for contrition and repentance in order to achieve salvation. The Bible tells us that sin cannot be avoided and death is the result of our transgressions; we are all guilty of sin. In Romans 3:10-12, we are told, "There is no one just, there is no one who understands, there is no one who seeks God. All have gone astray; all alike are worthless; there is not one who does good, not even one." "Father, I have sinned against you and am not worthy to be called your son. Be merciful to me, a sinner" (Luke 15:18). Our mothers are blamed for creating us in sin: "Behold, I was shapen in iniquity; and in sin did my mother conceive me" (Psalms 51:5).

The Judeo-Christian concept of Original Sin is the most preposterous religious abstraction in the history of philosophical ideas. It makes no rational, ethical or ideological sense. Its survival to the modern age is inexplicable from any objective viewpoint. Yet it remains a central doctrine of Christianity. The Council of Trent (1545-1563) reinforced the dogma of Original Sin, stating that only with God's help could its consequences be overcome.

It is time to disengage from the belief that humans are inherently sinful and should be made to feel guilty and regularly punished for even minor transgressions. The notion that we are born with the stigma of a corrupt essence is irrational. The idea that sin is passed from one man (Adam) to all of humanity is illogical. I think we should hold Adam (and Eve) blameless. Instead, let's blame Paul, who wrote that Adam's sin — and Eve's — brought death with it as punishment.

Christianity indoctrinates believers with a morbid sense of stoic tolerance for the vagaries and suffering of life on earth while emphasizing rewards accruing to the righteous in some imagined afterlife.

Since Original Sin, also referred to as "Ancestral Sin," is alleged to be responsible for suffering and death in the world, it deserves thoughtful, critical scrutiny. According to Jesuit theologians Ervin Nemesszeghy and John Russell,

> Every human being is born into this world with a nature that is imperfectly integrated and inadequately oriented towards its final end . . . Before the grace of Christ, man lives in a state of separation from God, a plight of darkness, futility and disorder.

This was not God's original plan. He, from the beginning, called man to integrity and fulfillment. The disorder came through the sinful act of Adam.

This is a difficult concept to grasp. God's original plan has gone astray because of Adam — who He created?

The lineage of Original Sin is not difficult to trace. It begins with Paul's letter to the Romans (5:12) assigning Adam's transgression to all humanity and establishing the concept of collective guilt. This was interpreted by early church figures — Irenaeus, Bishop of Lyons, and Augustine, Bishop of Hippo — as the "fall of man" and responsible for the blemish of sin on all humans, including those in the future.

Interestingly, even though it's traced to the Garden of Eden and the "sin" of Eve, Original Sin does not have a Biblical origin. According to James Boyce, in *Born Bad, Original Sin and the Making of the Western World*, the word "sin" was not used in the creation story. The doctrine of Original Sin "was always theologically vulnerable because no scriptural passages straightforwardly supported it... The punishment for disobeying God was, for Eve, labor pains and submission to her husband; for Adam, it was toil and work. No one was damned. And nowhere in the Old Testament was there any suggestion that the wrongdoing of the very first humans was transmitted to their descendants."

Yet, this core concept of Christianity originates with the world's most famous fairy tale, a poetic "once upon a time" story of good and evil that I have entitled, "Calamity in The Garden." In Genesis' enchanted Garden of Eden, we encounter a vengeful, watchful but invisible God; a cunning, incorrigible, beguiling serpent of persuasive communication skills; a miraculous tree that dispenses the knowledge of good and evil in the form of its fruit; and the main characters, two naked people — Adam and Eve — living in a paradise. The crafty snake convinces Eve to eat some tasty fruit from the "tree of knowledge." Like a compassionate wife, she shares the fruit with Adam. Eating this forbidden fruit snack offends God and He makes them aware — and ashamed — that they are naked and expels them from the Garden, consigned to wear fig leafs over their privy parts. Obviously, fruit from the tree of knowledge was not on the healthy menu in the Garden of Eden!

ALL FISH HAVE BONES

In just 24 sentences, this fairy tale introduced the preposterous Christian dogma of Original Sin, the philosophical construct of collective, inherited guilt, and the idea that the misbehavior of one person enslaves every person at birth to a pandemic guilt that results in the eventual death of all humans. The story begins with trickery and ends with humans doomed to wander the earth in a perpetual state of sinfulness, guilt and contrition, in need of absolution. Humanity was seduced by the father of all snakes.

Thus was the "downfall" of man, tainting us all with the strange concept of Original Sin and stigmatizing everyone as sinners in need of divine help. This was a powerful and symbolic beginning to Judeo-Christianity, an epic event with a cataclysmic outcome for future humans.

This fairy tale alerts us to the concepts of disobedience, death, good and evil, guilt and modesty. We are introduced to a vengeful God who decides eating this forbidden fruit warrants stern, everlasting punishment — painful childbirth for women and manual labor for men. God told Adam he would toil all his life and return to dust. Eve was told that childbearing pain would "greatly multiply" (Genesis 3:14-19). These punishments appear to be vindictive, given out for a sin that an omniscient God would foresee happening. This astonishing fairy tale — in which a woman is blamed for evil — morphed into the beginnings of a worldwide religion.

One thing fascinating about this tale is its startling similarity to the saga of the "first" woman on Earth in Greek mythology, Pandora. Found in the poetry of Hesiod, Pandora was a virgin of dazzling beauty formed from water and clay by Hephaestus. She was unable to control her curiosity and opened a vase (incorrectly known as "Pandora's Box") and released into the world all the evils plaguing humans (Hamlyn, 1963).

So we have the Hebrew myth of Eve and the Greek myth of Pandora; two women, formed by gods, who succumb to their innocent curiosity about the world and commit commonplace acts to satisfy their wonderment and end up blamed for all the evils in the universe. These are classic examples of both the mythic creation of the first woman and the attribution of all evil to her; two creation stories with a coincidental anti-feminine bias. The androcentric tone of the Greek myth was, unfortunately, also present in the writings of the early Christian fathers and it remains vividly obvious today as foundational Christian doctrine.

William E. Phipps, professor of Religion and Philosophy at Davis and Elkins College, wrote in an essay in *Theology Today* (1988), "Hesiod expressed a hostility toward womankind that was endemic throughout Greek antiquity . . . The Greek theme of women being universally and inherently alluring, but disastrous, infiltrated Jewish thought when Palestine came under Hellenistic influence in the fourth century."

The regrettable outcome of these myths is that, even in modern times, clergy continue to preach that women are the cause of evil in the world. Augustine, whose theological influence on Christianity cannot be overstated, used the myth of Eve to subordinate women in his writings. "What is the difference whether it is in a wife or a mother it is still Eve the temptress that we must be aware of in any woman. I fail to see what use woman can be to man, if one excludes the function of bearing children" (Letters, 243:10).

The concept of Original Sin is an imaginative, ingenious construct. Mankind is morally corrupt, collectively guilty and in need of a Savior. Paul, the inventor of Original Sin, at first persecuted Christians. On his way from Jerusalem to Damascus, he was struck off his horse by a bright light from God, blinded for three days and converted in a redemptive epiphany from Judaism to Christianity. In epistles to the Romans (5:12-14) and Corinthians (1st Cor. 15:21,22), he begins explaining the concept of Original Sin.

A central tenet of Christianity was invented by a "saved" Jewish-Roman persecutor of Christians, who based his idea on a fairy tale in the Bible. What Paul invented was developed by Augustine into a central doctrine of Christianity. Augustine's inner search for the root cause of his own lustful experiences led him to believe that desire for sin was within everyone. He believed no human could escape the perversity of sin, because it infected every aspect of human nature. This preposterous "theory" — based on a mythological Bible tale — has survived for 2,000 years.

Original Sin is the antecedent of the Christian concept of all sin. Original Sin is an inherited curse passed on through thousands of generations from

Adam to the present, the only example of eternal sin transference. Because of the disobedience of Adam and Eve, eating from the Tree of Knowledge of Good and Evil, humanity was corrupted and destined to suffer and die. However, we know sin doesn't cause death; all living organisms die at some point.

Sin is an indispensable and effective requirement to the idea of a God. Without sin, there is no need to atone to God for forgiveness. Sinfulness is an explanation for natural occurrences such as sickness, suffering, and death. Sinfulness explains the vicissitudes of life and is a facile premise for a forgiving God; a perfect being, superior to mankind and source of forgiveness and redemption.

Humans who lived prior to Paul and two-thirds of those since have not been branded with the stigma of Original Sin. Original Sin is a unique doctrine exclusive to Western Christianity. It was only in the second and third century that Paul and Augustine formulated the idea. Humans who existed before that had no knowledge of Original Sin or its effect on their lives. No other religion — including Judaism, Islam, Buddhism, and Eastern Orthodox Christianity — has a belief in Original Sin. Judaism and Islam believe that Adam's sins are his alone. Irish monk Pelagius (360-420) denied the doctrines of Original Sin and predestination, defending innate human goodness and free will. Pelagianism was condemned as heretical by the Synod of Carthage ca. 418.

Original Sin is a cornerstone of Western Christian theological doctrine. It endures today in Christian teachings. Early Christianity branded itself with a self-inflicted ascetic stigma that continues today as a signature characteristic. Connecting an ancient and mythical event — that never occurred — to babies born today is a stretch of imagination difficult to comprehend.

"It was no small matter when the Roman church constructed a God who scorned a fallen world and condemned its inhabitants because of a primeval sin . . . So central has Original Sin been to Western Christianity that it is now difficult to imagine how the religion could have been preached *without* (italics in the original) a belief in the doctrine" (Boyce, 2015).

Original Sin is an ancient, irrelevant artifact and should be denounced, and consigned to theological eternal rest. It is precariously supported by the fable of the Garden of Eden that ensnared naïve people and tarnished the concept of a benevolent creator. It nullifies the concept of free will, burdening innocent babies with a profound symbol of evil over which they have no control.

In a way, it was a resourceful concept; incorporating the idea of inherited sin to explain human suffering and death and branding humanity with a collective guilt that could only be overcome through remorse, atonement, and homage to a creator. It is the essence of Western Christian religion. We are continually reminded from the pulpit on Sundays that we are all sinners and cannot escape this branding without faith in God. Christianity offers a structured approach to remove the bondage of Original Sin and a pathway to forgiveness and redemption.

The Western Christian God requires the existence of sin. Otherwise, there is no need for a forgiving God. Original Sin fulfills that requirement since sin occurs at birth and impacts everyone. According to Boyce, "If the West is ever to move beyond original sin, history suggests this will not begin with the discarding of the doctrine's view of human nature, which is now so ingrained that even atheists promulgate it. Rather it may involve rejecting the caricature of a God who can only be at home in a sanctified soul or lost paradise."

To decipher the litany of sins the Catholic Church has identified might require a taxonomist. In addition to Original Sin — the alleged cause of sickness, suffering and death — the catalog of sins includes mortal sins, venial sins, and capital sins. Mortal sins — the kind you go to Hell for — are defined in *Catholicism* (1981) as offenses that "fully engage the person." In other words, the behavior is sinful, you know it is sinful, and you decide to do it anyway. Venial sin, on the other hand, is a less serious infraction; ". . . there is a genuine decision to do this or that action but there is no decision to become this or that sort of person."

There are seven Capital sins: pride, covetousness, lust, anger, gluttony, envy, and sloth. These are some of the "fun sins." Theologians tell us that all of our sins find their origin in these Capital sins. Capital sins were never mentioned as such in the Bible but codified by Pope Gregory the Great (540-604) in the sixth century.

Apparently men and women sin differently. In February 2009, writing in the official Vatican newspaper, *L'Obsservatore Romano*, papal theologian Monsignor Wojciech Gietych observed that men commit sins of lust and gluttony while women commit sins of pride and envy. Committing male sins is probably more fun.

Ever-present evil is cited by nonbelievers as an argument for the nonexistence of God. Theodicy is "the vindication of divine goodness and providence in view of the existence of evil," a concept that seems contraindicated by the state of the world. A classic response to the question of God and evil was expressed by Epicurus. The "Epicurean Paradox" is:

> *Is God willing to prevent evil, but not able?*
> *Then he is not omnipotent.*
> *Is he able, but not willing?*
> *Then he is malevolent.*
> *Is he both able and willing?*
> *Then why do we have evil?*
> *Is he neither able or willing?*
> *Then he is not God.*

The atheistic answer to the existence of evil is that the universe is neutral and godless; therefore, humans are confronted with the random occurrence of evil events.

We often read or hear that we should fear God. Why should we fear a benevolent, loving God? Christianity teaches that sinners deserve God's punishment for their transgressions and only the Church knows the path to salvation. Sin and its corresponding punishment are central to Church doctrine. Reinforcing guilt is a method of power and control for the Church.

In chapters five and eight we began discussing the influence of Paul, Augustine and Jerome on Christian sexual doctrine. There is no ambiguity in their teaching and writings: sex is evil, depraved, sinful, unnecessary and best avoided if possible. Historically, the Catholic Church — ruled by celibate, cloistered males — has governed boudoir behavior and established what is permitted and what is disapproved.

Augustine believed that all sexual activity, even in marriage, was shameful (*The City of God*, 14:18). For Augustine, the ideal marriage would be without passion, "so the sexes should be joined together to beget and bring forth not out of lust, but in accordance with the right desires of the will" (*The City of God*, 14:26). Augustine's view was that sex is mechanical, impersonal, emotionless and solely for the purpose of procreation.

Human history reveals many tribal traditions, ceremonies, and celebratory customs, some more important and inspiring than others. However, one festive observance stands out from the rest, matrimony. In many cultures, marriage is a unique, lifetime commitment to love and live with another person, reproduce, raise a family, and contribute as partners to society. Yet, historically, marriage has never been particularly valued by the Catholic Church — it involved physical sex. Thomas Aquinas valued virginity over marriage but considered marriage a necessary remedy for sin for those unable to retain their virginity.

Hali Meidenhad, a Middle English treatise written in the 12th century by an anonymous author, extols the virtues of virginity over marriage. "Hence was wedlock legalized in holy church, as a bed for the sick, to catch [in their fall] the unstrong, who cannot stand in the high hill, and so near to Heaven, as the virtue of maidenhood." The author admonishes that, "Maidenhood is that treasure that, if it be once lost, will never again be found. Hence it is a loss that is beyond recovery." Virgins will have an exalted status in Heaven since virginity is "so very dear to God, and so acceptable." Virgins will sing songs that only they are allowed to sing.

Marriage is considered a "distraction" from the worship of God. From the infancy of Christianity to present day, the Catholic Church has sanctioned marriage as one of the Seven Sacraments, but historic opposition to marriage, regulations surrounding the marriage contract, and current policy on sexual issues only reinforce the position of the Patristic writers that marriage was a "second best" option for humans if they were unable to adapt to chastity. Subordination of sexual desire is the preferred lifestyle. Medieval theology viewed marriage as an inferior choice compared to virginity and celibacy. This Medieval attitude continues in modern times to influence Catholic Church sex and marriage doctrine.

Rather than facilitate marriage— a happy event for most people — the Catholic Church makes the procedure arduous. "Mixed" marriages (marriage to a non-Catholic) are discouraged. A non-Catholic spouse might influence the Catholic partner to abandon their faith. Marriages are not allowed during Lent since celebratory occasions are counter to the penitential mood. Divorce is highly discouraged and there are a multitude of restrictions of access to church benefits after a divorce. Remarried couples who haven't had their first marriage annulled are considered to be committing adultery.

As recently as July 1, 2016, the Associated Press reported that the Archbishop of the Roman Catholic Archdiocese of Philadelphia declared that divorced parishioners who have remarried should abstain from sex and live like "brother and sister" if they want to receive Holy Communion. reaffirming the Catholic doctrine that remarried Catholics who have not had a previous marriage annulled are living in an adulterous relationship. He further advised those in same-sex relationships to avoid sexual intimacy.

The publication of Pope Frances' "apostolic exhortation" *Amoris Laetitia* (The Joy of Love) in April, 2016, has caused a kerfuffle among the Catholic hierarchy. In September, 2016, four Cardinals, concerned that the Pope was relaxing the ban on divorced Catholics receiving Holy Communion, asked the Pontiff for clarification of the ambiguity and contradiction of prior Church teachings in the document. He declined to respond to their request, remaining silent on the issue. This is just one more example of the theological quagmires that historically plague the Catholic Church.

When my fiancé returned early from a European commitment to marry me, our priest interviewed us separately. He asked if I was being coerced into marriage, assuming my fiancé was pregnant and returning to the U.S. to get married. That was hardly the case; our first child was born 15 months after we were married.

In Mark 12:25, we learn there is no marriage in Heaven!

Paul believed a celibate life was more conducive to worship of God, but allowed that men could marry if they needed to satisfy their desires. In 1st Corinthians 7:32-35, Paul suggests virginity is a virtue and the preferred way of life for men *and* women so they will not be "distracted from the Lord." He applauds the unmarried and widowed in 1st Corinthians 7:8. He says, "It is a good thing for a man not to touch a woman" (1st Corinthians 7:1). But he says in 1st Corinthians 7:9 that if "... they (men and women) cannot exercise self-control they should marry, for it is better to marry than to be on fire."

But wait — there are strict rules regulating extinguishing that fire. As previously explained, the Catholic Church regards the conjugal act — as designed by nature — primarily for begetting children. Fecundity is the only purpose of sexual activity. Church doctrine allows sex in marriage as long as the motivation is procreation. This doctrine was reinforced — in 1968 — by Pope Paul VI in his encyclical, Humanae Vitae, in which he declared; "The Church, nevertheless, in urging men to the observance of the precepts of the natural law, which it interprets by its constant doctrine, teaches that each and every marital act must of necessity retain its intrinsic relationship to the procreation of human life." This seems a pretty strong condemnation of sex as a method of bonding, pleasure, or quenching fire.

I have advanced what I believe are three compelling arguments for the nonexistence of a supernatural deity. The Bible is not the infallible word of God, but a compendium of stories how an ancient people thought, believed and conducted their lives. It contains both historical and mythological information. It is insufficiently factual to function as foundational material for a worldwide religion and lacks probative evidence of the divine nature of Jesus and the existence of God.

Evolution explains the development of all living organisms, including a plausible scientific explanation for the appearance of humans on the planet. It establishes humans as only one component of the biosphere and not a special species that has been exalted over nature. It is a perturbation for religion as it offers a coherent explanation for life without divine intervention.

ALL FISH HAVE BONES

The redemption narrative of sin, punishment, atonement and salvation has been demonstrated to be a flawed concept based on dubious documentation. There is zero evidence for the existence of the burning fires of Hell or the celestial wonders of Heaven. The concept that bloody sacrifice of humans or animals is somehow appropriate atonement for evil human behavior has been shown to be warped logic. The illogical concept of an afterlife, a centerpiece of religion, is without evidence.

Conflating these three issues — the Bible, evolution, and the illogicality of sin and salvation — demonstrates beyond doubt that there is no mysterious deity in the sky who created us, continually monitors our daily activities, has any interest in our welfare, judges our earthly behavior at death, or decides our eternal reward or punishment. As Carl Sagan writes, ". . . why should God be so clear in the Bible and so obscure in the world?"

To buttress these arguments, we add the prediction of Jesus in Matthew that the Kingdom of God would appear before some in his audience died! This is a failed prophecy. We also add the improbable capacity of a deity to track the behavior of seven billion humans and their daily activities. We likewise examine natural events in history for signs of a benevolent deity.

Scientists tell us that there have been as least five mass extinctions on earth that wiped out at least 50 percent of all living organisms each time. If there is a supernatural deity in the universe, it seems strange, illogical, cruel, counterproductive and insensitive to periodically deliberately destroy a significant number of the living organisms it created.

Religion is the ultimate fantasy in the pantheon of imagination. All religious concepts and doctrines are imaginary, and I suspect most believers attend a variant of the "Church of the Imagination." We imagine God, Heaven and Hell, an afterlife, the devil, angels and answers to prayers. We imagine our own sinfulness, even though we can't remember sinning. We imagine a God outside time and space even though we don't know what that means. Religion is a game of make-believe that extends into adulthood.

Apparently we are incapable of finding our way in life without divine guidance, so we accept, at face value, allegorical musings of Biblical writers, though we don't know who they were, their motives for writing or the basis for their assertions. Religion is mysterious and opaque, a metaphysical uncertainty. We depend on philosophers and theologians to interpret minutia in ancient texts using obtuse semantics and magical illusions to guide us toward wisdom and understanding.

So far, theologians have been unable to express themselves in a language that is intelligible and meaningful. When critically examined, religion is a product of the imagination. Religion and belief in a supernatural deity elevate hope and faith over objective reality and common sense. Hoping and wishing does not produce ponies for little girls, and faith and expectation do not result in the existence of a supernatural being. Imagination and desire combined do not produce a magic elixir that is God.

Religion, stripped of its assumptions, pretentions, customs and traditions, is essentially an abstraction supported by three powerful emotional forces: fear of death, fear of eternal punishment, and human wonderment and awe at the wonders of the universe.

We are simultaneously awed and confused by our environment. How did mountains, lakes, butterflies, lichens, trees, planets, galaxies, bushes, birds, fish, radishes, the moon, space, lions, tigers, cats and dogs come to exist? It's difficult to imagine that this happened by accident, but more difficult to imagine that an invisible, really, really smart being that has always existed designed and implemented the universe!

Religion is an attempt by the mind to interpret and make sense of humans and their locus in the environment. The facile explanation for early mankind was a supernatural force with immense power. This was understandable for primitives, but perplexing in an enlightened age of interpretations for natural phenomena that are obvious, provable and self-evident. The promise of an afterlife and the thought of a supreme creator of the universe combined might explain the continuance of Christianity, even though there was no real documentation of its origin, its human founder was killed, and his followers were uneducated.

Religion has become culturally embedded due to institutional structures, traditions and practices and these conditions will assure its continuance for some time. Still, it's puzzling in the empirical world we inhabit, that the halo effect of superstitious religious doctrine still prevails.

Christianity had a bizarre and eccentric beginning, a morally ambiguous intellectual and physical history and a questionable beneficial influence on humankind. A distillation of the history of Christianity leaves us beholding an eccentric fraternity, founded by a man, ruled by men and led by an invisible, unknowable male leader. This boys' club has an obscure, mystical origin, a history of barbaric acts against their fellow humans, anti-feminist leanings, and little empirical evidence supporting its mysterious doctrines. A glance at the human wreckage left behind by historic Christianity in absolute loss of life and the emotional consequences of anxiety and fear substantially eclipses any of its message of peace and love.

Scrutiny of religion reveals:
    Ineffectual outcome of prayer.
    No authentic indications of an afterlife.
    No observable value in the forgiveness of sin.
    No obvious benefit in church attendance.
    Mysterious, opaque religious doctrines.
    No visible or tangible rewards for believers.
    Puzzling and rigid rules and regulations for living.
    Nominal effect of preaching on human behavior.
    Betrayal of trust by holy, religious leadership.
    Illogical and inhuman punishment for misbehavior.
    Lack of conclusive evidence for its doctrines.

Religion seems inclined to servile allegiance to past ecclesiastical edicts. Clergy seem inattentive to the real lives of their flocks. To preach ancient mythology and rituals of uneducated and superstitious people as verities in modern times is baffling. Christian theology has been static for centuries. The scholarship of Christianity is afflicted by nimble theologians, unable or unwilling to reconcile ancient doctrine with the discoveries of modern science, emphatically reinforcing ancient dogma to a dwindling, disinterested audience. We are centuries distant from the geocentric cosmos of preliterate societies, yet cloistered Vatican minds continue to tenaciously embrace archaic beliefs, refusing to evolve and employ modern advancements in science and philosophy to Christian doctrine.

Christianity is presented to its followers as a comprehensive guide to life with an explicit theme of love and salvation. However, the nine beliefs outlined below appear to be a litany of contradictory doctrines that tend to diminish the integrity of its ideology.

• A novel contradiction in monotheism is the idea of an all-powerful God and an opposing satanic force; conflict between good and evil, competition between God and the Devil. We are taught that God is omnipotent, yet He is purportedly in a constant battle with Satan. It's illogical to have a superior force facing an archrival and unable to do anything about it. An omnipotent, beneficent force should have no problem in quietly and quickly dispatching an evil Satanic force. The illogicality of this power struggle is seemingly overlooked by the majority of believing Christians.

• The concept of continually fearing and appeasing a friendly, loving God seems inappropriate. If He loves us, why do we fear Him?

• Protestants and Catholics disagree on conditions necessary for salvation. Protestants believe professing faith in God is sufficient for salvation while Catholics feel faith must be supplemented with good works.

• According to Scripture, all persons were created equal. Yet Christianity is male dominated and women are subjugated and devalued.

• Sex is a natural function — an evolutionary, powerful drive to reproduce — yet the Catholic Church promotes virginity over marriage. Married Catholics can have guilt-free sex — without sin — as long as their purpose is to produce a child and the encounter is not pleasurable. J.N.D. Kelly points out in *Jerome* that early Christian writers and thinkers believed that, "... marriage is, on the most favorable interpretation, a poor second best; virginity is the original state willed by God, and sexual intercourse came in only after the Fall."

• Evangelical doctrine teaches that only those who believe in Jesus will be saved and enter the Kingdom of Heaven. Everyone else is condemned to

Hell for eternity. However, Pope Francis recently declared that even atheists might be welcome in Heaven if they are good and do good things!

✦ Christianity is marketed as a religion of peace and love, yet historically it has exhibited a militaristic, violent face.

✦ According to Christian belief, all humans are born with the stain of Original Sin and have a corrupt nature. Yet, with the grace of God, these sinners can be saved!

✦ Mankind is a component of nature, yet scripture exalts humans over nature.

These implausible, contradictory, doctrinal assertions present Christian believers with a confusing mixture of incompatible doctrines that are inconsistent in a Christian ideological framework.

Contemporary Catholic orthodoxy is woefully dissociated from reality. Original Sin, sexual abstinence, and eternal punishment in the fires of Hell are three of the most mindless theological concepts ever entertained in the imagination of mankind. And Catholicism has embraced all three and enshrined them as the nucleus of the Catholic Church. The rigidity of the past is replaced by the rigidity of the present. Clerics are so consumed with protecting doctrine that they have neglected the needs and desires of their congregations. For change to occur in the Catholic Church, the clergy may have to become uncomfortable and examine basic doctrines.

When we examine the world around us, it becomes readily apparent that our planet is not being administered and maintained by an outside cosmic force. The scientific discoveries of the past few hundred years are ample evidence that there is an alternative explanation for the universe other than a supernatural being. Carl Sagan underscores this when he writes,

> I think it is striking how poorly religions, by and large, have accommodated to the astonishing truths that have emerged in the last few centuries. Belief in a supernatural deity who created the universe, monitors all human activity, and acts as the sole and final arbitrator of good and evil behavior with the power of eternal damnation or everlasting happiness is the illogical result of delusional thinking.

Religion has become dogmatic, antiquated and irrelevant. Monotheism is a failed hypothesis which we are unable to truly test because of its mystical character. According to Harari, ". . . monotheism, as it has played out in history, is a kaleidoscope of monotheist, polytheist, and animist legacies jumbled together under a single divine umbrella." The ancient dogmas of Christianity and simpleminded interpretations of Scripture need to be re-examined to determine if the original concepts of Christianity have utility and relevance for 21st century consumption.

After examining all the evidence, an obvious question is, how can a modern civilization believe in the supernatural? For modern religious leaders to ignore 2,000 years of increased understanding of the universe, scientific discoveries, advances in modern biblical exegesis and critical archeological discoveries is incomprehensible, intellectually irresponsible, and a disservice to men and women living in the 21st century.

Looking to the future, will advancements of science and silence of the gods combine to enlighten mankind? I'm optimistic but unsure. After all, I have no access to revelation. The future of Christianity is impossible to predict. However, growing indicators of decline may be harbingers of the future. The current model, frozen in time, may not survive. The failure to modernize and become relevant may hasten the decline.

Has this chapter *proved* that God doesn't exist?

No.

Have we presented sufficient evidence to indicate that God's existence is *highly improbable?*

Yes.

ALL FISH HAVE BONES

CHAPTER TEN
LIVING WITHOUT GOD:
A NEW BEGINNING

What is the meaning of your life? It is the truth that you will discover as you strive, through your daily choices, to create yourself as an authentic individual, committed to enhancing the lives of others, fulfilling your own unique potential, and attuning yourself to your spiritual nature and the mysteries of the universe.
— *John Chaffee*

We can choose — don't let the inertia of life take you down a path that is not meant to be.
—*Oscar Wilde*

Is religion dispensable? I believe it is. Once belief in a supreme deity has been expunged from our philosophy, we are emancipated from religion. The next step is to seek a new paradigm to guide us. We are now liberated from

Biblical sexual mores, rigid scriptural interpretation of the concept of sin and unbending religious rules of behavior. We have concluded there is no God, no eternal life, no intrinsic purpose or organic meaning to existence. Gone is the expectation that God will momentarily arrive on Earth in a fiery cloud — accompanied by choirs of singing angels and blaring trumpets — to judge our behavior. We may be disappointed to not be greeted by St. Peter at the Pearly Gates of Heaven, but we can be consoled that neither will Satan be waiting for us with his pitchfork at the fiery gates of Hell!

We can abandon the quest for salvation and replace it with a more pragmatic approach to life. That there is no intrinsic goal for existence does not preclude fabricating goals and objectives to enhance our quality of life on Earth. In this country, we have been taught that we should never quit — it's considered a sign of weakness. But I believe it's alright to quit religion if you find it no longer serves a beneficial purpose in your life.

Christianity offers few solutions to serious problems facing the world. A question for modern Christians is can we liberate ourselves from the mythical legacy of our ancestors or do we continue to believe there will be a future miraculous intervention? Are we squandering our intellectual and practical future by tenaciously embracing the current vision of Christianity?

Humans have the ability to communicate with each other, but also often exhibit a xenophobia that hinders productive engagement with other cultures and religious beliefs. Liberation from isolating doctrines of religion opens the potential for productive communication with others. Eliminating competing gods lays a foundation for peaceful planetary co-existence.

The journey toward liberation from religion and search for a secular identity begins with a temporary sense of confusion, frustration and loss of direction. Replacing God and religion with the concept of an existence with no intrinsic meaning creates an emotional void that can be spiritually distressing. We may even harbor concerns about our apostasy. Religious dogma makes indelible impressions that are difficult to dislodge from our psyches. Discarding the illusions of religion and God may briefly confront us with a nihilistic world apparently bereft of meaning and a dilemma with the reality of permanent death, but it also furnishes us with an opportunity to discover a more reality-based approach to life. Abandoning cherished beliefs of a lifetime and the security of religion may be momentarily uncomfortable but there is no reason to become despondent. We can search for a new meaning in life outside the umbrella of religion.

During the intellectual emancipation from belief to nonbelief, it is helpful to remember that pleasure is not a bad thing and suffering does not have to be embraced as a prelude to happiness in the next world. Suffering should not define your life.

Health issues may intrude, but you do not have to add the additional anxiety of mystical religious belief. Your philosophy of existence will no longer be an abstraction but a tangible and rational approach to life and happiness.

We live in a bifurcated universe; a cosmos governed by natural laws understood by science, and a spiritual world requiring a leap of faith to understand. Each person should be free and have the opportunity to believe in any god or not believe in any god, but ancient religious superstitions need not be the foundation for our belief system in the 21st century. Everyone should independently examine the the mysteries of life and the universe and make an effort to resolve the puzzle of life with conclusions that are rational, plausible, and personally comfortable.

Both the scientist and the layman devote their lives to seeking clarity about how the world works. It is a Sisyphean endeavor. Life is a gift; unplanned, unpredictable and without goals, destination or identifiable giver. We are not here for a reason; we are a chance collision of sperm and ovum. We began as a zygote, a random product of the sexual union of our mother and father. We have neither control over our entry into the world, nor our exit. There is no prescribed objective or goal. Life just is. The universe just is. Discarding God opens a new direction for our lives, one not contingent on someone else for decision making.

Accumulating facts about the physics of the universe, biology of nature, and psychology of humans can move the needle on our intellectual gas tank from empty to full and furnish us with foundational data with which to make informed decisions. Science has provided us with remarkable insights on human behavior and the functions of nature.

Harvard biologist Edward O. Wilson writes,

> Human existence may be simpler than we thought. There is no predestination, no unfathomed mystery of life. Demons and Gods do not vie for our allegiance. Instead, we are self-made, independent, alone, and fragile, a biological species adapted to live in a biological world. What counts for long-term survival is intelligent self-understanding, based upon a greater independence of thought than tolerated today even in our most advanced democratic societies... The best way to live in this real world is to free ourselves of demons and tribal gods.

We may suffer from an overabundance of religion. At this stage in our brain evolution, we may be overwhelmed by the immense variety of available gods and ideologies and unable to process a meaningful religious philosophy. There are more than 4,000 religions in the world; Christianity, Islam, Judaism, Buddhism, Hinduism, Confucianism, Taoism and many others, each with their own definition of God and existence.

Imagine living in a world where religion was a private affair with no need for public expression. Each individual maintained, in their own mind, his or her own existential belief and respected contrary views. There would be no need for cathedrals, temples, synagogues, mosques, churches or shrines. With no public expression of religious views or practice of faith in an organized way, individuals could still believe in God or some variation of a cosmic force minus the liturgy and ritual of organized religion.

There are essentially two approaches to the questions, *Why am I here?* and *Why is there something instead of nothing?* They are scientific discovery and religion. Religion is arrogant, portraying God as the answer to everything, like a *Cliff Notes to the Universe*. Science is more modest. It admits that not everything about the universe is known and understood, but offers the titillating possibility that many mysteries will be comprehended through scientific discovery.

In chapter four, we began a discussion of the inquisitive nature of the human race. Humans seek order and certainty in a non-ordered and uncertain world. We are uncomfortable when traditional patterns of behavior are disturbed. We continually seek answers to questions about where we came from and how we got here. Philosophers, cosmologists and physicists spend entire careers attempting to determine the origin of the universe and a rationale for human existence.

Science has made significant progress in answering these questions, but it's far from offering an ultimate resolution. There are no definitive answers and sometimes little agreement among researchers. For many of us, scientific rhetoric is not particularly meaningful as we attempt to cope with the travails of everyday life.

Should we care about these questions? Are they important to our well-being? Yes and no. Inquisitive science contributes to a better understanding of our life on Earth and adds meaning to our existence. However, obsessive concern impedes dealing with the pragmatic nature of life. It may be an intellectually interesting academic question, but it may not be pertinent to humans interested in the more mundane topics of day to day life.

Science is governed by natural laws while belief in God is ultimately a matter of faith. Science has many answers, but will probably not answer the ultimate question of how we got here. It is unlikely we will ever discover a "theory of everything" that will answer all existential questions. Life, as we know it, will probably always be partly profound mystery. However, it seems reasonable to examine the present and compare it with the past.

The debate over the existence of God has polarized atheists and theists for centuries. Religion had its beginnings in ancient superstitions and mystical traditions that have little relevance in the modern world. With today's scientific tools and intellectual achievements, it seems a natural progression to compare the modern world with ancient history and see if there is a story to be told. Is it possible to replace ancient spiritualism with a modern ideology?

Since we are alive, we should be interested in these questions, but it may be more prudent to nibble at the edges of these enigmas than to be driven to despair if a satisfactory answer is not immediately found. Richard Dawkins estimates that there are between 1 and 30 *billion* planets in our own Milky Way galaxy and about 100 billion other galaxies in the universe. Carl Sagan estimated the number of galaxies at "hundreds of thousands of millions."

Most of us are quite unaware of where we really live. We inhabit an insignificant planet located in an infinitesimal part of a vast universe that is only beginning to be understood. There is always the potential for life somewhere else in the cosmos.

There are two certainties in life, birth and death, the bookends of life (for the sake of this argument we will not discuss taxes). Robert R. Ehman points out the obvious in his book *The Authentic Self* (1994), citing the German philosopher Heidegger's quote of a Medieval thinker, "As soon as we are born, we are old enough to die."

Ehman writes that, "A radical awareness of the possibility of death does serve to break down the unthinking assumption of permanence, security, familiarity in the everyday world that stands in the way of our experience of the precariousness of things and therefore of a proper appreciation of them. The sense of death prevents us from taking things for granted and draws our attention to them."

One of the frightening concepts in Christianity is the resolute embrace of Armageddon, the apocalyptic end of life on earth, ushering in a celestial reward in Heaven with God and his angels. Humans have a finite yet incalculable existence. Old age, sickness and death are inevitable. We are unique among fauna in *knowing* that we will die, however, none of us has any real notion of when, where or how it will happen. The certitude of death is as inescapable as the anxiety of dying. Death is unavoidable, the timing indeterminate and the result permanent. It is our ultimate destiny.

Nature has a birth, growth and death cycle for all organisms. Most of us develop coping mechanisms to try to make sense of our existence and escape reflecting on a meaningless life. For many, the explanatory mechanism is religion. Belief in a supernatural deity who has promised an afterlife fosters hope and creates a sense of meaning, harmony and security in this life.

That afterlife is essentially an unknown unknown. Will there be fishing streams, golf courses and hiking trails? Will we eat, drink and have sex? Will all our infirmities be cured? Will we enjoy encountering relatives we never liked? The creation story in Genesis is silent on this issue. Jesus himself never mentioned the conditions awaiting us in Heaven.

At this stage of evolution, we still harbor some hope that the life we are experiencing is not all there is. In *The Accidental Universe* (2013), Alan Lightman expresses his feelings on an afterlife: "To my mind, it is one of the profound contradictions of human existence that we long for immortality, indeed fervently believe that something must be unchanging and permanent, when all of the evidence in nature argues against us." We need to learn that we are but one part of nature, not elite and separate.

The Catholic Church teaches that death is the result of sin. The New Testament is explicit and unequivocal about the origin of death: "For the wages of sin is death..." (Romans 6:23). If you have read this far in the book, hopefully you have discarded the idea that death is the result of sin, even though we all die. Death is a constant reminder of our mortality, the fragility and impermanence of life. The catchy title of a book by L. A. Nik says it all: *Life is Short, Then You're Dead Forever.*

We are a part of nature, with no exemption from the birth and death cycle. We are born, experience sorrow and joy, likely undergo suffering, and die. A few lead lives of chronic misery, some self-inflicted, and some not. Within this framework, we need to extract a philosophy to live by.

As the existential clock ticks on, the thought of death intrudes more on our consciousness. We may change our diet, begin an exercise program, and curtail our drinking habits, but we still face a predictable fate. Inevitability and fear of when and how we are going to die occupies an inordinate amount of our time on earth. Fixating on souls damned for eternity can distract us from enjoying the only life we have. Reaching a satisfactory understanding of life includes arriving at an acceptable comprehension of death.

ALL FISH HAVE BONES

Suffering as a pre-requisite for a heavenly afterlife no longer has to guide our thought processes and activities. Thomas Hobbes, a 17th century English philosopher, described life as "solitary, mean, nasty, brutish and short." This Hobbesian "view of nature" may have been an accurate assessment for his time, but grief, misery and despair need not characterize our life on modern Earth. Death is not the result of our sin or the "Original Sin" of our ancestors, but a naturally-occuring event for all living things. Fear of death is inherent in our genetic make-up. It allowed our ancestors to escape predators, procreate and produce modern humans. However, obsessive preoccupation with death and placement in an unknown afterlife is morbid and counterproductive to the search for the good life.

All livings things eventually die: grizzly bears, pine trees, monarch butterflies, mallard ducks, dolphins and radishes. For the nonbeliever, death should not be a major worry.

If there truly is a benevolent, merciful God, He shouldn't have a problem with people who honestly and intellectually don't think He existed. If He's not benevolent and merciful, then we're *all* in trouble! We should be grateful we have the opportunity to experience life and therein seek purpose, meaning and happiness.

Religion offers a metaphysical palliative to counter the hardwired fear of death — an afterlife of celestial bliss. The irony is that if immortality was the certainty preached by clerical zealots, funerals would be more celebratory and less melancholy. Many religious folks must have doubts about life after death or coping with death would be much easier. The sorrow and grieving that accompanies the loss of a loved one demonstrates a lack of certainty and commitment to one of the basic tenets of religion.

I believe the key to attaining happiness in life requires addressing and then disarming two fears. We fear dying as well as the possibility of being punished in an afterlife. Confronting these can help achieve harmony in our lives.

Fear of death is hard-wired into our brains and contributes to survival of the species by allowing humans to recognize and avoid danger. The second fear, apprehension over punishment after death, is the self-inflicted "siren song" of religion. Fear is the attractant for religion and salvation is the product. Realization that a judgmental deity and Heaven or Hell are myths should neutralize the second fear and help us attain happiness now. If there is a good life after death, we will have something to enjoy; if not, we won't care!

Zuckerman (2014) eloquently puts death in perspective:

> For most of us, the lack of a belief in immortality and the sober embracing of death's finality make living all the more urgent, love all the more important, authenticity all the more warranted, and time with friends and family all the more precious. To the secular sensibility, life is not illusory, nor is it riddled with sin, nor is it the less significant precursor to some other more resplendent, pearly, or fiery realm. Rather, life is here, it is now, it is real, it is hard, it is soft, and it is ever so finite.

In an imaginative essay on growing older written by Roman statesman and historian Cicero, Cato the Elder (234-149 BCE) — who lived 100 years earlier — is portrayed as lecturing two young men. Cicero's Cato presents a rational and dignified approach to growing old and dying.

> Everyone hopes to reach old age but when it comes, most of us complain about it. I follow nature as the best guide and obey her like a god. Since she has carefully planned the other parts of the drama of life, it's unlikely that she would be a bad playwright and neglect the final act. And this last act must take place, as surely as the fruits of trees and the earth must someday wither and fall. But a wise person knows this and accepts it with grace. *How to Grow Old* (2016).

When life ends it should end with decorum and dignity. We watch our elderly and terminally ill spend their final days in pain and suffering because we won't address the issue of euthanasia (or assisted suicide). When we depart the world it should be on our own terms and not hindered by emotional religious sensibilities. Even in death, we are hamstrung by ecclesiastical authorities and their ossified interpretation of scripture.

ALL FISH HAVE BONES

During our existence on Earth, we will encounter situations that are both wonderful and ugly. We live in an impersonal world and remain relatively unknown in the grand scheme of things. We are, however, not just a meaningless lump of protoplasm. We may be a speck in the universe, but we are our own special speck. We are able to cogitate and make choices. Life is a gift and even if we know not from what, we are the recipient. We can avoid the boxes and classifications of sociologists and philosophers. We can enjoy our commonalities and celebrate our differences. Can we discover a meaningful approach to life in this chaotic world without relying on a god? Is it more realistic to personally confront the realities of life than having faith in a mysterious, invisible, supernatural entity?

Religion and the doctrine of perpetual guilt can be replaced with a realistic and common sense approach to life. Rather than living with the dubious illusion of a benevolent creator, we are liberated to search for other opportunities to experience the joy of life without the strictures of religious doctrine. Religion can be replaced with the actualities of life. In pursuit of a meaningful life, reason and common sense are more valuable than mystery and faith.

Bertrand Russell, in his book, *Why I Am Not a Christian*, observes that, "Religion is something left over from the infancy of our intelligence. It will fade away as we adopt reason and science as our guidelines."

Replacing scripture readings and boring Sunday homilies with pursuit of individual identity requires observation and imagination. Engaging one's intellect facilitates deciding what one wants from life and how best to experience it. In the grand scheme of things, we may just be a replaceable cypher. Our legacy may be unknown except to immediate family. We still possess our own individuality that we and our family and friends recognize, and we can search for happiness and develop our own authenticity.

French philosopher Jean-Paul Sartre (1905-1980) declared there is no creator and humans have no purpose, no "essence." Sartre and Nihilism, the belief that life is meaningless may lead some to despair. But, since there is no intrinsic purpose to human life, each person has the responsibility and opportunity to conduct a search for a meaning that is comfortable and appropriate for them. Religious spirituality can be replaced with a fulfilling, secular spirituality.

British philosopher A.J. Ayer, a member of the "Vienna Circle" (a group of philosophers meeting at the University of Vienna in the early 1900s), believes our morality is up to us. Ayer is quoted in Peter Watson's, *The Age of Atheists* (2014): "The purpose of man's existence is constituted by the ends to which he, consciously or unconsciously, devotes himself. . . In the last resort, each individual has the responsibility of choice, and it is a responsibility that is not to be escaped."

The Christian message of punishment for evil and reward for goodness resonates with many. We are continually reminded from the pulpit on Sunday that a wonderful place called Paradise awaits those of us who are "good." But we don't know what Paradise is, or where it is, and we have to die to get there. This has limited appeal.

Promising salvation after atonement for sin is the main marketing mechanism for religion. Once we come to realize that the concept of everlasting damnation is mythological and senseless, we can stop worrying about life after death and begin to enjoy fulfillment with the life we have.

Our immortality may best be thought of as the legacy of memories and deeds we leave with family, friends and colleagues. According to Timothy 6:7, we brought nothing into this world and leave it with nothing. Your life is your story, and what you leave behind. If you don't write it, others will. What you believe may be a product of inattention or a lack of motivation but a philosophy of life is too important to be accidental, or the accretion of the ideas of others.

Earlier, I spoke of the lack of purpose in our lives. Perhaps we could adopt an attempt to live in harmony with nature as our purpose. It would be fitting that a harmonious existence with nature might resonate with such a significant portion of humankind that we could extend the life of the planet while creating a pragmatic ideology of existence. Abandoning our impulse to control nature could lead to a reversal of destructive practices and a scientific paradigm beneficial to humans and our fellow inhabitants of the planet.

If, after reading this book, you still find yourself believing, like Martin Luther, that God is utterly unknowable and you have been unconvinced by the arguments against the existence of God, you can employ Pascal's wager. Blaise Pascal (1623-1662), a French physicist and philosopher, posited that a rational person might live as if God existed. If He does, you win a heavenly reward. If He doesn't, you haven't lost anything! This is a timorous position to take on life's most important issues but it is an attractive and charming argument for some.

CHAPTER ELEVEN
SEEKING A GOOD LIFE

True happiness is to enjoy the present, without anxious dependence upon the future, not to amuse ourselves with either hopes or fears but to rest satisfied with what we have.

— *Seneca*

For centuries, Christianity, driven by the musings of a wandering Jewish prophet, has anxiously awaited the fulfillment of an ancient promise — the Divine Kingdom of God, either here on Earth or in a supernatural realm. Since there is no discernable time frame for this celestial event, perhaps it's prudent to fashion a more practical, secular version of happiness.

The timeline in the Gospel of Matthew has long since lapsed. The span of time from Jesus' prophesy to the present is surely sufficient for this promise to have come true. Hope is not a dependable strategy for living your life. Secularism suggests that divine intervention in human affairs is unlikely.

Many writers and philosophers have offered their characterization of the good life. The Dali Lama believes, "The purpose of our lives is to be happy." The Greek philosopher Epicurus (341-270 BC) also taught that the goal of life was happiness. He believed that living modestly and gaining knowledge of the workings of the world could lead to tranquility, freedom from fear and absence of bodily pain. By eliminating the fear of death and punishment, people could enjoy peace of mind and pursue pleasure.

Abraham Maslow, in *Motivation and Personality* (1954), argues self-actualization is the ultimate goal of man, once basic needs are met. Mitchell Stephens writes in *Imagine There's No Heaven* (2014), "... in Albert Camus' silent universe, God is replaced by everything – by the dirt, the plants, the sky, the sun; by our creatures; by women and men; by our inextinguishable passions; by the myriad wondering little voices of the earth."

A secular good life is neither a point in time nor a particular destination. It is an internal realization of contentment with one's life. A religious life, on the other hand, downplays the importance of life on Earth and focuses on the hereafter. For religion, the good life is a *destination*: paradise.

The good life is a self-described condition that may appear at any time in your life. A good life is a meaningful life, an intellectual experience that liberates one from traditional societal constraints and allows thinking and acting according to a personalized set of values. If, after evaluating your values and principles, you are comfortable with who you are and what you believe, you are enjoying the good life.

People will always manifest varying degrees of happiness and misery, pleasure and pain, while navigating life. Achieving serenity is a creative journey during which individuals accumulate experiences, both pleasant and unpleasant, that can be assembled into an authentic image reflecting an emotional state of contentment. Happiness is not an ordained state of ecstasy, a constant feeling of elation, or a continuous state of bliss and an ever-present smile. It is a comfortable blend of pragmatism and tranquility; a contentment with and an understanding of life. It is an inner sense of peace and satisfaction with who you are and what you are doing with your life. It is the centerpiece of Buddhism.

Harari, in his book *Sapiens*, describes happiness as, "subjective well-being, something I feel inside myself, a sense of either immediate pleasure or long-term contentment with the way my life is going." Today, it is often represented by the emoticon of a happy face.

Daniel Dennett effectively captures this in his book, *Breaking the Spell* (2006).

> ... let your *self* go. If you can approach the world's complexities, both its glories and its horrors, with an attitude of humble curiosity, acknowledging that however deeply you have seen, you have only just scratched the surface, you will find worlds within worlds, beauties you could not heretofore imagine, and your own mundane preoccupations will shrink to *proper* size, not all that important in the greater scheme of things. Keeping that awestruck vision of the world ready to hand while dealing with the demands of daily living is no easy exercise, but it is definitely worth the effort, for if you can stay *centered*, and *engaged*, you will find the hard choices easier, the right words will come to you when you need them, and you will indeed be a better person. That, I propose is the secret to spirituality, and it has nothing at all to do with believing in an immortal soul, or in anything supernatural.

We are all imperfect beings, so it is unlikely that we will ever attain a state of perfect happiness. Happiness is an elusive goal. How will we know when we get there? I am unaware of a happiness scale. That does not preclude seeking contentment within our lives. Contentment is probably a better metric to apply to our emotional state than happiness.

Thomas Aquinas described happiness as the Beatific Vision and happiness here on Earth as transitory. According to Aquinas, happiness is attained by dying and entering an afterlife where you are mesmerized by staring at God. Religion promises a "better life after death." Living a life of chronic dependency on an illusory promise of an afterlife is irrational, unpleasant and unproductive. This impedes the quest for happiness here on Earth, the only certainty we have.

ALL FISH HAVE BONES

All the ingredients for seeking happiness and discovering the good life may be close at hand. Family, friends, community and satisfying activities are all within reach and can be explored for meaning and purpose. Reason, science and common sense offer a framework that can lead to a practical, rewarding, comprehensive approach to life.

The world we experience is not illusionary but controlled by the laws of nature. Gravity keeps our feet on the ground but our imaginations are free to fly. We will experience times of merriment and misery, hope and despair, faith and doubt, justice and injustice. We will meet nice people and smart people and some not-so-nice and not-so-smart. We have family, friends and enemies. We are alive and that is good — but we will not live forever and that is frightening. Cicero wrote, "No man is so old that he does not think himself able to live another year." While we are alive, it is our life to live and we are free to experience it any way we choose that is legal and not harmful to others.

It is essential to identify our "happiness triggers," those pursuits and friendships — self-centered or altruistic — that bring us pleasure. Happiness is not a point-in-time phenomenon, but a consequence of accumulating fortunate and unfortunate life events and drawing from these experiences to arrive at an acceptable view of living. Buddhism teaches that the source of happiness is inside, not from the outside.

There is nothing shameful in seeking happiness as long as the quest does not cause unhappiness in others. The quest for happiness is not thoughtless, indolent or self-centered but a pursuit of self-realization and an attempt to determine one's true identity.

Happiness is a choice; you have to decide if that is a path you want to take. If you wake up in the morning with the sun shining, no health issues, a happy family and living in a democratic country where you have freedom to do what you want; just maybe you are experiencing the good life.

We are told paradise awaits us when we die. I propose that we are experiencing paradise right here, right now on the planet Earth! We very well might be living in the only paradise we'll ever know. Reframing our concept of paradise may uncover new vistas; introduce us to new ways of knowing, new approaches, new concepts and different expectations.

Those of us who live in modern Western cultures may comprehend the good life by the number of creature comforts we have acquired or the amount of money we have accumulated, but the recipe for a good life has many interpretations. It's instructive to explore history and discover what other cultures perceive as the good life. We can gain wisdom from indigenous Americans who express their spiritual identity through respect for natural phenomena. Native Americans have a spiritual relationship with our planet and many of their myths and rituals pay respect to this sense of kinship. "Every phenomenon and every aspect of creation within the Native American cosmos has a spiritual dimension, but the earth, which is home to all living things, is regarded as having special sanctity" (*Mother Earth, Father Sky*).

For Indian cultures in the American Southwest, the good life is symbolized by the brightly colored, blue-green gemstone turquoise. Turquoise is the color of the sky and a symbol for water. A plaque in the Santa Fe, New Mexico, Museum of Indian Arts and Culture captures the meaning of the stone. Turquoise "... stands for all aspects of a good life and, more explicitly, it symbolizes water, sky, rain, sun, bountiful crops, and healthy, happy children." It is difficult to imagine a more fundamental compilation of the necessary ingredients for a good life.

The symbolism of turquoise may contain an important message for those of us living in the modern world. Turquoise was also prized by the Egyptians, Persians, and Tibetans of antiquity. The good life we seek may not be one with modern conveniences and luxuries. The turquoise representation of the good life offers a more profound approach to what we need to exist and enjoy life. The symbolism of turquoise reconnects us with our origin in nature and reminds us of our primal connection to the cosmos.

We can also learn the spirit of Aloha from indigenous Hawaiians. "Aloha" is understood today to mean both "hello" and "goodbye" in Hawaiian, but it also embodies the connection with nature and fellow humans.

Richard Carlson, in his delightful little book, *Don't Sweat the Small Stuff — and it's all small stuff* (1997), points out that an excellent measure of happiness is: "the differential between what you have and what you want. You can spend your lifetime wanting more, always chasing happiness — or you can simply decide to consciously want less. This latter strategy is infinitely easier and more fulfilling."

Since religion holds paradise in high regard, let's compare a secular and religious view of paradise. Here are some of my versions of paradise: Hiking to an alpine lake for a picnic. Attending a Verdi opera or Tchaikovsky ballet. Listening to the sublime and enchanting Adagio from Beethoven's 9th Symphony. Hearing a Mozart or Chopin sonata. Drinking vintage port and eating Stilton cheese in an English flat overlooking the Thames River in London. Fly fishing for trout in the Yellowstone River in Montana. Watching the sun go down over the ocean from your Hawaiian lanai while sipping single malt scotch. Having a beer or glass of wine with a good friend at the end of the day. Falling in love. Watching your children grow and mature into adulthood. Doting on your grandchildren. Simply being alone with someone of whom you're fond.

The religious view of paradise is spending eternity enjoying the Beatific Vision. You choose.

Introspection of our individual history may unlock the secret to the good life and emotional fulfillment. Recalling past pleasurable experiences, emotions, feelings and actions may be the starting point for identifying "happiness triggers" and serve as a framework for building a belief system.

A.C. Grayling eloquently argues for humanism as the answer to the search for meaning.

> As a broad ethical outlook, humanism involves no sectarian divisions or strife, no supernaturalism, no taboos, no food and dress codes, no restrictive sexual morality other than what is implicit in the demand to treat others with respect, consideration and kindness. It requires no commands from divinities, no promises of reward or threats of punishment, no myths and rituals, either to make sense of things or to serve as a prompt to the ethical life.

Seeking a Good Life

"Live in the moment" is a commonly heard phrase. "Savor the moment" may be an appropriate mantra to create and cultivate the foundation for the good life. Happy for sure, here and now, may be preferable over potential happiness after death.

I recommend humanism as an appropriate philosophical foundation for coping with the world and leading a happy life. *Humanist*, the magazine of the American Humanist Association, describes humanism as:

> ...a rational philosophy informed by science, inspired by art, and motivated by compassion. Affirming the dignity of each human being, it supports liberty and opportunity consistent with social and planetary responsibility. Free of theism and other supernatural beliefs, humanism derives the goals of life from human need and interest rather than from theological or ideological abstraction, and asserts that humanity must take responsibility for its own destiny.

These three of their 21 "principles" encapsulate the humanist message:

> We are committed to the application of reason and science to the understanding of the universe and to the solving of human problems.
>
> We affirm humanism as a realistic alternative to theologies of despair and ideologies of violence and as a source of rich personal significance and genuine satisfaction in the service to others.
>
> We believe in optimism rather than pessimism, hope rather than despair, learning in place of dogma, truth instead of ignorance, joy rather than guilt or sin, tolerance in the place of fear, love instead of hatred, compassion over selfishness, beauty instead of ugliness, and reason rather than blind faith or irrationality.

These are affirmations of a commonsense approach to life. Humanists are critical thinkers, they believe in evidence-based reasoning and the scientific method. Humanists believe in freedom of inquiry — everything can be examined. Humanism has no doctrines, no secret texts, and no authority figures. It is doubtful that the spread of humanism or secularism will result in universal moral decay and chaos.

Everyone has a comfort zone. If we give up on the endless quest for the improbable goal of everlasting life and evaluate what we have, it may become apparent that the holy grail we seek is already ours. Experiencing Sunday as a day for yourself is an exhilarating feeling. Sunday now belongs to you. Your church donations can be redirected to a charity of your choice and not to an everlasting mortgage on a significantly underused shrine erected to preserve a medieval concept; an antiquated monument to an ancient past and a dubious future.

The secular life is not a life of despair and lament over the knowledge that this life is the only one we have. Phil Zuckerman offers an interesting and unique perspective in viewing life in his book, *Living The Secular Life* (2014). ". . . secular men and women value reason over faith, action over prayer, existential ambiguity over unsupportable certitude, freedom of thought over obedience to authority, the natural over the supernatural, and hope in humanity over hope in a deity." He believes the term "secular humanist," as descriptive as it is, doesn't completely describe how he feels. So he calls himself an "aweist."

"Aweism encapsulates the notion that existence is ultimately a beautiful mystery, …that life is a profound experience."

By my count, we have discussed at least eight "isms" in this chapter, and I'm not sure I want to be labeled with an "ism." They are mostly invented by scholars writing in academic journals, hoping to burnish their professional credentials by adding another category of human behavior to academic literature. I harbor no hostility against inventors of "isms," but I have no interest in adding another. There may be virtue in living "ism-free," an idea that appeals to me. Rather than letting philosophers or professors decide who we are, we can decide ourselves.

It is difficult to categorize humanity in any meaningful way. It is highly unlikely any group with an "ism" label will be homogenous. Our individual natures make accurate labeling difficult. Rather than seeking commonalities and trying to pigeonhole people into collections where they don't completely fit, maybe we should concentrate on and applaud their differences.

Evangelicals may fear that moral chaos is going to engulf the American landscape, but the republic is not in grave danger from those who do not believe in God. This book debates an existential problem of human authenticity and philosophy of life. Hopefully the debate will continue in a civil manner, even though there appears to be a toxic intolerance in the U.S. directed toward those who don't profess belief in God. Religious believers seem to harbor antipathy toward those who don't believe in some version of a religious doctrine. Atheism has not received any welcome among faith communities, but it is just one more belief system among many.

The Catholic Church even states in Vatican II (1962-1965) that the atheist can be justified and receive salvation if the person acts within their conscience. *Catholicism* (1981) notes, " ... it is possible for a normal adult to hold an explicit atheism for a long period of time, even to life's end without this implying moral blame on the part of the unbeliever."

Unfortunately, the fundamental faithful have a perverted and myopic view of a growing number of our fellow humans, the nonbelievers. Admitting unbelief in God is considered unacceptable, inappropriate and leads to status as a pariah. In the U.S., people who don't believe in God are portrayed by fundamentalist clergy and laity alike as amoral, unpatriotic and a menace to society — an undeserved stereotype.

The opprobrium and contempt unleashed on atheists is unwarranted and unnecessary. It's rational and acceptable to *believe* in an invisible, unsubstantiated, and improbable supernatural being, yet considered offensive and unacceptable to *not believe*? Apparently, having an imaginary belief triumphs common sense.

Atheists, freethinkers, agnostics and nonbelievers have become a convenient piñata for religious folks who are ill-informed of the intellectual orientation of these groups and their agenda. This peevish animosity and bigotry has little factual foundation and appears to be a defense mechanism.

To stifle expression because it is incompatible with mainstream thinking goes against the principles that Americans have cherished since the founding fathers set us on a path to free speech. Intolerance for controversial ideas impedes human intellectual progress. Human evolution and growth can grind forward only if we sift through new concepts and theories and analyze and discuss controversial ideas. Exposure to contrary ideas and philosophies is how people become educated and mature intellectually.

Atheists, like Christians, come in many stripes, but they can be divided into two major categories; those that simply don't believe in God and those who expand their nonbelief to include the view that organized religion has an insidious and destructive effect on the human community. Atheists have no threatening agenda. Some are hostile to religion but most are indifferent.

In emotional defense of Christianity, evangelical zealots often resort to offensive criticisms. The vitriolic rhetoric hurled by Christians at atheists is disproportionate to the threat. No one can show that atheists are dangerous or violent. Atheists are no threat to society or to the way of life enjoyed in the U.S.

Fundamentalist commentary directed at nonbelievers violates the concept of individual dignity and freedom of speech and religion, basic principles of our republic. Critics of unbelief need to evaluate their rhetoric and determine if it encourages better understanding, or if it is offensive and undermines attempts at detente.

Being an atheist does not mean one has an absence of values. Atheists do not exist in an intellectual vacuum. They are people who believe science and reason triumph over mystery and imaginary beings. The great majority of atheists are not attempting to eliminate religion, only to reduce its influence in the public arena. They are interested in influencing the public with reason and scientific evidence. They feel life in the U.S. should conform to the ideals of the framers of our republic. People should be free to worship — or not worship — as they choose.

Opposition to prayer at civic gatherings and teaching Creationism as science in schools are two lighting rods for the anti-atheist lobby. The loss of religious rituals at public gatherings will not doom the republic. Removing the idea of God from the public sphere does not proscribe religious practices outside of the public arena. The irony in the anti-evolution movement is that in its attempts to eliminate the teaching of evolution in schools it has *evolved* from Creationism to Creation Science to Intelligent Design!

The mutual mistrust between the secular and the religious is a major impediment to any hope of co-existence. Believers feel sorry for atheists, since they are metaphysically clueless and destined to burn in Hell for all eternity, but why the abusive language and apparent contempt? There is nothing intrinsically evil about atheism. Very simply, atheists are people who have decided to not believe in an illogical concept. They are not depraved whackos, but people who have engaged their intellects and arrived at a different conclusion about the existence of God than religious folks.

Non-belief in God is portrayed by Christians as a cold, meaningless life, isolated from divine guidance on how to live. A majority of believers have little empathy for nonbelievers. A Pew Research Center survey seeking the views of the American public toward religious groups (conducted between May 30 and June 30, 2014) found atheists rated 41 on a scale of 1 to 100, with 1 being "coldest" and 100 "warmest." Jews, Catholics and Evangelical Christians all rated 60 plus. Given the pluralism of our diverse culture in the U.S. and operating under the assumption that the 1st Amendment gives everyone the right to worship or not worship, atheists should be viewed no differently than Lutherans, Baptists, Catholics, 7th Day Adventists or Quakers.

It appears reasonable that atheists should be judged on their behavior, not a misinformed conception of what constitutes an atheist. Religious persons tend to regard atheists as immoral. Without God to guide them, they will end up committing evil deeds and disrupting the tranquility of society. Notice on Sunday morning — as many believers go to church — the vast numbers of joggers, walkers, cyclists, golfers, fishermen, swimmers, picnickers and gardeners are simply enjoying their day and not committing violent, immoral acts or disrupting society. They raise their children to be respectful, are gainfully employed, participate in civic activities, and donate to charities just like religious folks.

I don't see a chance of unification between theism and atheism at this time in history. The philosophical differences are enormous. Fundamental believers don't just dislike atheists, they despise them. Psychologically, Christians have a visceral reaction to the implications of atheism. Atheists are looked upon as immoral threats to the Christian fabric. Believers impute, without evidence, a caricature of nonbelievers as unemotional, coldhearted, unenlightened and obtuse. Atheists and religious believers both think, with certainty, that they have discovered the truth and the other side obviously has an irrational and imperfect understanding of the issue.

Will there ever be understanding between the protagonists? I believe there is room for some modest appreciation of opposing viewpoints. Atheists also have their baggage. They could tone down the rhetoric when advocating their belief system. Harsh denouncements and lampooning of other beliefs by leading atheist writers, *ad hominem* attacks on church leaders, and denigrating believers does little to ingratiate atheists to church goers.

The stealth growth of unbelief mentioned in chapter three has emboldened a minority to become more vociferous in demands for eliminating prayer at public gatherings and removal of Christian icons from public venues. However, the majority of unbelievers are content to maintain their belief in private and hold no animosity toward those who believe in religious doctrines. Secularists do not despise religion; they just don't want to participate.

Atheists could strive to avoid combative denunciations of Christian doctrines. Much of atheist literature is strident and arrogant. Although this may have once been effective in spreading the basic message of atheism, it does little to convince nonbelievers of the efficacy of nonbelief. Atheism's intemperate demands for the removal of all Christian artifacts and traditions that are a significant part of the history of America show little sensitivity for U.S. religious history and only deepens the alienation between the groups.

American atheists should refrain from disparaging a religious heritage of historical significance. These attacks anger the religious community and malign U.S. religious history. Mutual understanding and co-existence between these opposite philosophies of existence will happen when the parties recognize that neither side will prevail due to the unprovable nature of the center of the debate — the existence or nonexistence of God.

Intolerance for religious views other than your own appear to be an essential element in religion. However, the first step in any rapprochement is for sides in a debate to engage in civil discourse and recognize that the other party may have valid arguments. Controversial issues can be productively debated by Christians and atheists if both parties understand and respect the history and tradition of the other. Hurling incendiary rhetoric across debate lines does little to advance detente.

The history of the U.S. embodies a fundamental principal of vigorous, yet civil, debate over complex issues and acknowledges a respect and accommodation for those who hold contrary views. If the goal of religious debate is seeking truth, abusive, combative rhetoric contributes little to the conversation.

In *The European* (July 4, 2013), Albrecht Durer writes, "In a secular society that places obstacles before religious groups, and thus impedes their ability to contribute to societal discourses, secular pluralism ceases to function. The idea loses its credibility."

Nonbelievers should recognize the religious community for its valuable contributions to mitigation of human suffering; ministering to the poor and underserved; and charitable work in under-developed countries with education, healthcare and infrastructure development. Ministries with abandoned and mentally ill children, abused women, prison reform, rehabilitation of criminals, the homeless and civil rights are beneficial contributions to humanity.

In turn, religious folks should become familiar with the basic precepts of nonbelievers, treat these beliefs and the people who hold them with respect, and develop the aptitude to discuss secular issues objectively.

Because of the sociocultural influence of Christianity in the U.S., it is doubtful that detente and harmony will ever break out between believers and nonbelievers, but it is a worthy endeavor for each side to try to understand the visceral commitment of the other and work toward lowering the volume of the rhetoric and antagonism. A significant advancement in the history of religion — and humankind — would occur if each belief system would remain insular and discontinue assaulting "infidels" who profess differing viewpoints. However, it is highly unlikely, in the near future, you will hear a spontaneous chorus of *Kumbaya* burst forth from an encounter of believers and nonbelievers.

As an advanced human society we have abandoned draconian practices of stoning, guillotines, crucifixion and witch burning as punishment for apostasy, infidelity and other bad behavior. It's time to recognize that those who don't believe in God simply have an alternate approach to life. They are exercising their freedom of non-religion and are not dangerous to the general population. Hopefully, the animus and rancor that exist between believers and nonbelievers will become less pronounced and lead to a more cordial co-existence where every individual can arrive at their own conclusion about faith.

I sincerely doubt that we will ever completely abandon religion in favor of secularization, but I would hope that one day we could reach a degree of accommodation among faith communities that would allow nonbelievers to simply be viewed as holding an alternate philosophy of life.

For readers wishing to further examine atheism, I recommend recent books by Richard Dawkins, Sam Harris, Daniel Dennett, Christopher Hitchens, and Victor Stenger. I also recommend Bart Ehrman, who is a prolific writer on problems with the Bible. *Free Inquiry* is an informative bi-monthly magazine dedicated to advocacy of the nonreligious life.

This may have been a difficult chapter to read, so perhaps it's time for an examination of the lighter side of life. When my children were young, I read to them from children's books and my all-time favorites were by Richard Scarry. He had a wonderful and rare talent to write on two levels; one for the enjoyment of the children and the other to bring a smile to the parent reading the book. My best-loved story was about the pig who had a hole in the roof of his house. When asked why he didn't fix it, he replied that when it was raining it was too wet to work and when the sun was shining it didn't need fixing! Maybe this easygoing approach to life has a message for those of us who occasionally find life a little too tedious and depressing.

Along those same lines I was once scolded by a good lady friend of mine who found me muttering over a project that wasn't working out quite like I anticipated. She said; "You're too old for perfect." I have adopted that phrase as my new mantra and find it quite satisfying as I age and doggedly continue to begin new projects.

One of the problems in adopting unbelief is the effect it has on relations with your friends and family. Expressing atheism, non-belief, agnosticism, humanism or secularism creates a conundrum for a new unbeliever. Though many quirky religious beliefs are tolerated, nonbelief is stereotyped as unnatural and abnormal. Communicating your newfound belief system may produce awkward and embarrassing encounters with friends, colleagues, and relatives. Because of this, I have developed increased empathy for the LGBT community.

It's a good idea to have a plausible response ready when you are asked why you stopped going to church after many years of faithful attendance. When my wife and I stopped going to Mass, it raised questions among fellow parishioners. They noticed our absence and inquired to our whereabouts. Their interest in our wellbeing was laudable but we didn't have a ready answer. Our initial response was that we "were taking a break" from church, or "we're taking a sabbatical."

I have only recently begun to mention to some acquaintances and family members my unbelief. Reaction has been varied. Some who I suspected were fellow nonbelievers reacted positively. In others, I sensed there was already some skepticism toward religion, and I found interest in discussing the issues. When this book reaches publication, I will have to develop an explanation that satisfies my wife and me and isn't offensive to others. Being reluctant to pull the trigger and admit our unbelief to others, we choose to euphemistically deal with the situation. I imagine this situation will eventually be found unworkable.

If you are one of many who have spent much of life believing a particular religious doctrine and participating in its rubrics and programs, it may be troublesome to forsake all of its practices. Nonbelievers do not have to give up all religious traditions. De-emphasizing God in your life doesn't have to result in abandonment of all long-held religious practices. Participating in social outreach programs of religious organizations may still be possible and rewarding. It can still be an opportunity to enjoy family and friends without the religious overture.

My wife and I have redirected our former financial commitment to our church to a volunteer organization in our town that provides health care to the underserved in the community. Instead of Christmas, one can substitute Saturnalia, an ancient Roman holiday celebrating the winter solstice. There may be opportunity to minimize the gift giving aspect of Christmas, which has commercialized the holiday to the extent that it is barely recognizable as a Christian holiday.

Reexamine the role of Santa Claus. Most kids learn the truth from older peers, causing unnecessary angst for them at Christmastime when they feel they have to fake belief in Santa Claus. Diminishing the commercial and religious connotations of Christmas may offer families an opportunity to develop their own traditions: food festivities, ski trips, sleigh rides, winter hikes, and visits to winter parks. Spend less time in box stores at midnight, elbowing your fellow citizens out of the way in order to grab the latest toy or electronic gadget. This is primitive behavior for what is supposed to be an advanced species celebrating a Christian holiday.

Tom Flynn, in *The Trouble with Christmas* (1955), argues for completely abolishing the Christmas holiday, but from my perspective (and that of retailers), his extreme view is not likely to soon be implemented. But it is an interesting study of the origins of Christmas and the holiday practice today.

Perhaps a fitting way to end this chapter — and the book — is to hear Henry David Thoreau's famous guidance from the conclusion to his seminal work, *Walden* (1854): "If a man does not keep pace with his companions, perhaps it is because he hears a different drummer. Let him step to the music he hears, however measured or far away. . . . if one endeavors to live the life which he has imagined, he will meet with a success unexpected in common hours."

Applying the fish metaphor is appropriate here. Many of us go through life without seriously examining our basic beliefs. If we critically examine our lives and engage our intellects, we might detect the cadence of our own drummer and live not a life of misery and frustration awaiting a "promised land," but a life of contentment here and now appreciating what we have.

True and authentic happiness cannot be contingent on a future event. Enjoy what is, and don't fantasize and agonize for what might be. Take pleasure in the present. The future is always problematic. The past is a memory and the future will become the present, so live in the now. Life is a gift; cherish it. Enjoy the one you were given and don't become preoccupied with an improbable next life.

ALL FISH HAVE BONES

EPILOGUE

Someone once said that if you don't know anything about a subject, write a book about it. This seems counterintuitive, to be sure, but I found it to be true. I was familiar with much of the material, but researching a book continually uncovers information you are unaware of which leads to many new avenues of thought. Putting together a book questioning theological propositions, the existence of God and the efficacy of organized religion was a humbling experience and not for the faint of heart. At times I questioned my sanity, but forged ahead, confident of my convictions. Periodically, though, I harbored trepidation about the reaction of family and friends. The process has been a meaningful event in my life.

Writing is essentially a solitary endeavor. When you begin a manuscript, you have no guarantee that it will ever be published or read. I was fortunate with my first, a graduate school textbook. It was accepted by the publisher after I submitted the first chapter. I have edited two books and written chapters for inclusion in several others as well as numerous articles on program evaluation for humanities' journals. However, the last article I submitted for a peer-reviewed journal in the humanities was soundly rejected by all reviewers; an ignominious way to retire from academic writing.

Writing is fun for me. Publication of the result is satisfying but not the goal. The objective is to convey some knowledge to potential readers and to learn more about myself in the process.

For me, words are fascinating. Words are engines of progress for humanity. Ideas, thoughts, opinions, views, theories, concepts, philosophies, discoveries and hypotheses increase in meaning and become useful only after they are formally documented by conversion into written words and widely disseminated. Without transforming oral conversations and private thoughts into written words, there is no record, no history, no lasting form of communication to exchange with others. Imagine, for instance, what Christianity might look like if we had the personal thoughts of Jesus and his apostles in their own writings.

Hopefully, this book has alleviated some of the anxiety that comes with the aging process. Chronologically, I am deep in the cold and snowy "winter of life" and apparently have been for some time! But "winter" is, to a certain extent, a state of mind. With some health luck and the right attitude, one can thaw winter out somewhat and make it seem more like fall or late summer.

The elderly do things more slowly but we have more time. Napping is an acceptable and necessary pastime. "Living the moment" is not a cliché but a way of life. Yesterday is gone and tomorrow is a long way off. Enjoy your family and friends. Life is a gift to be appreciated and savored.

My goal for this book is to stimulate people to perform an objective analysis of their lives and to critically examine thought processes and beliefs — particularly childhood religious beliefs — to see if they reflect the true essence of the individual. On balance, I believe non-believers are more secure and positive in their non-belief than faithful Christians in their belief. The non-believer's arguments are based on empirical evidence, common sense, and reasoning, whereas the faith community is forced to rely on the metaphysical and the supernatural.

Epilogue

One of the underlying themes of this book is empowerment; the idea that individuals can seek advice and input from others but reserve the ultimate decision making for themselves. My sincere hope is that I have, in the preceding pages, established that a good life is available here on earth and that it can be discovered and enjoyed by observation and listening while thinking for yourself and making your own decisions. Most of us have at least a dollop of common sense and intelligence to do research, cogitate, and make decisions that resonate and are logical. Place a high value on your own judgment. A good life is the ability to continually process the complex realities of existence in an authentic and satisfying manner to the individual. John Paul Sartre eloquently describes a secular approach to a good life. "Life has no meaning (*a priori*)—it is up to you to give it meaning, and value is nothing but the meaning you choose."

Remember the "fish." Life does not have to be dull, boring and anxiety ridden; look around, examine your environment, carve out your special space, relax and enjoy the life you were given and ignore the "afterlife" you have been promised. Hiking the pathway of life is more meaningful and rewarding if the trail you take is designed, built, and maintained by you.

ALL FISH HAVE BONES

Acknowledgements

Writing is a solitary endeavor but no book has ever been written without the help, assistance and advice of friends, associates, and family. This book is no different.

My interest in academics and writing began when my FBI boss and friend, John Glover, prodded me into attending graduate school so I could increase my professional skills and apply them to the work I was doing at the Bureau. It was in graduate school where I began to learn the craft of writing.

Ray Rist — who worked at the General Accounting Office and later at the World Bank — invited me to participate in annual conferences of an international evaluation group that he chaired.

Joe Wholey, my doctoral thesis advisor, was instrumental in teaching me how to write academically acceptable prose.

This book has benefited from being read by my wife, Sally, my publisher, Sandy Compton at Blue Creek Press, and my friend Ray Rist. They have been influential with their constructive criticism and advice. Sandy and Ray gave me direction after reading a first draft with rambling content. I am indebted to them for their guidance. Their observations and advice were instrumental in crystallizing my thought process and clarifying the theme of the book.

Sandy has been very helpful in guiding me through the book publishing process and preparing the manuscript for publication. His skillful editing has significantly improved the quality of the book.

My daughter, Jennifer Sonnichsen Parker is a professional graphic artist in Seattle and she designed the stunning cover. She was also the technical guru who I called on to decipher computer problems that I didn't understand.

I appreciate the proofreading skills of Britta Mireley who improved the quality of the manuscript by pointing out typographical errors and stylistic inconsistencies.

Finally, I am indebted to my wife, Sally, who put up with my writing obsession on a controversial subject for the last several years.

About the Author

After graduating from Forestry school, Dick Sonnichsen worked in the woods for a year before being drafted to serve in the U.S. Army. He served in the Counter Intelligence Corps from 1961 to 1963. In 1964, he joined the Federal Bureau of Investigation and served for 30 years as a Special Agent investigator, Inspector and senior executive. He retired as the Deputy Assistant Director in charge of the Office of Planning, Evaluation, and Audits.

In 1996, he received the Alva and Gunnar Myrdal Award for Government Service from the American Evaluation Association "in recognition of his career contributions toward making internal evaluation both valued and useful."

After retiring from the FBI, he did management consulting work and taught evaluation and social science research methods at the University of Southern California Washington Public Affairs Center as an adjunct faculty member. He has written one book and co-edited two others on evaluation, written numerous articles on internal evaluation and chapters for eight books. He has been a member of the American Evaluation Association, the

ALL FISH HAVE BONES

International Working Group on Evaluation, served on the editorial boards of three evaluation journals, and has spoken and presented evaluation papers in the United States, Canada, and Europe.

He received his undergraduate degree in Forestry from the University of Idaho and Master's and Doctorate degrees in Public Administration from the University of Southern California.

Dick has three adult children. He and his wife, Sally, divide their time between North Idaho and Maui.

BIBLIOGRAPHY

Armstrong, Karen. *The Case for God*. New York: Knopf, 2009.

Augustine. *On Christian Doctrine*. Chicago: Great Books of the Western World, Encyclopedia Britannica, Inc. 1952.

Barker, Dan. *How an Evangelical Preacher Became One of America's Leading Atheists*. Berkeley, CA: Ulysses Press, 2008.

Barr, Jane. *The Influence of Saint Jerome on Medieval Attitudes to Women*. In *After Eve*, (Ed.) Janet Martin Soskice. London: Collins Marshall Pickering, 1990.

Bellah, Robert N. *Religion in Human Evolution*. Harvard College: 2011.

Benedict, Gerald. *The God Debate*. London: Watkins Publishing, 2013.

Berns, Walter. *Religion and The Founding Principle*. In *The Moral Foundations of the American Republic*. Robert H. Horwitz (Ed.) University Press of Virginia: 1986.

Berry, Thomas. *The Great Work: Our Way into the Future*. New York: Bell Tower, 1999.

Birx, H. James. *Interpreting Evolution: Darwin & Teilhard De Chardin*. Buffalo, New York: Prometheus Books, 1991.

Bloom, Howard. *The God Problem.* New York: Prometheus Books, 2012.

Bloom, Paul and Weisberg, Deena Skolnick. "Childhood Origins of Adult Resistance to Science." *Science* 316, Pg. 996. Washington, D.C.: AAAS.

Boyce, James. *Born Bad: Original Sin and the Making of the Western World.* Berkeley, California: Counterpoint, 2015.

Boyer, Pascal. *Religion Explained: The Evolutionary Origins of Religious Thought.* New York: Basic Books, 2001.

Breining, Greg. *Super Volcano.* St. Paul, MN: Voyageur, 2007.

Brown, Raymond. *The Virginal Conception and Bodily Resurrection of Jesus.* Mahwah, NJ: Paulist Press, 1972.

Carlson, Richard. *Don't Sweat the Small Stuff… and it's all small stuff.* New York: Hyperion, 1997.

Cicero, Marcus Tullius. *How to Grow Old.* Translated by Phillip Freeman. Princeton, NJ: Princeton University Press, 2016.

Chaffee, John. *The Thinker's Way.* Boston: Little, Brown and Company, 1998.

Coyne, Jerry A. *Why Evolution is True.* New York: Penguin Books, 2010.

Crossan, John Dominic. *The Birth of Christianity: Discovering What Happened in the Years Immediately After the Execution of Jesus.* San Francisco: Harper San Francisco, 1989.

_____ *The Historical Jesus: The Life of a Mediterranean Jewish Peasant.* San Francisco: Harper, 1991.

_____ *Jesus: A Revolutionary Biography.* San Francisco: Harper, 1994.

Davis, Kenneth C. *Don't Know Much About History.* New York: Harper Collins, 2003.

Darwin, Charles. *The Origin of Species.* New York: Signet, 2003. Dawkins, Richard. *The God Delusion.* New York: Norton, 1997.

Davis, Mike. *The Atheist's Introduction to the New Testament.* Denver, Co.: Outskirts Press, 2008.

Dennett, Daniel C. *Breaking the Spell: Religion as a Natural Phenomenon.* New York: Viking, *2006.*

_____ *Darwin's Dangerous Idea.* New York: Simon & Schuster, 1995.

De Waal, Frans. *The Bonobo and the Atheist.* New York: W. W. Norton & Company, 2013.

Bibliography

Diamond, Jared. *Collapse*. London: Penguin, 2005.

Durant, Will. *Caesar and Christ*. New York: Simon and Schuster, 1944.

Dwyer, John C. *Church History: Twenty Centuries of Catholic Christianity*. New York: Paulist Press, 1998.

Eagleton, Terrey. *Reason, Faith, And Revolution*. New Haven: Yale University Press, 2010.

Ehman, Robert R. *The Authentic Self*. Buffalo, New York: Prometheus Books, 1994.

Ehrman, Bart D. *Misquoting Jesus: The Story behind Who Changed the Bible and Why*. New York: HarperOne, 2007.

_____ *How Jesus Became God: The Exaltation of a Jewish Preacher from Galilee*. New York: HarperOne, 2014.

Feuerback, Ludwig. In *Wikipedia, The Free Encyclopedia. February, 2016*.

Finkelstein, Israel & Silberman, Neil Asher. *The Bible Unearthed*. Touchstone: 2002

Flynn, Tom. *The Trouble with Christmas*. Buffalo, New York: Prometheus Books, 1992.

Fox, Matthew. *Original Blessing*. New York: Jeremy P. Tarcher/Putnam. 2000.

Freud, Sigmund. *The Future of an Illusion*. In *The Portable Atheist*, Ed. Christopher Hitchens. Philadelphia: Da Capo Press, 2007.

Furnivall, F. J. (Ed.) *Hali Meidenhad*. New York: Greenwood Press, 1922.

Gould, Stephen Jay. *Wonderful Life: The Burgess Shale and the Nature of History*. New York: W. W. Norton & Company, 1990.

Goldman, Emma. *The Philosophy of Atheism*. In *The Portable Atheist*, Ed. Christopher Hitchens. Philadelphia: Da Capo Press, 2007.

Greeley, Andrew. *An Autobiography: Confessions of a Parish Priest*. New York: Simon and Schuster, 1986.

Greyling, A. C. *The God Argument*. New York: Bloomsbury USA, 2013.

Hamlyn, Paul. *Greek Mythology*. London: Westbrook House, 1963.

Harari, Yuval Noah. *Sapiens*. New York: Harper Collins, 2015.

Harris, Sam. *The End of Faith: Religion, Terror, and the Future of Reason*. New York: Norton, 2004.

_____ *Letter to a Christian Nation.* New York: Knopf, 2006.

Hayden, Tom. *The Lost Gospel of the Earth.* San Francisco: Sierra Club Books, 1996.

Hofmann, Melissa. *Virginity and Chastity for Women in Late Antiquity, Anglo-Saxon England, and Late Medieval England: on the Continuity of ideas.* TCNJ Journal of Student Scholarship, Vol. IX, April, 2007.

Henning, Clara Maria. *Cannon Law and the Battle of the Sexes.* In *Religion and Sexism,* (Ed. Rosemary Radford Ruether). New York: Simon and Schuster. 1974.

Hitchens, Christopher. *God Is Not Great: Why Religion Poisons Everything.* New York: Twelve, 2007.

Jerome. *Against Jovinianus.* NPNF2. *Jerome: The Principal Works of St. Jerome.* Christian Classics Ethereal Library, www.ccel.org, Internet download.

Kelly, J.N.D. *Jerome.* Peabody, Massachusetts: Hendrickson Publishers, Inc., 1998.

Kramer, Heinrich Godfrey. *Malleus Maleficarum (The Hammer of Witches).* Cambridge, England: Cambridge University Press, 2009.

Krulonis, Greg. & Barr, Tracy. *Evolution for Dummies.* Hoboken, N. J.: Wiley Publishing, Inc., 2008.

Kurtz, Paul. *Afterthoughts.* In *Science and Religion,* Ed. Paul Kurtz. Amherst, New York: Prometheus Books, 2003.

Leakey, Richard. *The Sixth Extinction.* New York: Anchor Books, 1996.

Lightman, Alan. *The Accidental Universe.* New York: Vintage Books: 2013.

Lippmann, Walter. *The Public Philosophy.* New York: New American Library, 1955.

Loftus, John W. *Why I Became an Atheist.* Amherst, New York: Prometheus Books, 2008.

Lovelock, James E. *The Earth as a Living Organism.* In *Learning to Listen to the Land,* Bill Willers (Ed.). Washington, DC: Island Press, 1991.

Lowenstein, Tom & Vitebsky, Piers. *Mother Earth, Father Sky.* London: Duncan Baird Publishers, 1977.

Martin, Louis. *Anti-feminism in Early Western Thought: St. Jerome, Evolution, and Culture.* https://politicsandculture.org, April 29, 2010.

Bibliography

Maslow, Abraham. *Motivation and Personality.* New York: Longman, 1987.

Mathers, Norm. "The Pauline Model of Atonement in Romans 3:14-31" Faculty Publications and Presentations Paper 180. Liberty University, 2012.

McBrien, Richard P. *Catholicism.* San Francisco: Harper & Row, *1981.*

McCormick, Matthew S. *Atheism and the Case Against Christ.* Amherst, New York: *Prometheus Books, 2012.*

McLaughlin, Eleanor Commo. *Equality of Souls, Inequality of Sexes: Woman in Medieval Theology.* In *Religion and Sexism.* (Ed. Rosemary Radford Ruether). New York: Simon and Schuster, 1974.

Meier, John P. *A Marginal Jew: Rethinking the Historical Jesus.* New York: Doubleday, 1991.

Mithen, Steven. *The Prehistory of the Mind.* London: Thames and Hudson Ltd., 1996.

Morris, Bonnie J. *Women's History.* Hanover, New Hampshire: Danbury, CT: For Beginners, 2012.

Nagel, Thomas. *What Does It All Mean, A Very Short Introduction to Philosophy.* New York: Oxford University Press, 1987.

Nelson, Richard, *Words that made American History.* London, Stationary Office, 1978.

Naroll, Raoul. *The Moral Order: An Introduction to The Human Situation.* Sage Publications, Beverly Hills: 1983.

Nemesszeghy, Ervin & Russell, John. *Theology of Evolution.* Fides Publishers Inc., Notre Dame, Indiana: August, 1972.

New American Bible, Nashville, Catholic Bible Press, 1987.

Nik, L. A. *Life is Short then you're Dead.* Cartus Press: 2013.

O'Faolain, Julia and Martines, Lauro, Eds. *Not in God's Image: Women in History from the Greeks to the Victorians.* New York: Harper & Row, 1973.

Pandian, Jacob. *The Dangerous Quest for Cooperation Between Science and Religion.* In *Science and Religion,* Ed. Paul Kurtz. Amherst, New York: Prometheus Books, 2003.

Phipps, William E. *Eve and Pandora Contrasted.* In *Theology Today,* Vol.45, 1, 1988.

Pinker, Steven. *How the Mind Works.* New York: W.W. Norton & Company, 1997.

Pius X. *Vehementer Nos* (Encyclical: Libreria Editrice Vaticana, February 11, 1906.

Radford Ruether, Rosemary. *Religion and Sexism.* New York: Simon and Schuster, 1974.

_____ (Ed.) *Religion and Sexism: Images of Woman in the Jewish and Christian Traditions.* New York: Simon and Schuster, 1974.

Ring of Fire. In *Wikipedia, The Free Encyclopedia.* Retrieved 10-19-16.

Rodriguez, Pedro. *The Hierarchical Constitution of the Church.* Catholic Position Papers: *The Primacy of the Pope in the Church,* September, 1981, Japan Edition.

Rosenberg, Alex. *The Atheist's Guide to Reality.* New York: W.W. Norton & Co., 2011.

Roszak, Theodore. *The Gendered Atom.* Berkeley, California: Conari Press, 1999.

Ruse, Michael. *Atheism: What Everyone Needs to Know.* Oxford University Press, 2015.

Russell, Bertrand. *Why I Am Not a Christian.* New York: Simon & Schuster, 1950.

Scott, Eugenie C. *Evolution vs. Creationism (2nd Edition).* Westport, Connecticut: Greenwood Press, 2009

Smith, George H. *Atheism: The Case Against God.* New York: Prometheus Books, 1979.

Smith, Wilfred Cantwell. *The Meaning and End of Religion.* New York: Mentor Books, 1964.

Spinoza, Benedict De. *Theological-Political Treatise.* In Christopher Hitchens, *The Portable Atheist.* Philadelphia: De Capo Press, 2007.

Spong, John Shelby. *The Sins of Scripture.* San Francisco: Harper One, 2005.

_____ *Eternal Life: A New Vision.* San Francisco: Harper One, 2009.

Stark, Rodney. *When Sin Began.* In US News and World Report, *The Mysteries of Faith.* March, 2010.

Stenger, Victor J. *The New Atheism: Taking a Stand for Science and Reason.* New York: Prometheus Books, 2009.

_____*God and the Folly of Faith: The Incompatibility of Science and Religion*. New York, Prometheus, 2012.

Stephens, Mitchell. *Imagine There's No Heaven*. New York: Palgrave Macmillan, 2014.

Stewart, Matthew. *Nature's God: The Heretical Origins of the American Republic*. New York: W.W. Norton and Company, 2014.

Taylor, William. *A Tale of Two Cities: Mormons-Catholics*. Pocatello, Idaho: self-published, 1980.

Tarnas, Richard. *The Passion of the Western Mind*. New York: Ballantine Books, 1991.

Talmon, Shemaryahu. *The Old Testament Text*. In: Ackroyd, P.R. and C.F. Evans (Eds.). *The Cambridge History of the Bible*. Cambridge: The University Press, 1970.

Thoreau, Henry David. *Walden*. New York, Peter Pauper Press, 1966.

Turner, James. *Without God, Without Creed*. Baltimore: The Johns Hopkins University Press, 1985.

Tyson, Neil DeGrasse. *What Science is and How and Why it Works*. In *Skeptical Inquirer*, Vol. 40 No. 5, September/October, 2016.

Wasson, Donald L. *Janus*. Ancient History Encyclopedia. Last modified 2/6/15. http://www. ancient.eu/Janus/.

Watson, Peter. *The Age of Atheists*. New York: Simon & Schuster, 2014. Liveright Publishing Corporation, 2014.

Wilkes, Paul. *The Good Enough Catholic. A Guide for the Perplexed*. New York: Ballantine, 1996.

Wilson, Edward O. *The Meaning of Human Existence*. New York: Liveright Publishing Corp., 2014.

Zuckerman, Phil. *Living the Secular Life*. New York: Penguin Press, 2014.

Made in the USA
Columbia, SC
23 April 2017